CW00688547

NO JUSTICE WITHOUT A STRUGGLE

The National Unemployed Workers' Movement in the North East of England 1920-1940

DON WATSON

MERLIN PRESS

Published in 2014
by Merlin Press Ltd
99B Wallis Road
London
E9 5LN

www.merlinpress.co.uk

© Don Watson, 2014

ISBN. 978-0-85036-618-1

Catalogue in publication data is available
from the British Library

The right of Don Watson to be identified as author of this work
has been asserted in accordance with the Copyright, Designs
and Patents Act 1988

All rights reserved. No part of this publication may be
reproduced, stored in a retrieval system, or transmitted,
in any form or by any means, electronic, mechanical,
photocopying, recording or otherwise, without the
prior permission of the publisher.

Printed in the UK by Imprint Digital, Exeter

CONTENTS

ILLUSTRATIONS

Between pages 122 and 123

ACKNOWLEDGEMENTS

The publication of this book was made possible by a generous grant from the Barry Amiel and Norman Melburn Trust. I am very grateful to the trustees for their support. An early version of Chapter Nine appeared in *Socialist History* no. 40 in 2012 and I appreciate the permission to use the material here. I would like to thank Gateshead Local Studies Library for the use of images from the Jim Ancrum photograph collection. The photograph of the meeting at Newcastle's Bigg Market appears courtesy of Newcastle City Library.

I am also very grateful for the practical support given to me by fellow members of the North East Labour History Society while this book was being researched and written. The Society was established in 1967 and details of its activities can be found at www.nelhs.org. Peter Brabban had kept the tapes from the interviews he had carried out with NUWM veterans in Sunderland and Stockton for his student dissertation more than thirty years earlier. Peter's generosity in sharing this material meant that additional voices from the movement are heard in this book, and I was able to use more first-hand accounts as evidence than would have been possible otherwise. Kevin Davies is a tireless worker among the newspaper and other archives of the region, and indeed in the National Archives, and I owe him a debt for his help in tracking useful references and material.

Matt Perry very kindly copied many of the files he had made for his own research for me, thus saving me a great deal of time, and he has continually encouraged my efforts. Lewis Mates was always keen to pass on references and discuss progress. Archie Potts recalled his father Ernest's accounts of the unemployed movement in Sunderland in the 1920s for me, and Billy Vincent gave me some useful information about the Sunderland rent strike of 1939. The late Val Duncan introduced me to her father, Bill Reynolds, who shared memories of his brother Harry, who marched with the NUWM and was killed in Spain.

Willie Thompson read and commented on a draft of the book and I am very grateful indeed for the time he gave up to do so. Willie, like John Charlton, has been another consistent source of encouragement and advice along the way. Thanks are also due to Jane Coulter for her compilation of the index.

Colleagues in the International Brigade Memorial Trust have also been a great help. Duncan Longstaff gave me the transcript of one of his interviews with his father, John, in which he describes taking part in the 1934 Hunger March. Jim Carmody, the IBMT volunteer archivist, was an invaluable source of information about International Brigade members from the North East and about the difficulties involved in using the surviving records of the British Battalion. Sheila Gray shared the family information about her mother's two brothers, Bill and Ed Tattam, who were killed in Spain. Jim Carmody, Richard Baxall and Danny Payne read over a chapter for me and they too have been a great source of encouragement.

The reader will see that I have made much use of the County Archives for Tyne and Wear, Durham, and Northumberland, as well as the North East's various Local Studies Libraries. They have all been unfailingly helpful. A special mention is due to John Boothroyd and the team at Gateshead Local Studies Library for their help and support. I would also like to thank Jo Bath, who when she worked at the Beamish Archive identified and supplied me with transcripts of interviews with activists in the unemployed movement.

I appreciated the help of staff and volunteers at archives outside the region too. The Labour History Archive and Study Centre, the TUC Library at London Metropolitan University, the Working Class Movement Library and the Marx Memorial Library are invaluable resources for the labour historian and we must ensure that they continue to be viable.

Finally, I should mention that over the years I knew four of the people, all no longer with us, who appear in these pages: Charlie Woods, Frank Graham, John Henderson, and Len Edmondson. This book is an evaluation of the efforts that they, and many like them, made to improve the lot of the unemployed and to change the conditions that gave rise to mass unemployment and poverty. I hope their experience will prove useful to those who continue to make that effort.

ABBREVIATIONS USED

BLSA	British Library Sound Archive, London
BMSA	Beamish Museum Sound Archive, Beamish, County Durham
DCRO	Durham County Record Office, Durham
GLS	Gateshead Local Studies Library, Gateshead
IWMSA	Imperial War Museum Sound Archive, London
LHASC	Labour History Archive and Study Centre, Manchester
MML	Marx Memorial Library, London
NA	National Archives, London
NCRO	Northumberland County Record Office, Woodhorn, Northumberland
NLS	National Library of Scotland, Edinburgh
TUC	Trades Union Congress Library, London Metropolitan University
TWAS	Tyne and Wear Archives Service, Newcastle
WCML	Working Class Movement Library, Salford
WIHM	Welcome Institute for the History of Medicine, London

Chapter One

INTRODUCTION

The trade recessions of the inter-war years caused a sharp contraction in the staple industries of the nineteenth century, the ones on whose growth the urban and industrial development of northern England, South Wales and much of Scotland had been based. This was a catastrophe for the working-class people who depended on these industries. Mining, shipbuilding and repair, merchant shipping and all the other occupations related to them took the brunt. Although there was a tradition in County Durham of moving to another colliery village to work if necessary, or of signing on in the merchant navy as an alternative, these were not options when most of the villages in the county were in the same position and the merchant ships were idle. The pattern of industrialisation in the previous century had been to create single-workplace towns, and now the reason for their existence had been removed.

For socialists like Jarrow MP Ellen Wilkinson, mass unemployment was capitalism in action:

> In capitalist society vast changes can be made which sweep away the livelihood of a whole town overnight, in the interests of some powerful group, who need take no account of the social consequences of their decisions. These are the facts at the base of the modern labour movement.[1]

They are also the facts at the base of this book. Mass, long-term unemployment and poverty were significant features of the economic landscape at this time, but organised resistance to it was a significant feature of the political landscape too.

By 1920 local trades councils were forming unemployed committees both to advocate for their members and to lobby elected representatives about unemployment. They formed the National Unemployed Workers' Committee Movement to co-ordinate activity and to work with the Trades Union Congress and the Labour Party for national action. The NUWCM was well to the left of the labour movement and by 1929 through a combination of factors – the failure of the General Strike and the miners' lockout of 1926, an ultra-left policy imposed on the international Communist movement, dissatisfaction with the Labour and TUC leaderships – the Communist Party was in control of its successor, the National Unemployed Workers' Movement. It has been estimated that at its peak the NUWM had 50,000 members, which would make it the biggest single radical working-class organisation of the 1930s.[2]

The NUWM sought to unify the employed and the unemployed as a force to overthrow capitalism, the system that had produced mass unemployment. Therefore its work was always in the broader context of the militant left in the inter-war years and how the wider labour movement of the time reacted to it.

What is the point of a local study of this, and why of the North East of England in particular? Local accounts can provide a better understanding of the dynamics of working-class politics than national accounts, and can also add to the exploration of national issues. Richard Croucher, author of the first really analytical account of the NUWM, does admit that national accounts cannot do justice to the lively *local* branches of the organisation or the breadth of their work. He has also stated that we need to know more about the sociology of unemployed movements, who participated in them and who was active in different ways. A local focus is a useful way to contribute to this.[3] The perception of unemployed struggles in the North East of England is inextricably linked with the Jarrow March, but for me it is a question of context; neither the decision in Jarrow to organise a march of the unemployed to London nor, crucially, the opposition of the Labour and Trade Union leaderships towards it can be explained without an understanding of the National Unemployed Workers' Movement up to 1936. The basis of this inextricable link is the creation of a favoured status for the Jarrow March because it was a 'non-political' event and not because it had any impact at the time.[4] Nevertheless the link *is* inextricable and so there is all the more need to examine a local unemployed movement that was political and which receives far less attention.

There were of course other marches. Peter Kingsford provides an extremely useful study of the Hunger Marches in Britain;[5] unemployed men, and later women, from the North East took part in each of the NUWM National Hunger Marches to London in 1922/3, 1929, 1930, 1932, 1934 and 1936. The information available about these marches is uneven but there is a need to examine the regional organisation of these marches and where the local sources of support, and opposition, came from. There were also a number of local demonstrations, rallies, lobbies of local authorities and labour exchange managers in the region. These are much less well-known than the national marches but they were important to the work of the NUWM in the North East; they also made a significant contribution to the success of the campaign against benefits cuts in 1935. Some NUWM demonstrations included the most violent political crowd disorders seen in the region between 1920 and the miners' strike of 1984/85.

Marches, demonstrations and lobbying was one aspect of the movement's work. Another was casework for individuals, help with claims and representation at appeals. As one of the historians of the welfare state in Britain has said of the 1930s, 'Applicants for benefits needed to cut their way through a jungle of bureaucratic obstacles...'[6] Charlie Woods, a Communist miner from Blaydon, was active in both the NUWCM and the NUWM, and he is one of several veterans whose testimony is included in this book. He recalled this case work:

> The history of case fighting on the North East coast was a prodigious history, if it could have been compiled into a single volume, and there was enough for one, then it would have been a demonstration of the degree to which we had experts, working-class lawyers, on unemployment acts. We had in each branch, particularly in the bigger branches, men devoting their time to this particular work. This was all done on a voluntary basis because we had no funds except the penny a week that was being paid in contributions by each member and this was barely enough for organisational expenses. The work that was involved has been forgotten. It's sad that we don't have a record of some kind that could have been written up, and would have been a credit to the lads who put in a lot of time to this kind of activity.[7]

The NUWM is justly credited by historians for the effectiveness of its 'working-class lawyers' and so their work in the North East ought to be assessed. Nevertheless the NUWM did not have a monopoly on advice and representation work and so the role of the local trade unions, trades councils and the Labour Party in representing, and indeed organising, the unemployed also needs to be assessed and compared.

During the 1930s the Communist Party had six councillors elected in the region, from Blyth, Houghton le Spring, and Felling. The Party almost won a seat on Tynemouth Council too on different occasions. This provided most of the real electoral challenge to Labour from the left, and each of these CP councillors was a well-known local activist in the NUWM. How far it was their record of providing practical support for unemployed people that got them elected, and what they were able to do once elected, needs to be understood.

The NUWM had an important role in the opposition to organised fascism in the region, both directly and by denying fascist organisations the opportunity to recruit or influence the long-term unemployed. The significant part played by local NUWM activists in the International Brigade in Spain deserves to be examined. This involves hitherto unexplored detail about the role of political education in the unemployed movement and the extent of members' involvement with the International Brigade. The effect on the unemployed movement of having so many of its activists involved in the campaign for the Spanish Republic needs to be discussed.

It might be expected that a movement of unemployed workers in a region noted for mining and heavy industry would be purely a men's movement, but this was not entirely the case. Life for the unemployed on the original Poor Law relief, and under the Means Test that took over from it, had an impact on the domestic sphere traditionally managed by women, and so how far they were represented in NUWM protest marches and other activities needs to be discussed. A few women became notable leaders of the local unemployed in their own right and their story should be included.

The NUWM was active in the region until early in the Second World War but with a shift of focus from its previous patterns of national agitations and local activity. This does not mean that the movement at this point can be dismissed. It was active in the Sunderland Rent Strike in 1939 (which is examined here in detail), in the campaigns for additional winter payments, and ensuring that special war work preparations and schemes took unemployed people on at trades union rates.

It is not my intention to spend time on events and issues that have been thoroughly covered elsewhere and so the reader is directed to those sources. There are several accounts by Wal Hannington, the leading figure in the movement for twenty years, and although they include important material they are very much the 'official history'.[8] His books and pamphlets do not deal with the frequently problematic relations between the NUWM and the Communist leadership. This book has been able to make use of the minutes of meetings of the Central Committee of the CPGB in the 1930s, and recent research related to them, to draw this out and discuss the consequences.

Clearly the unemployed movement developed in a political context. The years immediately after the end of the First World War were ones of acute stress for the British establishment, both at home and overseas. The Irish War of Independence between 1919 and 1921 and the persistent nationalist movement in India – the massacre at Amritsar had taken place in 1919 -were direct threats to imperial hegemony. The Bolshevik revolution in Russia had overthrown the accepted order of things and installed a government that seemed intent on exporting its success throughout the capitalist world. The British government had committed a large armed force to try to suppress the Bolshevik government but the revolution had aroused interest and sympathy in sections of the British labour movement. This included Newcastle, where public meetings expressed 'outbursts of resentment' about the government's effort to stifle the new socialist state by force. The Newcastle and District Trades Council wholeheartedly backed the 'Hands Off Russia' Movement and also the cause of Irish independence, and this was by no means unusual in the labour movement. Worse, between 1920 and 1921 several revolutionary socialist organisations had come together to form the Communist Party of Great Britain, a formal section of the Communist International, the Comintern, and which received funding from it.[9]

One result was that for several years after the First World War all local police forces were required to submit regular reports – co-ordinated, in the North East, through a superintendent at Felling Police Station – to the Home Office, and in turn these were submitted as digests to a Cabinet Committee. The reports supplied information about any activities by the 'unemployed, Communists, Red International of Labour Unions and Workers' Committees, Independent Labour Party members, travelling agitators, foreign seamen and stowaways acting as couriers'. In addition, they must monitor the activities of 'extremists in the Co-operative Societies, circulators of revolutionary literature, and seditious speeches'.[10] These records show that a number of local militants from Communist-Labour and the ILP were under observation, and that the police provided reports on local unemployed activities to the Home Office. The more militant organisations of the unemployed were also monitored throughout the 1930s, and the NUWM was a regular target for police informers.

The unemployment benefit system on which many working people had to rely had not been designed to deal with and could not cope with persistent and structural unemployment. Between 1929 and 1934 for example the international trade slump reduced coal exports from County Durham by almost 40 per cent as well as substantially reducing output in the shipyards. Unemployment in the shipbuilding and ship repair industries of Tyneside, consequently, was estimated to be 59 per cent in 1923, falling to 30 per cent a year later but rising again to 60 per cent by 1926. In 1928 some 27,000 fewer miners were employed in Durham than two years previously. Between 1929 and 1934 unemployment in Durham and Tyneside more than doubled, and later into the 1930s the official figures showed unemployment far in excess of the English average. 25 per cent unemployment in Durham and Tyneside by1937 could be welcomed as an encouraging reduction from previous years, although these are regional averages which conceal the position in individual towns: the 80 per cent unemployment in the Jarrow of 1932 had not changed significantly five years later.[11]

The benefits system was a compromise between the century-old Poor Law administration and the 1911 National Insurance Act for which the labour movement had campaigned. The Act covered a comparatively small section of the workforce who paid contributions that after a set period would entitle them to a period of weekly benefits in the event of involuntary unemployment. After that those still unemployed had to seek 'outdoor relief' under the Poor Law from the local Board of Guardians. These Guardians were elected, but statutorily separate from elected local authorities although it was possible to be a member of both. Although 'Relieving Officers' were employed for the day-to-day work the Guardians were responsible for the nature and level of relief to be paid, and often the circumstances in which it could be paid at all.[12] Traditionally recipients of Poor Law relief were regarded as 'paupers' and to be in that position was a source of shame for many working-class people. Claimants were often not trusted to be paid money but were paid 'in kind', by vouchers for local shops; cash could be given but often only as a loan, thus storing up future debt problems; Guardians could impose unpaid 'test work' on claimants as a condition of relief. Thus the system served to reinforce stigma, the ultimate of which was the denial of relief and admission to the workhouse. Where claims were denied an appeal could be made to a regional Umpire and then to the Court of Referees.

The money available to Guardians was derived from the local rates and during structural unemployment this created another problem. Working-class towns had a low rateable value at the best of times but were now facing higher demands for services and relief. For example between 1914 and 1928 Jarrow experienced a 186 per cent rise in rates per head of population compared to 43 per cent in middle-class Whitley Bay. In 1928 too it was reported that Newcastle was spending as much per week on relief as it was spending per year in 1914.[13] There were of course political limits to how far rates could be raised, and the alternative was to request overdraft facilities from the Ministry of Health, which oversaw Poor Law Guardians; the Ministry tended to insist that every possible economy was made on relief payments before this was granted.

The Boards of Guardians were elected and on occasion they became a political arena. The Poplar Board in London demonstrated this in an iconic struggle from 1919. The Poplar Board of Guardians became dominated by Labour councillors elected from a destitute borough; they insisted on paying a decent level of relief, challenged the rating system and embarked on a collision course with central government. Eventually they won some success but only after a spell of imprisonment and the mobilisation of the local community in their support.[14]

British governments between the wars made several major changes to this system. The purpose of each was always twofold: reducing expenditure on unemployment at the expense of those who were out of work, and reducing and then removing the element of local democratic participation. Conservatives believed that local influence over the level of benefits, particularly in Labour areas, resulted in over-generous rates being paid, and that it was too vulnerable to campaigns and lobbying. The Poor Law Guardians were abolished in 1929 and later replaced by Public Assistance Committees and later still Unemployment Assistance Boards, both of which screened eligibility for benefit through a rigorous and intrusive household Means Test. As far as the organised unemployed were concerned these were the same issues recurring in different guises, and their collective action continued in response.

Finally, Richard Croucher's study was researched and published when many parts of Britain were undergoing the economic recession of the 1980s. At time of writing parts of the country seem to be repeating that experience. Although circumstances are never repeated exactly it is possible that an account such as this might have contemporary relevance as well as historical interest. In any event there is no doubt that the NUWM slogan of 'no justice without a struggle' will never lose its importance and force.

Notes

1   Ellen Wilkinson, *The Town That Was Murdered: The Life Story of Jarrow*, (London: Victor Gollanz Left Book Club 1939, p. 7).

2   Sam Davies, 'The Membership of the National Unemployed Workers' Movement 1923-1938,' *Labour History Review* Vol 57 No.1 (Spring 1992, pp. 29-37).

3   Richard Croucher, *We Refuse to Starve in Silence: A History of the National Unemployed Workers Movement 1920-1946* (London: Lawrence and Wishart 1987); see also his editorial 'History of Unemployed Movements', *Labour History Review* Vol 73 No.1 (April 2008, pp. 1-19).

4   This is examined in detail in Matt Perry, *The Jarrow Crusade: Protest and Legend* (Sunderland: Sunderland University Press 2005).

5   Peter Kingsford, *The Hunger Marchers in Britain 1920-1940* (London: Lawrence and Wishart 1982).

6   Charles Webster, 'Health, Welfare and Unemployment During the Depression', *Past and Present* No105 (November 1985, p. 227).

7   Charlie Woods, interview with Peter Brabban 1979.

8   Wal Hannington, *Unemployed Struggles 1919-1936* (London: Lawrence and Wishart 1977), *Never on Our Knees* (London: Lawrence and Wishart 1967) and *Ten Lean Years* (Wakefield: EP Publishing 1978).

9   Home Office Report to Cabinet 18 September 1919 (NA: CAB/24/88/21); J.F. Clarke and T.P. McDermott, *Newcastle and District Trades Council 1873-1973: A Centenary History* (Newcastle on Tyne: Frank Graham 1973, p. 26); Willie Thompson, *The Good Old Cause: British Communism 1920-1991* (London: Pluto Press 1992).

10   Copy Correspondence, Superintendent at Felling to Chief Constable of Durham 20 March 1922 (TWAS: T148/7).

11   Henry Mess, *Industrial Tyneside: a social survey made for the Bureau of Social Research for Tyneside* (London: E. Bell Ltd. 1928, p. 55); *Newcastle Journal* 30 July 1928; D. Euart-Wallace, *Report of Investigation into the Industrial Conditions in Certain Depressed Areas: Tyneside and Durham* (London: Ministry of Labour 1934, p. 72); Commissioner for the Special Areas: *4th Report* (London: Ministry of Labour 1937, p. 21).

12   A discussion of the system is provided by Noreen Branson, *Britain in the Nineteen Twenties* (London: Weidenfield and Nicholson 1976, pp. 69-91).

13   Mess, *Industrial Tyneside* op. cit. p. 162; North *Mail* 29 February 1929.

14   For a full account of this see Noreen Branson, *Poplarism 1919-1925: George Lansbury and the Councillors' Revolt* (London: Lawrence and Wishart 1979).

Chapter Two

1921-1926 – A MOVEMENT EMERGES

The unemployed agitations of the 1920s seem to have been overshadowed by the events of a decade later.[1] The 1930s saw the Means Test, most of the National Hunger Marches and the Jarrow Crusade, and so it is as if those years have been assumed to be the crucial ones. Yet for the North East 'the depression' began well before then, certainly by the summer and autumn of 1921 when unemployment in the traditional staple industries had grown rapidly. The unemployed agitations that emerged at that time were important events in their own right and repay study for their own sake and not just as the prologue to some main event. Some forms of protest, political and organisational issues, and campaign themes emerged that were to continue until the outbreak of war in 1939. The five years after the first national miners' lockout in 1921 provides a starting point in the development of the organised unemployed movement; the lockout itself is relevant too.

The 1921 Miners' Lock-Out

When this dispute began the Miners' Federation of Great Britain (MFGB) argued that the owners had in fact locked their members out. There was a feeling even in establishment circles that they had a case, and the miners always referred to the dispute as a lockout and not a strike.[2] Therefore they believed that miners should be eligible for unemployment pay and lodge secretaries were urged to liaise with employment exchanges about claims. Sunderland was used as a test case when a large group of miners attempted to sign on there in April 1921.[3] These claims were turned down however and the MFGB lost its appeals to both the Court of Referees and the Umpire. The legal position since 1900 was that Poor Law Relief could not be paid to able-bodied men who were on strike or locked-out, only to their wives and children if they had them. Single men would not normally be eligible.

Boards of Guardians still had obligations for the relief of miners' families and in the North East there were marked variations in how these were interpreted. Newcastle would not make relief available, although later this was modified; Easington provided it 'in kind' (vouchers for provisions) to miners' families; Bishop Auckland provided cash relief but only on loan; Gateshead though provided cash relief and argued that this was within the rules, because they were empowered to 'have regard to special circumstances which they deem expedient'. This was a popular decision: 'when the news spread the number of applications rose to hundreds, and the offices were overwhelmed'. The Durham Guardians too provided relief 'in kind' but only until they could agree an appropriate cash rate. This meant operating on an overdraft and risking being individually surcharged by the Ministry of Health, but this they were prepared to do 'to look after the children and starving people'.[4]

In a number of areas however a reluctance to claim was noticed. Although the soup kitchens were 'supported by other trade unionists and by those who were in favour of the men's side of the fight' many 'would not use them until their own money was exhausted...Relief and charity, where accepted, have produced a very natural feeling of humiliation'. In Consett for example 'people who were legitimately entitled to poor relief had not deigned to ask it...this aversion to poor relief has in some cases nearly led to tragedy'.[5]

The report of the Durham County Medical Officer for 1921 also provides information about the attitudes of miners' families to claiming support from the authorities. This was done through the Child Welfare Centres managed by the County Council, where milk and baby foods were made available free or at a subsidised cost depending on the parents' financial circumstances. The Centres were certainly busy - 'The Medical Officers and Health Visitors found it very trying and almost impossible in some districts to deal with the large numbers who flocked to the Centres- this was especially felt in Birtley and Blaydon...' Expectant mothers had problems over nutrition until they contacted the Centres or Relief Committees; also:

> A certain number of applicants undertook to repay the cost of the milk, but as the weeks of the dispute spun out, some of these asked to be released from their promise; they evidently saw a load of debt piling up ahead which they would be unable to tackle.[6]

At this point the fact that Durham, uniquely for an English County Council then, was Labour controlled, and that the prime mover in the Labour group was the Durham Miners' Association, became crucial. The 'Feeding of Necessitous Schoolchildren Act' had been passed in 1907 and enabled local authorities to provide a free meal for those schoolchildren who, in the professional opinion of the School Medical Officer, were too malnourished to take advantage of the education provided for them. School meals are usually considered in terms of the history of education, but in the North East they should be seen in terms of the history of the miners' struggles. The 1921 lock-out provides the first example, when Durham County Council implemented the Act and used its discretion over eligibility, so that the deciding factor became family income and not health. By the first week of July 1921 773,000 meals had been provided. As the lockout wore on other authorities followed their example.

All this caused controversy with the vociferous right-wing ratepayers' associations in the region who objected to the mining families receiving any form of assistance through the rates. The elections to the Boards of Guardians in April 1922 saw candidates fielded by the Newcastle Business Group and the Gateshead Property Owners' and Ratepayers' Associations as a direct result. The Durham County Ratepayers' Association had invoked the historic stigma of the Poor Law to attack the miners, who 'should be ashamed to take parish relief' and 'ashamed of themselves for allowing their wives and children to become paupers'. Clearly in some cases although not in others this shame was still a very real factor.[7]

In terms of the development of the unemployed movement in the North East the 1921 lock-out has some interesting factors. There is some evidence that unemployed groups worked to ensure that the unemployed were not used to break the lock-out. 'No black-legging the miners!' was a slogan at the end of one unemployed meeting in Gateshead in April 1921. This was the first industrial dispute in the region where Poor Law relief was an issue even though recourse to it might initially be avoided. The organisations of ratepayers protesting at the payment of relief and the imposition of additional rates for it, either on principle or on grounds of cost, were to offer a political and legal challenge to Labour throughout the decade.[8]

Almost immediately after the miners' return to work the wider labour movement responded to the unemployment crisis in different ways that can be examined area by area.

North Tyneside

Events in North Shields during the autumn of 1921 illustrate what might be called the mainstream trade union response to the unemployment crisis. Early in September 'a fairly large number of unemployed men' who were 'fortunately very quiet and orderly' gathered at the bottom of Howard Street in the town centre for a mass meeting after a demonstration through the town. Local Boilermakers' Society Secretary and Labour Party branch official Fred Lonie, one of the organisers, explained that Tynemouth Borough was lagging behind others in both providing relief and public work schemes to relieve unemployment. The Feeding of Necessitous Schoolchildren Act had been implemented during the miners' lock-out but this school feeding had stopped when they returned to work. This should be re-introduced and the unemployed should get their claims in to press for it. A deputation would be made to the Council for relief work schemes and to the Board of Guardians for relief payments. The chair of a local Amalgamated Engineering Union branch commented that:

> It is the women who are suffering in this battle: it is the women who have to face the landlord, the butcher, the grocer etcetera and we must do our best to help the women'. It was agreed to send a deputation made up of union branch secretaries – but aiming to represent non-members also – to put demands for work schemes to the Council and for relief to the Board of Guardians. It was believed that the threat of a large number of men seeking admission to the workhouse 'would go a long way towards moving the Board of Guardians' towards paying relief.[9]

Three days later a 'crowded mass meeting' heard a report from the deputation, which had in fact only been able to discuss public works schemes with the Town Clerk. Another deputation to the Council itself was agreed, along with a commitment to 'use moral persuasion and not cause trouble; to act in an orderly fashion but let the Council know that they would not be fobbed off with promises'. A proposal for a mass demonstration to the Board of Guardians was voted down because 'that's how disorder starts'; the results of the deputation should be known first. 'Disorder' was more than likely a reference to the clashes between the police and the unemployed that had occurred elsewhere in the country, and which were reported in the local press.[10]

The Board of Guardians also received a deputation on behalf of the Wallsend unemployed – 'sensible men, not the militant type at all' – and assured both them and the North Shields representatives that they had no intention of using the workhouse for the genuinely unemployed. Wallsend Town Council had undertaken to increase the rates to provide temporary and part-time work schemes. The Board decided to grant relief to single men and women and those with dependents, on a scale to be approved by the Ministry of Health and at least half of which would be paid 'in kind' (vouchers for provisions), any cash to be repaid at some future date. The chairman remarked on 'the splendid way the unemployed had conducted themselves up to this time'. At the report meeting the next day the deputation announced that between 500 and 600 men would be placed on Council work schemes; the Council 'had had to have pressure brought to bear before acting'. It emerged though that some people who had exhausted their unemployment benefit didn't know how or where to claim, and were in dire need. The branch officials collected names. There was a clear voice from the unemployed that relief should be in cash and not 'in kind', because that 'placed wives in the humiliating position of having to deal with tradesmen with notes from the Guardians'.[11]

Representatives of the Willington Quay unemployed warned the Tynemouth Guardians that 'there had been a dangerous clamour for some time from the unemployed, particularly ex-servicemen, and things were assuming dangerous proportions…people had given an undertaking of good behaviour until the result of the deputation was known'. However all this seems to have secured was an expressed determination by the Board to see that tradesmen did not overcharge when customers presented Guardian vouchers.[12]

In the same week another mass meeting was held in North Shields at which further grievances were revealed. There was criticism that those who were being taken on by public works schemes were not necessarily in the most need; single men were still being offered workhouse tickets; married men with dependents were required to present proof of their circumstances, which they resented. A few days later Lonie organised another deputation to the Board of Guardians. He criticised the 'inquisitorial methods' of the Relieving Officers and how demeaning it was for claimants to be put through questions about their personal circumstances. As an alternative the names of applicants for relief could be put forward by their union branch secretaries, because many had held the role for over twenty years and knew their members' circumstances very well. The Board agreed to issue cash relief to single men on a loans basis and to review its practices about questioning claimants. At a further mass meeting in Howard Street unemployed men repeated that they would not allow Relieving Officers into their homes because of their attitude to claimants; and, in view of the high local rents that had to be paid, the Guardians' scales of relief were too low.

Another mass meeting was held in Howard Street to hear the latest proposals from the Guardians. They would make a modest increase in the relief scales and, although they were obliged to have some questions asked of claimants they were prepared to modify them. The unemployed responded by agreeing an Unemployed Committee consisting of Lonie and four other union branch secretaries. Their role would be to work with the Guardians, in an office provided for them, to submit claims for the unemployed and thus by-pass the need for the 'inquisitorial methods' that had caused such resentment. The Committee would try to help those who were not trade union members. In addition a demonstration would be held to reinforce their case for higher relief scales.[13]

There are some interesting features to these episodes. They illustrate how the process of applying for relief to the Guardians could be a demeaning experience for the unemployed. They were skilled shipyard and engineering workers, probably high earners during the war years, now having to rely on the administration of the Poor Law for survival. They often weren't sure how to apply, they had no information; they were subject to personal questioning by officers whose attitude towards them was clearly high-handed; one of the resolutions passed called on the Guardians to 'dispense with the relieving officers in North Shields, and replace them with men who will show more consideration, humanity and courtesy in their business'. Successful claimants were issued with stigmatising food vouchers which could also leave them at the mercy of local shopkeepers. On top of this the amounts involved were less than adequate. Long serving trade union officers dealing with these issues were trying to rise to this new challenge of representing their members who were now out of work. The question was raised in North Shields about the position of unemployed workers who were not union members; the role of the union officers with them seems less clear.[14]

County Durham

Further and different examples of trade union responses can be found in the Durham coalfield, examples that also help to illustrate the situation of unemployed miners and their families. In October 1921 'a demonstration of unemployed miners from five collieries, with bands and banners' marched to a meeting of the Lanchester Board of Guardians. Their deputation of lodge officials put the case that 'if they could not get work they looked to the Guardians to see that they lived in decency'. They wanted relief scales to be increased and applied fairly; they were opposed to relief being granted in the form of loans and 'in kind' vouchers for shopkeepers, they wanted the freedom to buy what they needed for themselves. The system at the moment was that Relieving Officers issued vouchers for shopkeepers listing permitted commodities; rather than being granted things they might not want the unemployed should receive a note stating the amount of money that could be spent. Some families apparently were destitute, their children missing school because they had no boots, because they would not take Guardian loans they could not repay. Further, although there were legal issues, the deputation believed that the allowances the Durham Miners Association (DMA) was able to pay to its unemployed members should not be deducted from relief payments. There was no relief available for the 14-18 years age group and this should be reformed.

The demonstrators 'acted in a most orderly manner' and it was 'obvious that many inhabitants of Lanchester sympathised with them'. So did the Guardians, who made what were in the scheme of things important concessions: relief scales for married people were raised and a scale for those over 16 years introduced; no reduction would be made for DMA allowances providing the money was used for children's clothes and boots; loans would no longer have to be legally signed for, and vouchers would be 25% cash and the remaining amount listed rather than permitted commodities. Both the deputation and the demonstration it reported back to were pleased at the outcome, and before they dispersed the colliery bands played requests for the Board of Guardians.[15]

This success is interesting in that the example of the DMA allowances shows that even within the legal framework Guardians could have some freedom of action if they chose to use it. As in North Shields the issue was not only the scale of relief but how it was administered, how efforts could still be made to maintain the dignity of unemployed people.

Elsewhere in County Durham deputations of the unemployed were received by local authorities but without the same success. Whickham, and Stanley, Urban District Councils were urged to raise relief scales and, more importantly, to provide public works schemes. Similarly across the Tyne the Newburn District Council was urged by representatives elected by the unemployed to provide 'work not dole' public works and implement the Necessitous Schoolchildren Act. In all these cases the standard if sympathetic reply was that Councils were pressing central government to take these issues on as a national responsibility. Not all protests in the county mining areas were as amicable as these. It was in October 1921 too that 300 miners protested at the Durham Poor Law Institution, in the tactic of demanding mass admission. This was designed to encourage relief payment because that would be cheaper than the costs of large scale workhouse accommodation. The result here however was police action to disperse the demonstrators.[16]

Teesside

Such actions were becoming common across the region. Among the first was in early May 1921 when 'one of the most remarkable scenes in the history of municipal government in Middlesbrough' was witnessed. A march of the unemployed 'headed by several leaders of the Labour movement' marched to the Town Hall where they 'packed themselves into every inch of standing room' and 'the atmosphere seemed to be charged with electric waves'. Eventually the Council agreed to hear a deputation of five, who pressed mainly for public works schemes that paid adequate rates. The Council agreed to set up a relief fund and examine other actions it could take, decisions that were reported back to the main body of the demonstration in Middlesborough Market Square. In the second week of September 1921 1,500 unemployed people marched to the West Hartlepool Guardians where a deputation was led by officials from the General and Municipal Workers' and the Blastfurnacemens' Unions. They achieved an increase in their relief scales in line with those used by the Stockton Board, and the introduction of loans for single claimants. They were satisfied with this outcome.[17]

South Tyneside

The potential for 'disorder', and warnings against it, were a regular theme in the North Shields and Wallsend negotiations in the autumn of 1921, and may even have been a negotiating card played by the unemployed deputations. This was also the case in South Shields at the same time. The Board of Guardians there received two separate deputations in the second week of September, from Jarrow and South Shields. The Jarrow delegate told them that 'no-one could live and maintain a respectable appearance' on the current relief scales, and his Shields colleague, Mr Bradley, added that failure to increase allowances would mean 'the calling out of the whole of the unemployed of the town to demonstrate at the town hall'. This meeting achieved a modest increase in relief scales, but as was soon the case with many other Boards in the country the weight of numbers claiming relief created budgetary pressures. A mass meeting in Jarrow secured a special Council meeting to organise relief work for the unemployed following a deputation to the Town Hall.[18]

The following month the Guardians received another deputation from the unemployed led by Labour Councillor George Linney and Alderman Dunlop, members of South Shields Council. Linney urged the Guardians to ignore the Ministry of Health and pay what was needed to alleviate hardship; if necessary they should risk prison as their counterparts in Poplar had done. Unsurprisingly the Board members were not convinced. Dunlop was equally unsuccessful in arguing that relief should cover the rent payments that unemployed tenants could not afford. The Guardians rejected what one claimed was 'a move by the Socialist party'.

Labour Party figures were active at meetings of the unemployed elsewhere that month, the police observing that a chief speaker was Alderman Dunlop, himself an unemployed shipyard driller and according to the police 'an extremist', who had been urging the unemployed not to pay their rent.[19]

By July 1922 the South Shields Guardians responded to their budget problems by introducing new and lower relief scales, prompting a demonstration by more than 2,000 unemployed from Jarrow and Hebburn outside their Board meeting. Guardians complained of a 'menacing attitude' but the Chief Constable felt that he 'cannot find much fault with their demeanour'. He suggested that the Guardians meet a deputation, or at least explain their decision in a 'conciliatory statement'; this they refused to do, but the Chief Constable persuaded the demonstrators to disperse, and the police paid for the tram fares of 200 women protestors back to Jarrow.

The next day however 'a very large body of men' had re-assembled, blocking the streets around the Board room in Barrington Street. Again the Guardians refused to meet a deputation and complained of intimidating behaviour; after a few hours the police drew batons and forced the crowd back to a half mile away to allow the Guardians to leave the meeting. Twenty four men from Jarrow and Hebburn were fined for obstruction or assaulting the police and two women were bound over to keep the peace. The chairman of the Guardians blamed 'market place agitators' for the disturbance, and the Chief Constable commented on what seems to have been the standard method of protest by the unemployed at this time: he wondered why they 'couldn't have a deputation without three or four thousand people there'. Unfortunately no details about the 'agitators' were given, although the private police report named the Newcastle Communist George Wheeler as a speaker. A few days' earlier police had used batons to clear a mass picket of strikers at St. Hilda Colliery. On that occasion Linney and Will Pearson had been speakers; described in the same report as a 'communists' these Labour councillors would presumably have held dual membership.[20] At this point it was possible to be a member of both the Labour and Communist Parties at the same time. By 1923 Jarrow was particularly hard hit, with a quarter of its workforce dependent on Guardians' relief. The Jarrow Labour Party and Trades Council were active in promoting open-air rallies and marches in the area, addressed by MPs calling for government work schemes at union rates.[21]

A National Movement

Similar protests to those described in this section were taking place around the country. Centres of the engineering industry in Coventry and Birmingham were involved as well as the heavy industry areas and the major ports. Therefore in April 1921 Unemployed Committees in London organised a national meeting to establish a National Unemployed Workers Committee Movement (NUWCM) to which all trades council unemployed committees were urged to affiliate. Two leading activists who were about to join the Communist Party, Wal Hannington in London and Harry McShane in Scotland, were appointed to organisational positions on the National Administrative Committee; it is unlikely that either of them realised that this would be their key political role for the next twenty years. The meeting agreed national aims:

1. To organise the whole of the unemployed for the removal of the cause of unemployment, i.e. the capitalist system, and the substitution of a system of Workers' Ownership and Control of Industry
2. Work, or full maintenance, for the unemployed and partially unemployed workers at Trade Union rates of wages
3. As a means of finding employment for the unemployed in the trades with which they are associated, the immediate putting into operation of the Trading Agreement with Russia, and the recognition of the Soviet Government
4. All Unemployed Committees shall make the fullest demands of the local authorities, and Government Boards, such as will ensure full maintenance of all unemployed and their dependents.

Further meetings that year agreed a scale of benefits and relief payments as a national standard, free from local variations. These were: 36s a week for man and wife, 15s for young single people and 30s for older single people; 5s a week for each child, up to 15s a week for rent and a generous weekly allowance for coal or gas. How did these scales compare with what was actually being paid? In the North East Chester le Street Guardians were reputed to pay the most. In 1925, shortly before a reduction, these were 30s a week for a man and wife, 15s for single adults, 5s per week for each child to a maximum of 50s per week per family, the rent to be paid and a half of the relief to be 'in kind'. In contrast Sunderland Guardians were reputed to pay the lowest scales. Again in 1925, shortly before a small increase, they paid 15s a week for man and wife, 10s a week for single adults, 3s for each child. Any payments towards rents were discretionary; all payments would be reviewed every month and were paid strictly on a loans basis. As a police report noted, 'As the various unemployed committees link up they are becoming aware of the differing scales of relief, which gives rise to recrimination'. Recrimination in turn gave rise to campaigning when it was seen that other areas had improved their provision after lobbying.[22]

National assemblies also committed the NUWCM to assist workers in dispute through picketing and working against strike-breaking; asserted the intention to resist evictions, and pledged support to Labour candidates who supported the movement's demands. A movement newspaper, *Out of Work*, later *New Charter*, was published and at one point claimed sales of 40,000. Like the NUWCM National Administrative Committee base in London this was funded through member subscriptions and union donations. Both fluctuated in the coming years so that staffing and certainly a regular publication were both sporadic.

The NUWCM aimed to keep the organised unemployed as a part of the main and not the margins of the labour movement and thus sought to affiliate to the Trades Union Congress. This was turned down but the TUC did agree to joint working with the NUWCM and supported the first National Hunger March to London at the end of 1922 into early 1923. During this period separate contingents were organised by the Unemployed Committees in their areas to march down to London for a lobby of Parliament and the Prime Minister. During October a contingent of seventeen left from Newcastle and South Shields, to be joined later by twenty-seven from Tyneside. This was out of a national total of two thousand on the March. They were principally skilled engineering and shipyard workers, miners and labourers and like their fellow marchers from the rest of the country they included many ex-servicemen. One leader who emerged was Sam Langley, a miner from Houghton le Spring who had served in the Royal Navy throughout the war; he was to be prominent in the local and national unemployed movement until the next war.

Their demands included the NUWCM scale of benefits as the national scale and as a charge on central government revenue rather than dependent on local ratepayers; also for public works at trade union rates. The movement had lobbied local government and the Boards of Guardians, and now it turned to those in whose power it was to address the national issues. Once in London, sustained along the way by combinations of labour movement efforts and attempts by workhouses, which they resisted, to treat them as pauper inmates, their lobbying achieved some limited success. Historians have noted that the government agreed to form a committee to examine responses to unemployment at this time. The expectations of the NUWCM were not exactly high; but they did believe that the publicity and focus they had generated had made it politically impossible for the government to make further attacks on the living standards of the unemployed before the election of 1924 returned a minority Labour government. In the North East the close links between the CP and the NUWCM had not gone unnoticed; one newspaper editorial called the March 'futile' and claimed the marchers 'are being used to advance the subversive policy of the communists'.[23]

The NUWCM was clearly an organisation well to the left of the labour movement from the outset. At its first national conference at the end of 1921 it was reported that the North East had 66 affiliated committees, the largest of any area outside London. By February 1922 a North East regional structure of sorts was also reported to be in place, with a district council covering Newcastle, Gateshead, Wallsend, South Shields, Felling and Sunderland. Apparently seven members of the council of twelve were Communists. It is likely, as will be shown, that these structures could come and go along with the size and composition of the movement itself. One of the few reports of how a local organisation was intended to function comes from when Sunderland Trades Council and Labour Party established an Unemployed Workers Committee in 1925. Members were to be organised in ward groupings 'for political and financial purposes'; meetings would be held at Sunderland Town Moor on Monday afternoon and the West Park on Fridays; the branch would have a full Committee, and Executive Committee; affiliate to the Trades Council and Labour Party and send delegates to it; and be affiliated to the NUWCM.[24]

Sunderland: Agitation, Riot and Aftermath

By the middle of 1921 conditions in Sunderland seem to have been particularly desperate, so much so that in the April Sunderland Police had organised soup kitchens for out-of work families. Unemployment was most keenly felt in the shipyards – output in 1921 was half of that of the previous year – and particularly grating for the skilled men who had earned high wages during the war. The local NUWCM branch leader was Jimmy Lenagh, an Irish-born Communist and an unemployed shipyard plater; he was assisted by George Wheeler, an engineering lathe turner with a full-time regional role in the Communist Party.

The first week of August 1921 saw the start of a series of actions in the town, generally beginning with a rally in the West Park followed by marches and deputations to the Board of Guardians, the Mayor and the Town Hall. Lenagh was almost invariably one of the speakers and he is remembered as highly effective in this role. An interesting aspect of the Sunderland agitations in this summer and autumn is their regular, almost daily occurrence and the building of a momentum leading to a serious clash with the police in the town centre.[25]

In that week Lenagh led a demonstration from the West Park to the

Town Hall ('as done on several previous occasions') only to find that the Mayor, Councillor Walter Raine, was absent. He then led the demonstration to the Mayor's home in nearby Thornhill Park, where Councillor Raine discussed unemployment issues with them for an hour; despite the 'running accompaniment of questions, jeers and abuse' he did not apparently feel intimidated although Mrs. Raine later complained about the state the garden had been left in. The Mayor agreed to meet a deputation the following day. This deputation (supported by 400 demonstrators, whom the police refused to group together so that traffic would not be blocked) felt that it had gained nothing. The next week Lenagh had a crowd of 10,000 in the West Park, although the press claimed that many were sightseers. During the subsequent march to the Town Hall trouble nearly broke out when some demonstrators objected to being controlled by police horses pressed against them; meanwhile the deputation pressed the Council meeting for an expansion of the public works schemes. More relief work schemes were also the main topic when Lenagh met the Council and the Board of Guardians later that month, but little assurance seems to have been given to him.[26]

In the first week of September, during a NUWCM week of action, very large crowds gathered for NUWCM meetings in the West Park; at one, which marched in to the town centre with banner slogans like 'Fight or Starve', a group of 300 attempted to enter the workhouse. The idea was that their maintenance there would cost the Guardians more than paying relief would, so the prospect of that could lever some payment. They were turned back by the workhouse master and the police. A contingent led by Lenagh split off to demonstrate at the home of the councillor who chaired the Board of Guardians. In similar circumstances to the Mayor the previous month, the councillor stood on his garden wall to discuss issues with Lenagh: relief should be paid more in cash than 'in kind', single men and unmarried couples should have equality of treatment with married couples over eligibility for relief. A meeting with an NUWCM deputation was arranged for the following day.[27]

Accounts of what happened on that next day could still cause controversy in Sunderland more than forty years later. As usual a very large crowd assembled in the West Park for the demonstration to accompany the deputation into the town centre. There, probably importantly, Lenagh and a deputation went into the Board of Guardians office and thus effectively left the crowd unoccupied and without leadership. According to Chief Constable Crawley this was the latest in a series of episodes where the town centre was dangerously blocked to traffic, and so the crowd had to be moved; at the same time though he claimed to have information that the march was to 'mature into a violent attack on property' most likely from 'the younger section of the unemployed who were violently hostile to the police'.

In the official version the police were facing an increasingly aggressive crowd intent on breaking through their lines, and when this escalated into a hail of stones and bottles a baton charge cleared the street, 'officers using their batons freely right and left'. A number of arrests were made leading to imprisonment and twelve demonstrators were treated in hospital.

The unemployed saw things differently. Their version was that the police were waiting for them in the town centre, keen to establish control over the streets after the continuous large demonstrations had taken them over. The baton charge was violent and unprovoked; the hurling of missiles at the police was done through frustration and self-defence. Sunderland Council Watch Committee received letters of complaint from a local engineering trade union branch but after an investigation it fully supported Chief Constable Crawley's action. The level of thoroughness of a police complaint inquiry at this time is suggested by the recollections of a Sunderland police sergeant who took part in the baton charge:

> There was an outcry from some of the labour fanatics afterwards and each of us employed in the charge had to write reports supporting the Chief Constable.[28]

There were repercussions for the Sunderland NUWCM leadership. At the end of September 1921 George Wheeler was arrested following a speech at one of the West Park meetings; a detective constable, 'under the cover of shrubbery at the side of the park' had noted down his words, which included encouragement for the unemployed to form a Workers' Defence Corps. The court was told that Wheeler had spent the previous two months as a full-time organiser for the Northern District of the Communist Party, and that a raid on his home in Heaton had produced a wealth of Communist literature and correspondence. Lenagh, called for the defence, tried to explain to the court that the references to 'struggle' and 'fight' in this literature were in relation to industrial matters and not an effort to foment civil war. This did not work, and Wheeler was gaoled for a month for sedition.[29]

Interestingly, in the same first week of October when Wheeler was sentenced the regional press carried a short series on how 'a sinister movement was afoot' to exploit unemployment and bring about 'a similar state of affairs to that in Russia'; but 'thanks to the excellence of the secret service the plot was quickly known to the police' and danger, for the time being, averted; nevertheless 'the leadership of the unemployed had fallen into the hands of men who were simply agitators'. The source of this report was clearly the intelligence services and it shows an attempt to marginalise the leadership of the unemployed movement and distance it from mainstream politics and the labour movement.[30]

Unemployed men in Sunderland, who looked as if they were forming a group on the street, even just meeting and talking socially, were now routinely moved on by the police; their mounted colleagues had earned the nickname 'Crawley's cowboys'. A month after the disturbances and Wheeler's arrest the Home Office was informed that 'Meetings at which formerly three, four or five thousand people attended have now sunk to one or two hundred'. The Chief Constable though had to report that he had had to change his method of obtaining information about the organised unemployed. It was not safe for his plain clothes men to monitor public meetings, even under cover, after the circumstances of Wheeler's arrest. As he said, 'Police have been handicapped by not having anyone at the meetings who would dare to enter the witness box in a prosecution for sedition. A detective constable was the last to do this but he was badly assaulted and thrown down the embankment at the railway line'. But if the Sunderland unemployed could exact retribution for Wheeler their ranks also contained collaborators, as the Chief Constable continued: 'We have, however, been exceptionally well served by informants…I am in touch with persons who appear to be in a position to give reliable information respecting the movements and intentions of the unemployed organisation'.[31]

This was not the end of the Sunderland unemployed movement by any means. Four days after the baton charge Lenagh and a deputation continued their meeting at the Board of Guardians where they secured what the press described as 'important concessions' from them. Relief would be paid a third in cash rather than in kind and would include a rent allowance; it would also be paid to single persons, although there was still an expectation that it was on a loan basis. At the end of 1921 and into early 1922 the Chief Constable had to report to the Home Office that 'the extremist section of the unemployed is active' and that 'communists are making progress among the 20,000 unemployed in the borough'. As we have seen three years later an NUWCM branch was re-established by the Trades Council and Labour Party, and Lenagh himself continued to play an active role with the Sunderland unemployed movement at least until the early 1930s.[32]

Newcastle

Towards the end of September 1921 James Cameron, a Communist and unemployed engineering worker, chaired a rally of 1,000 unemployed in the

Palace Theatre in the Haymarket, Newcastle city centre. This followed, to a large extent, the pattern of other unemployed agitations in the region at this time but it also reveals some interesting political tensions in the unemployed movement. Cameron told the meeting that it was time the unemployed 'asserted their authority' as had been done in Sunderland, London and Liverpool, a reference to the large demonstrations that had recently taken place. He urged them to organise a demonstration to demand work or full maintenance, and to remember that the only real solution to unemployment was the end of capitalism, a point repeated by Labour Councillor Hurst. This apparently led to some protests from the floor about 'politics' and criticism of Cameron for distributing Communist literature. Jack Cogan, the Gateshead unemployed organiser who was an Independent Labour Party activist, claimed that he had been trying to unite the unemployed groups in Newcastle and Gateshead 'but had been boycotted because he was not a Communist'. This point will be discussed later, but in any event the meeting agreed a committee of twelve, chaired by Cameron, and to hold a demonstration and deputation to the Board of Guardians.[33]

After at least two other public rallies in the Haymarket addressed by Cameron and Councillor Oliver, and a Labour Party mass meeting addressed by local MPs, another rally at the Palace Theatre agreed the demands to be put to the Guardians. These were for relief scales in line with those advocated by the NUWCM, and for absolutely no payments to be on a loans basis. The Guardians though voted by a substantial majority in favour of only slightly increased scales with a limit to how much would be paid 'in kind'. At a report back meeting the next day the mood was aggressive: 'Comrade McNamara' supplied Cameron with the names of the Labour Guardians who had voted against the demands and J. Thompson proposed repeated deputations to the Guardians until they had satisfaction. During early and mid-October demonstrations of between 500 and 600 people took place in the city centre in support of 'immediate work or adequate maintenance', against relief loans, against public works that did not pay the union rate, and pledging mass action to resist evictions. Their demands though met little success. According to the press 'Comrade Charlton' denied that 'Communists were trying to capture the unemployed in Newcastle' and Cameron, probably their leading example, called on the movement to use 'legitimate and constitutional methods'. This was around the time of Wheeler's arrest in Sunderland, and in the context of widespread arrest of local Communist leaders around the country, and so possibly Cameron was trying to distance himself from possible criminal charges.[34]

Six months later in March 1922 however less constitutional methods were employed. The Newcastle tramwaymen were on strike and the NUWCM sought solidarity with them when they lobbied the Guardians. According to the police report:

On March 3rd about 1,500 of the Newcastle unemployed, headed by the band of the tramwaymen on strike, marched to the offices of the Guardians who received a deputation headed by a local communist named Cameron: the deputation carried into the Boardroom a banner bearing skull and cross bones and a few war medals: the demands of the National Administrative Council of the Unemployed were put forward. After the deputation had withdrawn the Board agreed to hold a special meeting on the following Monday: the crowd outside had meanwhile attempted to force an entrance, and had thrown bottles, stones and other missiles at the police, three of whom were injured. Several of the unemployed were under the influence of drink and the police were eventually forced to use their truncheons: some windows were broken, several persons were arrested for being drunk and disorderly and two, G.R. Price and W. J. Dadswell, were subsequently charged with endeavouring to disturb the public peace by inciting others to riot.

The unemployed had a different version, although it is the case that a number of shop windows in the Bigg Market area of the city centre were smashed. Cameron denounced unprovoked police attacks on the unemployed, described the injuries they had sustained and made unsuccessful demands for an inquiry. For much of that month joint demonstrations were held in Newcastle between the striking tramwaymen and NUWCM branches. In one case, according to the police:

On March 16th about 3,000 Gateshead unemployed joined the Newcastle unemployed in a demonstration, about 10,000 people including the tramwaymen on strike paraded the streets of Newcastle and after a short halt at the Guardians offices were addressed by J.E. Cameron at the Town Moor: no disorder occurred but my correspondent states that it would have needed very little persuasion to induce the men to attack the Guardians' offices or any other public property.[35]

Over the next two years the Newcastle Guardians were continually pressed to increase relief scales, a pressure they resisted despite lobbying from the local Labour MPs and others. This Board consistently had the smallest left-wing representation at this time and seem to have been the most persistently reluctant to increase relief scales.

The Newcastle NUWCM found other opportunities to show their commitment to trades union values. Claimants were obliged to collect evidence from employers that they had sought work from them in order to qualify for benefits; this was the 'genuinely seeking work' clause in the legislation. In March 1926 a group of 150 toured Newcastle together to meet this requirement and also demonstrate the futility of the exercise. They made a big point too of *not* visiting engineering works, in support of a lockout then in progress.[36]

Gateshead

As in North Shields the organisation of the unemployed was done by the trades unions and the Labour Party, which in Gateshead seems to have been considerably stronger. In response to the severe recession the trades council organised an Unemployed Workers Committee and by 1921 the *Newcastle Journal* reported that it had at least 1,200 members on its books, many of whom had no income at all. In April 1921 the Mayor of Gateshead agreed to chair a meeting between the Council, the local Tory MP and the Unemployed Workers Committee in the Town Hall. A speaker from the packed audience told them, 'amid cheers' that 'we followed the flag in 1914 but we're following a different flag now.' A number of unemployed ex-servicemen denounced the cost of the Gateshead war memorial compared to the pittance their families were now forced to live on. The audience agreed a resolution urging the Council to 'put into practice all possible means to alleviate the unemployment problems in the town and protest at the criminal policy of the government'. The message was repeated a month later when 'a large number of the unemployed packed the Council Chamber' to hear their delegates lobby the Council.[37]

In September 1921 what the *Newcastle Journal* described as an 'imposing demonstration' of 1,600 unemployed workers was held outside the Board of Guardians' Office on Prince Consort Road. Standing in ranks 8 deep, their banners included the slogan: '1914- Your King and Country Need You. 1921- Nobody Needs You'. Unemployed ex-servicemen were also to the fore that same month at a mass meeting in the Town Hall, 'an impressive scene' where the Council again agreed to hear from the unemployed. The Unemployed Committee Secretary told them that 'the heroes of 1914 are now on the scrap heap … you are playing with fire' and his colleague told the Councillors that '… many of you own the slums we live in'.[38]

Meetings like these passed resolutions calling on the Board of Guardians to implement higher benefits scales, on the Council to establish public works at trade union rates to relieve unemployment, and press the government to take over unemployment benefit as a national charge rather than a charge on local authority rates. Special government action was needed for the areas of high unemployment, but before Labour took control the Council did establish a distress fund (organised with the Unemployed Workers Committee) and extended free school meals for needy children to week-ends and school holidays.[39]

These September demonstrations appear to have taken place during a week of action called for by the National Unemployed Workers' Committee Movement. The scale of the response in the North East is illustrated in the table below, extracted from the Home Office Report to the Cabinet:

NUWCM Week of Action September 1921 – Numbers of Demonstrators

6th	Southwick	500
7th	Gateshead	1,500
7th	Southwick	300
7th	Sunderland	3,000
8th	Gateshead	1,500
8th	Sunderland	3,000
8th	West Hartlepool	600
9th	Gateshead	2,000
9th	Southwick	100
9th	Sunderland	3,000
12th	Sunderland	2,000
12th	North Shields	1,500

(Compiled from Home Office Report to Cabinet 15 September 1921 -National Archives CAB/24/128/123)

This indicates a total of 19,000 people on the streets, although obviously there is double counting because the same individuals would have attended different demonstrations in their towns. By way of comparison the same source states that during the same week Glasgow and Edinburgh together saw a total of 8,500 demonstrators while Cardiff and Tredegar saw 9,800.

In Gateshead the chairman and key organiser of the Unemployed Workers Committee, Jack Cogan, was definitely in touch with the NUWCM network by 1923 when he sought to contact 'like-minded comrades' through *Out of Work*. The paper had commented on the Gateshead agitation two years earlier. Cogan himself was an engineering worker and

AEU branch chair, an ILP activist and in the early 1920s an unsuccessful candidate for Labour in the Council and Board of Guardians elections. The secretary of the Committee, Alec Fullerton, was a Communist. There were, as was suggested earlier, close links between the Gateshead and Newcastle activities, or as the police put it 'George Wheeler and other Newcastle communists have aggravated the situation by participating in Gateshead meetings'. A few days after the disturbances in Newcastle in March 1922 the Gateshead Unemployed Committee organised a march to the Guardians about relief scales, a demonstration in which Newcastle unemployed took part; there was no attempt to break the police cordon, a move supported by the unemployed at a mass meeting later at the local 'speakers' corner', Windmill Hills. Cogan told them that any such effort would have given the Chief Constable the excuse he was looking for 'to break their organisation'. It would have been for intervention like these that the Labour Party had claimed that it was 'in good measure due to the advice of Cogan and his colleagues on the Unemployed Committee' that there had been such 'good order' among the Gateshead unemployed.[40]

There was some history here. In December 1921 the Chief Constable had refused to allow any more people than the actual deputation from the Unemployed Committee into the Town Hall, being obviously uneasy about the frequent large gatherings. The Committee protested to the Council Watch Committee that this was 'a class bias in all its naked brutality', the Chief had 'taken unfair advantage of his position' and they claimed their right to make their appeals 'without being deferred by bluff or threats'. The Council supported their Chief Constable after he 'read out extracts from some reports he had received as to the methods adopted and pursued by the leaders of the unemployed'. Nevertheless demonstrations continued, as we have seen. Newcastle and Gateshead Guardians had imposed supplementary poor rates to cope with the demands of the miners' lockout and the recession meant that demands for relief continued to grow after it. Increases in relief scales were not thought to be feasible politically and when the Ratepayers Association effectively took control of the Guardians in 1922 they were accused of trying to turn down as many needy claims as possible simply to save money.[41]

Interestingly although the Gateshead Committee (like the others in the region) appears to have been dominated by male skilled workers, reflecting the local employment characteristics, there is evidence that the movement was not purely a men's movement. In 1923 the NUWCM women's organiser Lily Webb reported that, '200 women, members of the NUWCM, have formed a women's section in Gateshead. A distress fund has been formed after organising a deputation to the town hall. Women here are taking up their own labour exchange and board of guardians cases'. This deputation - Mrs. Kirk, Mrs. James and Mrs. Coffey - to the Council from the Unemployed Workers Committee (Women's Section) had raised issues about the families of out of work men and out of work young women who were ineligible for benefits. In fact the Council's response – to refer the points raised to the existing Distress Fund Committee – was criticised by Labour Party branches as just a way of shelving the issue. This is one of very few references to the work of a NUWCM Women's Section in the region and unfortunately it is tantalisingly brief.[42]

This women's deputation was one of a regular series that the Gateshead Unemployed Committee sustained both before and after Labour gained control of the Council in November 1923. For example delegations in February 1923 had pressed for expansions in public works, and for trade union rates to be paid, and for extensions to free school meals provision given the evident malnourishment of children in the town. A deputation from those on public works schemes successfully lobbied the Labour Council over being paid trade union rates. This was an issue because the Ministry of Labour, who made grants available to Councils for works schemes specifically to relieve unemployment, made it a condition that only three-quarters of the normal wage rate should be paid. This cost reduction measure obviously caused resentment amongst the unemployed and trades unionists. Therefore a local campaigning point for the Unemployed Committees was the rate for the job, unfortunately at further costs to the rates where Councils such as Gateshead and Chester le Street supported them.[43]

Once Labour took control in Gateshead it did make efforts to implement the programmes of the local and national movements. Drastic cuts in funding for school meals by the Board of Education meant that free school meals for necessitous children had to be funded through the rates: this was done, the numbers of free meals rising from 80 to 400 a day within a year. Public works such as a council house building programme were expanded, the Unemployed Committee ensuring that trades union rates were paid. These projects all had to be charges on the rates (and thus, apart from anything else, limited) because central government funding was either absent or completely inadequate given the scale of need.[44]

Issues

This is to some extent a map of the active unemployed movements in the region in the early 1920s. One characteristic is shared by all, be they politically moderate such as in North Shields or as elsewhere in the region on the radical left. This is openness: representatives and delegates reported back to the public meetings from which their mandate was derived. The next chapter examines some other key themes. These are activity such as advocacy with claimants and tenants; electoral work and political relationships; the role played in the movement by ex-servicemen and their political responses; and the involvement of women in the unemployed committees. Finally the role played in 1926 by the NUWCM and other groups in the preparations for the General Strike and the miners' lockout are discussed in detail.

Notes

1   This point is explored in one of the few local studies of the 1920s, John Tanner: 'The Only Fighting Element of the Working Class? Unemployed Activism and Protest in Sheffield 1919-24', *Labour History Review* Vol.73 No.1 April 2008 p. 145-167.

2   Durham Miners Association Executive Circular 1 April 1921(GLS); *North Mail* 31 March and 1 April 1921; Peter Lee: 'A Lockout not a Strike ', *North Mail* 5 April 1921.

3   *Sunderland Echo* 8 April 1921; *North Mail* 9 April 1921.

4   *North Mail* 22 April and 18 April 1921.

5   *Sunday Sun* 22 May and 12 June 1921; *North Mail* 22 April 1921.

6   *Annual Report of the Medical Officer of Health for the County of Durham* 1921 (Durham: Durham County Council 1922).

7   *Chester le Street Chronicle* 22 July and 19 August 1921; *North Mail* 3 April and 5 April 1922; *Newcastle Daily Chronicle* 4 May 1921.

8   *Gateshead Labour Party and Trades Council Circular* No.55 15 April 1921 (GLS).

9   *Shields Daily News* 10 September 1921.

10   *Shields Daily News* 13 September 1921.

11   *Shields Daily News* 16 and 17 September 1921.

12   *Shields Daily News* 17 September 1921.

13   *Shields Daily News* 23 and 30 September 1921.

14   *Shields Daily News* 30 September 1921.

15   *Blaydon Courier* 15 October 1921.

16   *Blaydon Courier* 24 September, 22 and 29 October 1921; *Newcastle Daily Journal* 14 October 1921.

17   *North Eastern Daily Gazette* 11 May 1921; *Newcastle Daily Journal* 9 September 1921.

18   *Shields Daily News* 8 September 1921.

19   *Shields Daily Gazette* 6 October 1921; Home Office Report to Cabinet 27 October 1921 (NA: CAB/24/129/129).

20   *Shields Daily News* 14 and 15 July 1922; Home Office Reports to Cabinet 20 July and 24 August 1922 (NA: CAB/24/138/164 and CAB/24/138/169).

21   *North Mail* 7, 10 and 24 September 1923.

22 On the formation and the early days of the NUWCM see Wal Hannington: *Unemployed Struggles 1919-1936* (London: Lawrence and Wishart 1977) and *Never on Our Knees* (London: Lawrence and Wishart 1967); Richard Croucher: *We Refuse to Starve in Silence: A History of the National Unemployed Workers' Movement 1920-1946* (London: Lawrence and Wishart 1987); on the local Guardians' scales *Sunderland Echo* 17 July and 10 September 1925 ; Home Office Report to Cabinet 20 October 1921 (NA: CAB/24/129/128).

23 *North Mail* 5 January 1923. On the first National Hunger March see Peter Kingsford, *The Hunger Marchers in Britain 1920-1940* (London: Lawrence and Wishart 1982).

24 Home Office Reports to Cabinet 1 December 1921 and 2 February 1922 (NA: CAB/24/131/133 and CAB/24/132/141); *Sunderland Echo* 28 July 1925.

25 Information given by Mr Archie Potts, whose father Ernest Potts took part in the unemployed movement in Sunderland at this time.

26 *Sunderland Echo* 5, 11 and 20 August 1921.

27 *Shields Daily Gazette* 7 September, *Sunderland Echo* and *Shields Daily News* 9 September 1921.

28 Minutes of the Corporation of Sunderland Watch Committee 15 August and 12 September 1921 (TWAS: C.B. SU/65/30); *Sunderland Echo* 9 September 1921; James Conlin: *Symbol of Glass: The History of the Sunderland Borough Police Force* (Sunderland: James A. Jobling Ltd 1969 p. 75).

29 *Newcastle Daily Journal* 6 October 1921; *Sunderland Echo* 28 September, 5 October and 18 November 1921.

30 *Sunday Sun* 2 and 9 October 1921.

31 Information from Mr Archie Potts, from a recollection of his father Ernest; Minutes of the Corporation of Sunderland Watch Committee 12 September 1921 (TWAS: C.B. SU/65/30).

32 *Sunderland Echo* 13 September 1921; Home Office Report to Cabinet 23 March 1922 (NA: CAB/24/134/148).

33 *Newcastle Daily Journal* 21 September 1921.

34 *Newcastle Daily Journal* 28 and 29 September, 4, 5 and 15 October 1921.

35 Home Office Reports to Cabinet 9 and 23 March 1922 (NA: CAB 24/134/146 and CAB/24/134/148); *Newcastle Daily Journal* 6 and 7 March 1922; Minutes of the Corporation of Newcastle on Tyne Watch Committee 31 March 1922 (TWAS: MD/NC/274/14).

36 *Newcastle Daily Journal* 9 March 1926.

37 *Newcastle Daily Journal* 1 and 2 September 1921; *Gateshead Labour Party and Trades Council Circular* No.55 15 April 1921 (GLS).

38 *Newcastle Daily Journal* 1 and 8 September 1921.

39 *Gateshead Labour Party and Trades Council Circular* No 56 May 1921 (GLS).

40 *Out of Work* no 57 1923; *Gateshead Labour Party and Trades Council Circular* No 61 15 October 1921 (GLS); Home Office Report to Cabinet 26 January 1922 (NA: CAB/24/132/140; *Newcastle Daily Journal* 9 March 1922; *Gateshead Labour Party and Trades Council Circular* No 61 15 October 1921 (GLS).

41 Minutes of the County Borough of Gateshead Watch Committee 25 January and 17 February 1922 (TWAS: C.B. GA/57/14); *Gateshead Labour Party and*

Trades Council Circular No 84 September 1922 (GLS).

42   *New Charter* No.1 June 1923; *Gateshead Labour Party and Trades Council Circular* No.78 March 1923 (GLS).

43   *Gateshead Labour Party and Trades Council Circulars* No 77 February and No.78 March 1923 (GLS).

44   *Gateshead Labour Party and Trades Council Circulars* No.90 February and No.91 March 1924; *Gateshead Labour News* September and October 1924 (GLS).

Chapter Three

1921-1926 – ACTIVITIES AND ISSUES

Advocacy and Support

An appearance before a Guardians' Committee in defence of a claim or an appeal under the Poor Law was dreaded by unemployed people. As has been remembered:

> … they'd almost strip you naked … to draw from you all that they wanted. They were into your private affairs; it was just like, it was terrible going in front of these committees.

During the 1926 miners' lockout Labour Councillor Jack Kelly at Blaydon claimed too that 'men who had faced machine guns and death were afraid to face even members of the Board of Guardians'. This may have been an exaggeration for oratorical purposes but Kelly himself was a member of the Gateshead Board and would have witnessed how appearing before the Guardians was experienced by working-class people. These appearances must have assembled several nightmares all at once: the stress of poverty, the shame attached to the status of 'pauper', the indignity of having to endure the 'inquisitorial methods' of investigating claimants' circumstances. In addition claimants knew their fate to be largely at the discretion of Guardians and Relieving Officers and therefore they were in their power.[1]

As we have seen in North Shields, for example, a claimant's trade union could assist and act as an intermediary. This was the practice too with one of the region's biggest unions, the Durham Miners' Association, which in September 1921 was 'successfully handling claims for hundreds of miners'. Individual lodges took up claimant issues from members, and took cases for an entire colliery workforce to appeal at the Court of Referees and the Umpire. In Sunderland the Trades Council and Labour Party Unemployed Committee (affiliated to the NUWCM) addressed instances where 'unemployment relief was not being administered as it should be…the Committee would attend to the regulations and discover whether decisions relating to specific cases were legal or not'. It was aware that unemployed trade union members could find their membership lapsed if they stopped paying subscriptions because of financial pressures, and so urged constituent bodies to make lists of them to ensure they were helped if needed. In Gateshead too the Unemployed Committee took up practical issues such as 'in kind' vouchers being issued when shops were closed for two days – no small matter for people dependent on the vouchers for food – and liaised with the Trades Council and Labour Party about Guardians' decisions.[2]

In Sunderland and Gateshead the Trades Councils tried to ensure that their representatives on the Guardians and the Employment Committees operated as an organised group, voting the same way and supporting the same cases. Where claimants were dissatisfied with the behaviour or voting of these representatives – such as a case in Sunderland where one was said to be 'intimidating' – the people concerned were accountable to the Trades Council. Therefore although the NUWCM has justly earned a reputation for what is now called welfare rights advice and representation this was also within the scope of the mainstream trade union movement.[3] The question had been asked in North Shields about unemployed people who were not union members; their access to help from the union apparatus is less clear, a point to be borne in mind.

By 1923 the Communist Party paper *Workers Weekly* carried a regular column by 'A Communist Guardian', presumably a dual-membership activist, who gave advice on eligible claims under the Poor Law. The particular emphasis was on where Guardians had discretion over the administration of relief because it was obviously here that there was the most room for negotiation. This service must also have provided useful information about what had been granted in different parts of the country, something a national organisation was best placed to do. Support could be given for interviews at Employment Exchanges. In Newburn for example the Exchange was noted for harsh questions ('the trickiness of these questions gets men trapped') and so the NUWCM prepared a list of specimen answers to the likely questions, apparently with some success.[4]

Left-wing Guardians seem to have helped claimants too, partly through arguing their case at committee meetings and also with advice on how to arrange their claims. This was noticed by a Conservative Guardian in Newcastle[5] in 1926. In his experience:

… many recipients of relief understand all the moves on the board, together with the fact that they have the full help and support of a certain number of Socialist Guardians, whom, I make bold to say, help them to an extent which is tantamount to conspiracy against the ratepayer.

The organised unemployed movement developed a wider focus than agitations and claims work. Charlie Woods, a miner from Blaydon, was a First War veteran who joined the CP in 1922 and, three years later, the NUWCM. He had this comment about the early days of the unemployed organisation:

Because of the widespread poverty the movement covered a wide sphere of operation, it didn't just confine itself to demonstrations about relief and unemployment, it covered every aspect of what was affecting poverty-stricken families. Our support came from the poorest areas.

There are certainly examples of the NUWCM trying to deal with 'every aspect'. In Gateshead in October 1922 a crowd of about 500 unemployed blocked off a street and prevented court bailiffs from carrying out 'distraint', seizing household goods to cover rent arrears. According to the police report there was no disorder and 'a settlement was subsequently reached, enabling the family to retain its possessions'. In Newcastle in September 1923 a family found by the NUWCM to be living in a cellar were 'squatted' in a house until activists could arrange for them to take over the tenancy officially. This apparently had been achieved when all 'constitutional' methods had failed, a Tenants' Defence League formed and a 'more active' unemployed committee recruited. It is not possible to estimate how widespread these actions were but it does suggest that some imaginative approaches were taken to the issues thrown up by the poverty of the area.[6]

'Constitutional' methods were not ignored. Towards the end of 1925 the Chester le Street District Council of the NUWCM comprised branches in Annfield Plain, Tanfield, Burnhope, Stanley, Sacriston and Waldridge as well as Chester le Street itself. The Secretary, Jack Liddle, wrote to members of the Labour Council to protest at the eviction of an NUWCM member: '…you stand condemned as reactionaries…no class conscious man or body of men would or should lean towards evicting any members of his own class, not under any consideration or circumstances'. A month later, when the District Council appeared to have a new committee, R. Ward asked for a meeting with councillors to discuss a family of ten living in two rooms, whose name had 'been drawn in the ballot for a council house' but rejected because they owed some rates. As he put it, '…very few people who are miners will be able to show a clear rent book these last few years'. However even this more diplomatic approach did not achieve a result, even though the Council did invite the NUWCM to send delegates to a conference it was organising on unemployment.

Early in 1926 a new Chester le Street District Secretary, Mark Owen, wrote on behalf of NUWCM members threatened with eviction. It was 'not their fault they are in arrears, the fault lies with those who are preventing them from earning the wherewithal to pay the same'. Some were trying to pay their arrears, albeit by small amounts, so could the Council 'withdraw these harsh conditions, and so help to ease the already great mental burden they have?' A month later yet another District Secretary, W. Bailey, told the Council that low scales of relief meant that people in Council houses could not pay their rent. Could the Housing Committee find a way to help? In all these cases the Council was sympathetic but unwilling to change its procedures or make exceptions. Although the brief Labour Government of 1924 had launched some council house building schemes the projects were far too few to even approach the scale of need for re-housing in the North East. This NUWCM District is therefore an example of engaging with the politics of rationing as Councils struggled with criteria for the allocation of the resources they had. Whereas Wal Hannington has supplied exciting accounts of the 'unconstitutional' methods used to good effect by the unemployed the fact remains that more mundane approaches were also in use, and neither could be guaranteed to work.[7]

Nevertheless 'looking after the rights of the unemployed in a perfectly constitutional fashion' was the stated aim of the Unemployed Workers' Committee established by Sunderland Trades Council and Labour Party in 1925, and affiliated to the NUWCM. Similarly the Gateshead Trades Council and Labour Party contrasted its own 'peaceful and constitutional methods' with those of the Communist Party. Its solution to the large number of hardship cases rejected by the Guardians, brought to it by the Unemployed Committee, was to point out that 'the scales and rules of the Board of Guardians can only be altered by a new Board of Guardians', meaning a Labour majority at the elections. The use of Poor Law relief during the 1921 lockout had underlined the importance of the political control of the Guardians' policies.[8]

Electoral Activity

As democratically elected bodies the Boards, in the eyes of both the organised unemployed and the organised ratepayers, were there to be influenced. This was especially true where there were Labour members who could operate as a group or even as a majority. Charlie Woods claimed that in this early phase the emphasis was on influencing Labour:

> The idea that the NUWCM should get its own members elected to the Boards didn't come up at this time. We pressurised the Labour members and the Labour authorities as best we could, with deputations and meetings…at election times the unemployed movement provided the leg-workers for the canvassing during the election campaign. You had questions for Labour candidates at the hustings, efforts to get a commitment from them and deputations to candidates during elections over issues affecting the unemployed. These methods were used with some measure of effect at that particular time. [9]

His recollection may actually be a reference to council elections because at that time the left of the unemployed movement *were* standing in elections to the Guardians. By 1922 *Out of Work* was urging NUWCM contacts and 'suitable labour movement people' to stand, despite the legal handicap that people who had claimed relief within twelve months before their election could only attend and not vote at Guardians' meetings. Thus the police report about Sunderland in March 1922:

> Two communists, Alfred T. Wickham and Lewis Roberts, are standing for election to the Board of Guardians on April 3rd: the sixteen wards in the Borough would have been contested but for the fact that all the communists with the above exceptions have received poor relief.

Both these candidates ended bottom of the poll, as did Joe McCue who had stood as the 'unemployed and workers' candidate' for the Sunderland Board in November 1921. In the 1922 Board elections in Newcastle George Wheeler, James Cameron and Henry Morrison stood not as Communists but 'in the name of the organised unemployed'. Only Cameron came within 100 votes of his opponent, Labour's Tom McCutcheon, to whom he pledged the support of the unemployed 'if he carries on the class struggle inside the Board'.[10]

A particular coup for the movement, or a section of it, must have been the election of Jimmy Lenagh to the Sunderland Board in July 1925. He had stood as a Communist at least once before, such as in 1923 when he was unsuccessful but nevertheless polled 500 votes to Labour's 30. The press noted that he was 'the first Communist Guardian' in the region (a few others, such as Alec Henry at Chester le Street, were dual membership

Communists standing for Labour) although Lenagh appears to have left the CP for the Labour Party not long afterwards.[11]

The programme these candidates would have put forward was partly local and pragmatic, partly national and radical. They pledged to 'to serve the cause of the workers in the administration of relief and end the control of these institutions by your class enemies'. This meant NUWCM relief scales, and the end of the workhouse and its rituals. Unemployment relief would be a national charge on the Treasury and administered through working-class organisations like the trade unions. They were also clear that ending unemployment would require the overthrow of capitalism by the new socialist social order.[12]

Charlie Woods was accurate when he recalled that unemployed movement activists sought to gain support for their programme from Labour candidates. For example when Labour met to choose its candidates for the Chester le Street Board elections in 1922 the NUWCM sent a deputation. They compared the relief scales paid by this Board unfavourably with others in the region and urged the adoption of the NUWCM proposed national scale. A Labour Councillor and lodge secretary Jack Gilliland, responding to a colleague's call to 'feed the kids and damn the rates', explained that the proposed scales would bankrupt the Guardians. His position on this was to change during the 1926 lock-out but for the time being he was not supporting the unemployed movement's demands. In Gateshead the accountability of elected or prospective representatives to the unemployed movement seems to have been expected and not just confined to the local elections. Although in early August 1921 only a minority of the Guardians were Labour they were still obliged to defend their record at the open-air meetings organised by the ILP, Labour or the Unemployed Committee at Windmill Hills. This was Gateshead's Speakers' Corner and the assembly point too for the demonstrations to the Town Hall and the Boards of Guardians' office. In May 1921 the unemployed were said to be 'highly active' for Labour in the local elections, attending meetings where they marched in with their banners. Election literature too featured the candidates' records on work with the unemployed movement.[13]

However Gateshead Labour said it could not support certain positions 'put forward by a section of the unemployed' (i.e. the NUWCM) when it was selecting candidates for the Board of Guardians election that same year. The reason given was one that was to surface on several occasions during the decade, and that was the differential between the proposed relief scales and local earnings. The low levels of earnings in the town were being exacerbated by short-time working and to adopt the NUWCM scales would, some trade unionists feared, mean there would be no financial difference between work and unemployment. One of the selected candidates was the ILP organiser of the unemployed, Jack Cogan; clearly in practice NUWCM activists were standing on Labour programmes rather than that of the unemployed movement. As Charlie Woods also put it, 'Despite some criticisms of its policies, and shortcomings, the general attitude of the unemployed and left movement towards the Labour Party was one of support, particularly during election campaigns'.[14]

In local authority elections Fred Lonie in North Shields captured a seat for Labour on Tynemouth Borough Council in November 1921; his role with the unemployed must have influenced his success, despite disparaging references in the press to his being an activist of 'the orange box type', a speaker at open-air meetings. Success was never certain, of course; in April 1922 the Ratepayers' Association 'swept the board at the expense of Labour' in the Gateshead Guardians elections. The consistently low polls in Board of Guardians elections in the region were a concern across the political spectrum.[15]

Inter-Party Relations

Fielding candidates at elections underlined the issue of relations with the Labour Party and its affiliated unions. In Newcastle in 1922 Wheeler and Cameron had stood 'for the organised unemployed' against Labour candidates; both were well-known Communists by now, active in a party that was seeking to affiliate to Labour. At the time they criticised Labour for standing against the unemployed movement but the following year they claimed to have reached an agreement with Newcastle Labour Party to avoid a clash of candidates. Certainly when Wheeler and Thomas Black stood, unsuccessfully, for the 'Unemployed Organisation' for the Guardians then there were no Labour candidates against them. An interesting example of co-operation occurred in September 1923 when Newcastle Board of Guardians received a deputation 'on behalf of the Labour Party, with its affiliated organisations, and the organisation of the unemployed'. Its members included MPs Arthur Henderson (then on a regional speaking tour), C.P. Trevelyan and David Adams. The other four members included two well-known local Communists, District Secretary John Tearney and the NUWCM Hunger March leader Sam Langley. According to the Communist version Arthur Henderson was extremely reluctant to take part in this but had eventually succumbed to Labour rank and file pressure. In any event the disorder of the previous year does not seem to have impeded this joint activity.[16]

The Communist Party urged unemployed committees to support Labour candidates who were 'prepared to back the unconstitutional revolutionary activity necessary to carry out the unemployed programme...the full powers of the Council must be used to reduce distress and unemployment, all the resources of local administration should be used to meet the demand for work or full maintenance at trade union rates...The excuse that their powers are limited cannot be admitted here. If necessary, these limitations must be broken through and the workers' representatives take their stand with those of Poplar.' In practice all this seems to have meant trying to move Labour as far as possible to the left over unemployment and relief issues.[17]

An example is South Shields, January 1926, when the NUWCM organised a conference attended by the local unemployed committees, three miners' lodges and five trade union branches, the CP, ILP, Labour Party and Trades Council. Labour Councillors proposed – led by Linney, as we have seen possibly a dual membership Communist supporting the NUWCM – but against dissent by others on grounds of practicality, to press several demands on the Labour group on the Board of Guardians and the Council Education Committee. These represented the position of the NUWCM: full implementation of the Feeding of Necessitous Schoolchildren Act, an increase in all relief scales with nothing taken into account, allowances for single people, and coal and gas allowances. Further, a resolution was carried in favour of establishing a joint standing committee of employed and unemployed delegates 'to co-ordinate the activity of the working class in South Shields'. Whereas the Communists reported that this was a victory for political joint working there is evidence that it was not so clear cut as they claimed. Labour Councillor Donnelly, clearly not on the left, complained that the resolution 'was a Communist tactic that he would never agree to. Communist tactics meant disruption in the Labour Party...The Workers Unemployed Committee wanted to run the town as far as Labour was concerned'. Mr W. Hall, the first secretary of the Birtley Committee and a 'Labour man' would have sympathised; when a meeting he had organised offered to send a telegram to the NUWCM annual conference he stormed out claiming 'you're all communists here!'[18]

The impact of the Labour Party decision in 1924 to ban Communists from participating in its affairs was bound to be felt in the unemployed movement, although the ban mainly gathered pace after the 1926 lockout. Before that in 1925, though, the TUC had blocked affiliation by the NUWCM. There was similar official antipathy to the Minority Movement, the Communist-inspired network of left activists in each industry who could be organised to press for militant policies and leaders. One early local example of the ban in action is the expulsion of Jimmy Lenagh from Sunderland Labour Party ('after several months of internal dissension') for being a Communist. This he denied, and he began to retaliate by standing as an 'unofficial socialist' in Council elections. In Lenagh's case this could well have been just an attempt by Sunderland Labour to get rid of a nuisance. Elsewhere it was noted that Birtley CP branch had not been allowed to join the Labour Party May Day procession there in 1925, and there were attempts to exclude Communists from Wallsend Labour Party too at this time. Nor were relations with trade union leaderships necessarily straightforward. When the Follonsby Lodge checkweighman and revolutionary George Harvey spoke to a mass meeting of unemployed miners at Heworth in November 1921 the local lodge officials refused to lend the meeting the colliery band because 'extremists' were speaking. This was an example, wrote Harvey, of 'the knock-kneed leaders' in the DMA lodges.[19]

The Labour Party itself held unemployed meetings. In November 1921 the Labour agent in Gateshead organised a 'large gathering of unemployed' in a rally at Felling to demand Council public works; two years later, Labour and the NUWCM organised a mass meeting of the unemployed which was claimed to be 'the largest indoor Labour meeting held in the Felling area'. Nevertheless, if police reports are accurate, when the NUWCM established a branch in Felling in 1924 and held open-air meetings in Victoria Square, the Labour Party began holding meetings there as well 'to rebut the arguments of the communists'. Apparently the close connection between the NUWCM and the CP was becoming an issue for Labour.[20]

What can be made of Jack Cogan's statement that he faced obstacles to uniting the Newcastle and Gateshead unemployed because he was not a Communist? Was this an example of the CP and the ILP, inevitably rivals for the leadership of the left, competing for position in the unemployed movement? This certainly seems possible but at the same time as we have seen there were, after these early Newcastle meetings at least, several examples of joint activity between the branches and between Cogan and his Communist colleagues.

Ex-servicemen

Another political factor was the role of unemployed ex-servicemen in the movement. Some early stirrings had been visible in April 1919 when the candidate of the Discharged and Demobilised Soldiers' and Sailors' Federation, Frank Mellor, was elected as one of the Birtley representatives to Chester le Street Board of Guardians. The DDSSF branch held several rallies in Birtley that summer and rented a room to provide advice sessions on war pensions and benefits. Politically they made it clear that they 'were not sympathetic to Bolshevism' but at the same time they refused to participate in peace celebrations in protest against unemployment among ex-servicemen and the 'parsimonious' treatment of their widows and dependents. Labour had just recently taken control of Durham County Council and, perhaps sensing a potential challenge to this position, Councillor and miners' lodge secretary Jack Gilliland urged the DDSSF to 'link up with the trade union party'. Some such organisations certainly did, for example the Gateshead branch of the Ex-Servicemen's Association affiliated to the Trades Council and Labour Party, in line with the policy of their parent body, and after 1921 their contingents were a regular feature in May Day marches.[21]

As we have seen the organised unemployed in Gateshead included a significant number of angry ex-servicemen. At the Town Hall meeting addressed by the local Conservative M.P, himself a former senior officer, a man who stated that he had served under the MP during the war told him:

Look at me. Wounded five times and gassed twice, no pension, and having to keep a wife and five kids on £1 a week. You're building a war memorial over the other side of the town. We ask for bread and you give us stones. Isn't there a big enough memorial already in the crosses for the Gateshead lads on the Ypres salient?

In Sunderland, anecdotally, the ex-service presence among the unemployed is shown in the verses they sang to the tune of a popular song of the time, mentioning national politicians:

What was it for? We won the war
You can ask Lloyd George and Bonar Law.
We beat the German, the Austrian and the Turk
That's why we're marching
Down and out of work [22]

If the organised unemployed movement brought ex-servicemen and socialist militants together the relationship was not necessarily an easy one. The DDSSF members in Birtley as we have seen were not sympathetic to what they saw as 'Bolshevism'. The socialists had a very high level of political awareness compared to the others, even if the ex-servicemen were angry about their current circumstances. A good number of the Communists would have been members of the various Marxist organisations that came together to form a new party in 1920-21. Many of these groups had opposed the war and some had aided war resisters and conscientious objectors. *The Communist*, the CP weekly paper, advertised meetings of former conscientious objectors, to which 'all anti-militarists, regardless of their position on the war', were invited. Similarly the Independent Labour Party included many who had actively opposed the war, and it always contained a resolutely pacifist current in its ranks. This may not have sat easily with an ex-serviceman for whom having 'done his bit' was now a matter of pride; nor with the very large number of bereaved families for whom it was a source of consolation. Post-war working-class attitudes to conscientious objectors could be forceful: in 1919 for example miners at Whitburn colliery near South Shields walked off their shift in protest at two former objectors starting work there even though the DMA had approved their employment. The colliery did not produce for a day and the men returned with an assurance that the conscientious objectors would be removed. Silksworth Colliery near Sunderland too had a similar situation. There is some evidence that this attitude persisted into the 1920s. In the Durham colliery village of New Brancepeth, normally a Labour stronghold apparently, a colliery manager standing as an 'independent' took an Urban District Council seat from them in January 1926. The defeated Labour candidate had been a conscientious objector and his opponent, an ex-serviceman, made an issue of this; among usual Labour supporters 'emotions ran high and several angry scenes were witnessed' during the campaign.[23]

In contrast for some early Communists and NUWCM members who had fought, the experience and the post-war situation was part of their radicalisation. This was certainly true for Charlie Woods in Blaydon and Alec 'Spike' Robson in North Shields, both of whom were army veterans. At least two other local Communists who were to become national figures as well as local leaders in the unemployed movement (Jimmy Ancrum from Felling and Sam Langley from County Durham) had served through the war in the Royal Navy. They would all now have been regarding the war as an imperialist exercise. The Communist leader of the Sunderland unemployed, shipyard worker Jimmy Lenagh, made the politics of this clear when he was asked about his own war record: 'I had nothing to fight for. The only army I am in is the working-class army, and it is the only one I intend to be in.'[24]

In Sunderland these tensions seem to have caused a split in the movement, and prompted some ex-servicemen to form another Committee. According to Lenagh this was the work of 'reactionaries' led by a Tory councillor; given that Tory MPs were trying to fund right-wing ex-servicemen's associations at the time this claim is not implausible. This rival organisation told the Sunderland Board of Guardians when their deputation argued for higher relief scales that they were not 'members of Lenagh's party'. It seems they had been angered by what they took to be disparaging references by a Communist speaker in the West Park to their 'comrades dead in France and Belgium'. Their plea of respectability was in vain however; the Board turned down their request for higher relief scales. At least one of this group's meetings in West Park, addressed by a town councillor who advised against 'demanding things' as a tactic, dissolved in disarray as the audience drifted to a rival meeting elsewhere in the park. Towards the end of 1921 police observers reported that 'Ex-Service men in Gateshead are endeavouring to organise a group to oppose the communists who have obtained control of the unemployed' although as we have seen they were unsuccessful. The ILP's Jack Cogan (probably a 'communist' in police parlance) remained in place, and so did the actual Communist Fullerton until his premature death in 1924.[25]

The point here is that although bitterness among ex-servicemen was very real it cannot be assumed that this translated into some homogeneous or coherent political radicalism. The ranks of the NUWCM in the early days clearly benefited both in numbers and emotional impact from unemployed war veterans in the region, but any further generalisations should be made with care.

Women

In 1921 the NUWCM National Conference agreed Lily Webb as Women's Organiser and the importance of building women's sections of the movement. Women were 'the majority of the population and so they should be in the majority of the class struggle'. However Wal Hannington's histories of the movement he led make no references to Lily Webb or the work of the women's sections in the 1920s, underlining the suspicion of one historian that their work was not exactly a priority for him. In any case in the North East employment outside the home after marriage was rare for women and the major employment opportunity was domestic service. This sector was neither unionised nor covered by the National Insurance legislation.[26]

As we have seen Lily Webb was in Gateshead for a period, probably because her husband, Maurice Ferguson, had a full-time role with the Communist Party on Tyneside at the time. Nevertheless for whatever reason the action in Gateshead described earlier - 'women taking up their own cases' - is a very rare reference in the region. There are one or two vaguer ones. In July 1923 Gateshead Trades Council and Labour Party was encouraging trade unions to take up places on the Local Employment Committees, including the separate Women's Employment Committee, where they were legally entitled to equal representation with the employers' representatives. This was a means to ensure a fairer hearing for cases of hardship. Otherwise there is the occasional reference to cases of married women with national insurance contributions being deemed ineligible to claim, and investigations into the legality of this. The Gateshead NUWCM Women's Section held street collections to raise money for unemployed families' children's' events in 1924 and 1925, thus showing that the Section was alive and active even if in humdrum capacities.[27] The NUWCM organising these events is an example too of a wide range of activity.

Women were seen as victims of unemployment, as was clear from the comments of the trade unionists in North Shields; they were the ones having to deal with the stigma of approaching shopkeepers with vouchers from the Guardians. Poor Law relief therefore affected their domestic role as household managers on two levels, having to organise the home on a significantly lower income and being in the front line when it came to being 'paupers'. As Labour's Mrs. Lilley from Hetton said, 'it's time the men faced the landlord and the tallyman and went to the pawnshop'. It was because of that role they could find a place in the movement rather than through being unemployed workers themselves.

In 1922 *Out of Work* strongly urged the involvement of women in NUWCM public events: '...they should take an active part in demonstrations. Children should be brought into the processions when the march is only of a short duration. So long as the authorities see no misery displayed they will hold back relief'. It is difficult to judge the balance between propaganda manipulation and a genuine aim of inclusion here, but women and children definitely took part in some of the marches in the North East at this time. For example in Sunderland in 1921, and South Shields and Jarrow in 1922, women were noticeable among the demonstrators, as they were also in Felling early in 1926. 'Mrs R.A.' from Gateshead thought that 'It's no use sitting at home. It is your duty as mothers and wives to stand shoulder to shoulder with your husbands and sons and take part in the fight'. This was, as historians have recognised, also the attitude largely taken by miners' wives during the lockouts: women seem to have supported their men, often in the conviction that the cause for which the union was fighting was their cause too.[28]

In the light of Charlie Woods' recollection about the movement taking on 'every aspect of what was affecting poverty-stricken families' there is another relevant consideration. In Chopwell Emmie Lawther – often given the ascribed status as 'the wife of' Steve Lawther of the militant Lawther family, but in fact a left Labour activist in her own right – was an organiser for the Workers' Birth Control Group in the 1920s. This had some success in getting policies on contraceptive services adopted by the Labour Party and Co-operative Women's Guilds. Phyllis Short from Chopwell recalled he own part in this, illustrating how for political activists like her it was part of the overall struggle:

> … we brought up the issue of family planning, some organisations, they wouldn't touch it with a bargepole, you certainly couldn't have mentioned it to my mother, she thought you'd get a disease doing that. We went all over County Durham, every Labour Party Women's Section and Co-op Women's Guild, and had meetings on the question of birth control. And we had some rough times. We had meetings with unemployed workers wives, got them interested in these sorts of things. Speakers included Dora Russell, Dora Cox, and Marjorie Pollitt. We used to have discussions about this. We fought for the Councils to take this up. We sowed the seed for all the help they get now.[29]

In the North East the message of the women activists among the organised unemployed was for women to become involved, to take part, and this was to persist as a theme until the outbreak of the next war in 1939.

The 1926 Lock-Out Approaches

Government subsidy to the coal owners was due to expire in 1926; the left and the miners' unions knew that the employers would respond by wage cuts and increased hours to make up the difference. A major dispute throughout the British coalfield was likely if not imminent, and the implications for relief issues were well understood by the left in the North East. In July 1925 the Labour members of Houghton-le-Spring Guardians declared that 'we are going to see that our class is fed'; Sunderland Unemployed Workers' Committee predicted additional needs because of 'the forthcoming mining lockout'. In early August 1925 Labour members of the Gateshead Board of Guardians, speaking at an outdoor meeting, made it clear that 'the rates will be going up' and that they would defy the law if necessary so that 'the people they represent would be fed irrespective of whether there was a trades dispute or not'; if the coal owners were going to use the starvation weapon they 'will use the Board of Guardians weapon and beat them at their own game'.[30]

In the North East some collieries were out several months in their own local disputes before the 1926 lockout began. The case of the five collieries of the Consett Iron and Steel Company is a well-known example, the Harton Colliery in South Shields less so. In both the tactics of the NUWCM were visible.

In August 1925 during the Harton Coal Company lockout another Lawther, Andy, was living in Marsden and assisting with the soup kitchen for children. In the 1960s he wrote a personal account of one mass admission to the workhouse action and it communicates some of the 'feel' of such a protest. The DMA provided a coal allowance for single men but the Guardians were refusing to provide them with any relief payments. 'I decided to call a meeting' he wrote,'… and went round the colliery houses rousing them all to attend'. About 100 single men then marched from Marsden to the Guardians office in South Shields to apply for admission to the workhouse. A deputation of three went in while the rest 'waited outside in an orderly fashion'. They had come to the wrong office and had to march again to Laygate. Along the way they met a Lodge official who was a member of the Board of Guardians and tried to enlist his support; he refused to join them because he had not had notice from the Lodge. The police had covered the Laygate office but 'everything was completely under control'.

They were given tickets for admission to the workhouse but due to the numbers they had temporary beds of blankets on the floor 'There was little sleep on the first night, which was spent talking and telling stories'. The breakfast was disappointing for many but there was a good meal the next day, 'the men certainly felt the benefits of the food'. During the day they formed up and marched to the Marsden Institute, and later marched back for the night. They were joined by additional contingents from Whitburn and South Shields, and collections were held to raise money for some extra comforts, like sugar for the porridge. The Miners Joint Board organised a 'mass demonstration' in support of their claim for outdoor relief for single men. Eventually after eleven days of this they were successful, the Board of Guardians undertook to provide relief payments, and 'wild scenes of jubilation' greeted the news. On the last night the men put on a concert, apparently revealing quite an array of talent, and both police and the workhouse master joined in. The workhouse master praised their good behaviour throughout. South Shields Board of Guardians knew that some outdoor relief would be cheaper than large-scale workhouse admissions and they did not expect this particular dispute to be long, although it had still not been settled by January. The relief payments were in the form of food vouchers, which were an improvement on nothing at all.[31]

Lawther seems to recount this tactic as his own initiative whereas in fact as a tactic, as we have seen, it had been tried before by the NUWCM in

Sunderland and Durham. He also claims that it was a unique action; its success here, certainly, does seem to have been unique.

During the same month, in Sunderland, miners' representatives were involved in the NUWCM deputation that argued for the adoption of their national relief scales at the Guardians' meeting. They only managed to secure a comparatively minor increase, at which Lenagh accused the other Board members of being 'the guardians of the rates not the poor'.[32]

Some of the Consett Iron Company collieries were in the area covered by the Lanchester Board of Guardians, and as was common legal practice the miners' wives and children were paid relief but not the men. A large public meeting was held in Leadgate in February 1926, and 'after speeches a number of men set off for Lanchester, amid cheers, to demand admission to the workhouse'. The following afternoon another contingent, 'some hundreds strong' from the nearby villages marched off too, 'the streets of Leadgate being crowded with people who gave the men a hearty send-off'. Once again a tactic of the organised unemployed movement was brought to bear. A number of the men later returned at the request of the leaders who reportedly felt that the situation was becoming difficult to handle. The workhouse was now full and with around 500 waiting.

The more traditional form of protest took place a week later, in an echo of the successful action carried out during the 1921 lock-out. 'Thousands of men and women…several contingents marching with bands and banners flying' assembled at the Lanchester Board of Guardians meeting convened to consider paying relief 'to men for whom work was available'. This crowd displayed 'admirable fortitude and patience' standing outside in the cold and rain for several hours and remaining good-humoured. Inside the Board debated and heard a deputation led by the Lodge Secretary Jack Gilliand. He argued their case and added that the Board was not acting in the interests of the poor but in the interests of the Consett Iron Company, which he claimed had been lobbying them. The Board decided to continue with its current policy in order to avoid a legal confrontation with the Ministry of Health; however, it would instruct relieving officers to look sympathetically at individual cases of hardship.[33]

As the autumn of 1925 drew into early 1926 there were other examples of the left preparing the ground for this site of struggle against the 'starvation weapon'. When the Labour Chester le Street Board reduced relief scales following government pressure in January 1926, the Birtley Unemployed Organisation circulated a leaflet stating, 'Your scale of relief has been attacked and reduced…have Moderates succeeded where Labour reigns?… are the Guardians fighting your battles as they should?' The Birtley organisation organised a delegate conference at the end of January in the Co-op Hall, made up of miners' lodges, trade union branches and 'working-class political bodies'. Delegates agreed a new Committee 'more representative of the unemployed' and criticised the failings of those Guardians who had been 'sent there to look after their own people'.[34] This new Committee contained local Communists such as Alec Henry and Billy Hall as well as the ILP's Anthony Bolam, and it was from this meeting that the 'Labour man' W. Hall had stormed out.

In October 1925 the NUWCM organised 'some hundreds of unemployed', contingents from Wallsend, Blyth, Dudley and Annitsford – all, significantly, mining towns and villages – in a march to the Tynemouth Board of Guardians. They were joined by the North Shields Unemployed Committee. This was not affiliated to the national body but obviously willing to support this action despite the Blyth contingent singing the *Internationale*. Their deputation included a Labour Council candidate and it pressed for an increase in relief scales to bring Tynemouth into line with Gateshead and Chester le Street. This, for a non-Labour Board, was optimistic to say the least but the deputation did secure an increase, and refreshment and fares home for some of the demonstrators. It is to the credit of the deputation that they achieved an increase despite protests to the Board of Guardians shortly afterwards by both the Ministry of Health and all the prominent local ratepayers. At the end of March 1926, nearly on the eve of the General Strike, local NUWCM groups tried again to secure an increase from the Tynemouth Guardians only to be told that its standing orders did not permit a revision to relief scales within six months of an earlier revision.[35]

At the same time Gateshead NUWCM was less successful and exposed a division in its Labour support. Again at the end of March 1926 the Gateshead Guardians reduced its scales and discontinued rent allowances in order to prevent significant increase in its Poor Law rate. 30 of its 36 members were Labour but 20 of them voted for the reduction and this ensured that it went through. This was highly controversial in the town and during the meeting 'a force of several hundred unemployed, some of whom came from Chopwell, thronged the precincts of the Poor Law offices'. The Guardians heard from a deputation consisting of Harry Bolton, Jack Cogan and John Hesketh, who were supported by the Labour and ILP representatives on the Board Jim Stephenson and Jack Gilliland. These men had been the speakers at the August rally that had pledged Guardians' support during a trade dispute and they were incensed at the stance their colleagues were now taking. They threatened to 'expose' the Labour members who had voted for the reduction and assured that they would 'tell the demonstrators who was responsible', although they also persuaded the crowd to disperse pending future demonstrations. The reasoning behind the Labour members' decision lay in the short time working and low wages prevalent in Gateshead: as they had five years earlier, they argued that the incomes of men in work were now too close to the level of relief.

The threatened demonstrations certainly took place over the following three weeks. In the first week of April 1926 a mass meeting chaired by Jack Cogan resolved to take up the attitude of the Guardians with the Gateshead Labour Representation Committee; at least 200 Felling NUWCM members ('men, boys, women and children') rallied with 'an impressive banner' in Felling Square; 'several hundred men and youths' marched from Windmill Hills to the claims office in Shipcoate Terrace, where there was disorder after a benefits appeal was refused. Finally in the last week of April, just before the General Strike was called, the Mayor of Gateshead, 'following several demonstrations and signs of unrest in the town', addressed a mass meeting of the unemployed in the Town Hall. He pointed out what the Council was trying to do over work schemes and listed the difficulties placed in their way by central government. He 'asked for no discord in the ranks of the Labour Party at this juncture' and claimed that only elected Labour majorities at every level of government could deliver what the unemployed needed.[36]

At this stage, the eve of the 1926 General Strike and miners' lockout, it is useful to review the effect, extent and political complexion of the organised unemployed movement in the North East.

How successful?

One historian has suggested an essentially limited impact for these forms of protest:

> The Guardians usually expressed their deep concern for the problems of the unemployed, but were only prepared to act on a certain range of issues. Demands for more work were always met with encouraging replies, for it was the policy…to provide relief work wherever possible, but they persistently refused to pay the standard trade union rate which would have involved defying national government. Demands for higher rates of relief were generally met with sympathetically worded refusals, on grounds of their insolvency … requests which asked only for a small amount of practical help were invariably complied with, but complete policy changes – never. [37]

This verdict needs to be qualified. Some higher rates of relief had definitely been achieved by the middle of the decade, and if the sums involved seem small it is important to remember the impact that even small amounts could have on people on the breadline. Where a local authority was held by the left- such as Chester le Street, Blaydon by 1925, Gateshead from 1923 until 1926 – union rates for government-funded public works schemes could be achieved too. Nevertheless the sheer scale of demand created by structural unemployment overwhelmed their ability to sustain higher rates in the face of local political opposition as well as government restrictions. Defiance of national government by North East authorities did happen later, in fact, as we shall see in the next chapter.

Presence and Politics

The national historian of the unemployed movement suspects that as a formal organisation the NUWCM was 'just more or less surviving' at this time. The kind of mass agitations witnessed in 1921 and 1922 were not going to be sustainable activities and once local Boards of Guardians had settled on their scales and the procedures for their Relieving Officers the committee movement fell into abeyance. Does this verdict need to be qualified too?

At the first national conference of the NUWCM it was reported that the North East District had 66 affiliated committees, the largest of any area outside London. By the third national conference in 1923 this had reduced to 15 functioning committees (12 of which had Women's Sections) out of a national total of 250. In 1925 the admittedly hostile *Newcastle Journal* claimed that whereas the NUWCM could claim nearly 6,000 members in the city in 1922 it was now down to 400 members and that from an unemployment register of nearly 14,000. Clearly the high level of activity that marked 1921 and 1922 was not being maintained. Further, although some names are consistently present as NUWCM organisers, the frequent turnover seen in the Chester le Street District Committee secretariat suggests a lack of continuity in key positions as activists, for whatever reason, dropped away from activity.[38]

There are signs that NUWCM branches would be formed in response to a particular local issue and, as far as most members were concerned, activity would fade away when the issue had been resolved or an impasse reached. For example in Jarrow a branch claiming a membership of 150, and five months later 500, was formed in 1925 in response to some relief payments being stopped; in 1922 80 men formed a branch in Blaydon, assisted by Cogan, to take up issues with the Guardians. In both cases no further activity was reported for a few years.[39]

In the North East the impetus in 1920 and 1921 came largely from unemployed shipyard and engineering workers, centred in Gateshead, Sunderland, Wallsend, Jarrow and Newcastle, rather than from the coalfield villages. This was generally in line with the national picture. As the 1920s wore on though the picture began to shift. This was because both local industrial action and the anticipation of another national lockout in the coalfields were generating NUWCM activity if not branch structures.

The Unemployed Committees were not homogenous and it is important to recognise that. Some were active but chose not to affiliate to the NUWCM. In Birtley in January 1926, for example, Communist-Labour Guardian and lodge secretary Alec Henry had to stress to the local unemployed that the Unemployed Committee there 'was not connected to the Minority Movement'. Despite his best efforts the group kept apart from the NUWCM and this was not just because of 'the Bolshevik bogey' as he had explained a few months later. In their area Labour controlled the Parish, District and County Councils and the group was linked to them through a Labour Representation Committee. Good relief scales had been achieved including payments to those over fourteen years, and these 'made organisation seem less necessary'.[40] Nonetheless their activity was entirely in line with the NUWCM. In Newcastle at the same time the local press noted with approval that the unemployed had severed their connection with the NUWCM and were establishing 'a non-party organisation opposed to Bolshevism and seeking constitutional solutions…the Red influence that has held sway locally has been eliminated'. At the same time according to the Communist Party District Secretary John Tearney this was a split engineered by the right-wing; another committee affiliated to the NUWCM was still actively functioning. Again though there seems to have been more involved than politics. As was the case in Birtley, the unemployed did not want to contribute towards a headquarters and officials in London.[41]

Some local trades council Unemployed Committees were not necessarily affiliated to the NUWCM, for example North Shields and the original Birtley, and one in Newcastle, and some did not have a political focus either. This became clear in Blyth in February 1926 when the Council funded a recreational hut for the use of the Unemployed Committee. However the lease stipulated that the hut could not be used for political purposes, and this prompted a split in the Committee between 'moderates' who agreed to this and 'Communists' who did not; eventually the 'moderates' signed the lease.[42]

A contrast is provided by Sunderland. When the Trades Council and

Labour Party formed an Unemployed Workers Committee in 1925 the main speaker, Labour Party agent E. Gower, stated that whereas a previous Committee had not looked after their rights as it should have, they intended to 'set about looking after the rights of the unemployed in a perfectly constitutional fashion...any fool could go rioting'. This was clearly a critical reference to the events of 1921 in the town. Nevertheless the same Labour organiser successfully argued for the Committee to affiliate to the NUWCM, and pay the subscriptions the rules required. Many of the demands of the unemployed were national ones, he pointed out, and would need a national body to press them, and the national office would be an important source of advice and support. Interestingly, it was two weeks after the 'any fool can go rioting' reference that Lenagh was elected to the Guardians.[43]

The Party affiliations of the local NUWCM branches were not homogenous either. Clearly the fledgling Communist Party was heavily involved in the movement but did not have a monopoly over the leadership, and its relations with Labour and the Labour left could be a function of the wider relationships between these three, or could be more locally determined. By and large 'unconstitutional' methods were more likely to be adopted by Unemployed Committees on the left of the movement, whereas those around the centre were more likely to rely on the election of Labour majorities on Councils and Boards of Guardians to meet the needs of the unemployed.

On 3 May 1926 the General Council of the TUC called on all affiliated unions to strike in support of the miners and a new phase in post war class politics began.

Notes

1   Bill McNestry, interview in the *General Strike and Lockout Transcripts Vol.2* (GLS); *Blaydon Courier* 31 July 1926.
2   *Newcastle Daily Journal* 21 September 1921; *Sunderland Echo* 7 July 1925; *Gateshead Labour Party and Trades Council Monthly Circular* 15 July 1923(GLS).
3   *Sunderland Echo* 7th July 1925; *Gateshead Labour Party and Trades Council Monthly Circular* 15th July 1923 (GLS).
4   *Workers Weekly* 10 February 1923; *Workers Life* 10 February 1928.
5   *Newcastle Daily Journal* 3 June 1926.
6   Interview with Peter Brabban 1979; Home Office Report to Cabinet 12 October 1922 (NA: CAB/24/139/176); *Workers Weekly* 15 September 1923.
7   'Correspondence with Chester le Street Unemployed Association 1925-1938' (Durham County Record Office UD/CS 203/23-30); this file includes correspondence with NUWM branches.

8   *Sunderland Echo* 7 July 1925; *Gateshead Labour Party and Trades Council Monthly Circular* 15 December 1921 and 15 July 1923 (GLS.

9   Interview with Peter Brabban 1979.

10   *Out of Work* no 27 1922; Home Office Report to Cabinet 23 March 1923 (NA: CAB/24/134/148); *Sunderland Echo* 1 November 1921; *North Mail* 1 and 4 April 1922.

11   *Sunderland Echo* 12 April 1923; 22 July and 11 September 1925.

12   *Workers Weekly* 27 February 1925.

13   *Out of Work* no 31 1922; *Gateshead Labour Party and Trades Council Monthly Circular* no 56 15 May 1921 (GLS).

14   *Gateshead Labour Party and Trades Council Monthly Circulars* no 66 15 March and no 67 April 1922 (GLS); Interview with Peter Brabban 1979.

15   *Shields Daily News* 31 October and 2 November 1921; *North Mail* 5 April 1922.

16   *Workers Weekly* 24 February 1923; *North Mail* 26 and 27 March 1923; *North Mail* 15 September 1923; *Workers Weekly* 28 September 1923.

17   *The Communist* 28 January and 18 February 1922.

18   *Newcastle Daily Journal* 18 January 1926; *Chester le Street Chronicle* 29 January 1926.

19   Roderick Martin, *Communism and the British Trade Unions 1924-1933: A Study of the National Minority Movement* (Oxford: Clarendon Press 1969); *Newcastle Daily Journal* 13 January 1926; *Sunderland Echo* 27 February and 2 November 1926; *Workers Weekly* 8 May 1925; *The Communist* 19 November 1921. On Harvey see David Douglass, *George Harvey: Pitman Bolshevik* (Gateshead: Follonsby Miners' Lodge Banner Association 2011).

20   *Gateshead Labour Party and Trades Council Monthly Circular* 15 January 1923 (GLS); correspondence to Chief Constable of Durham (TWAS: T148-7) 31 August and 21 September 1924.

21   *Chester le Street Chronicle* 17 January, 4 April, 27 June and 12 July 1919; *Gateshead Labour Party and Trades Council Monthly Circular* no 55, 15 April 1921 (GLS).

22   *Gateshead Labour Party and Trades Council Monthly Circular* no 55, 15 April 1921 (GLS); other information from Mr Archie Potts, recollections of his father Ernest Potts.

23   *The Communist* 2 April 1921; *The Times* 7 May 1919; *North Mail* 14 January 1926.

24   *Newcastle Daily Journal* 2 September 1921.

25   *Workers Weekly* 28 April 1923; *Sunderland Echo* 18 November 1921; Home Office Report to Cabinet 24 November 1921 (NA: CAB/24/131/132).

26   *Out of Work* no 21 1921; Sue Bruley, *Leninism, Stalinism and the Women's Movement in Britain 1920-1939* (New York: Garland Press 1986, p. 220). Hannington's accounts do, however, mention the Women's Sections of the 1930s.

27   *Gateshead Labour Party and Trades Council Monthly Circular* 15 July 1923 (GLS); Minutes of the County Borough of Gateshead Watch Committee 26 March 1924 and 16 April 1925 (TWAS: CB.GA/57/15).

28   *Workers' Life* 14 October 1927; *Out of Work* no 33 1922; *Workers' Life* 26 August 1927.

29 Phyllis Short, interview with Peter Brabban 1979. See also Steve Lawther, *Emmie Lawther: A Tribute* (Gateshead: privately published 1964 - GLS).

30 *Sunderland Echo* 7 July and 31 July 1925; *Newcastle Daily Journal* 10 August 1925.

31 Andy Lawther, letter to Sam Watson 1 December 1966 (DCRO: Sam Watson Papers, D/MRP 8/4).

32 *Sunderland Echo* 10 September 1925.

33 *Blaydon Courier* 6 and 13 February 1926.

34 *North Mail* 15 January 1926; *Blaydon Courier* 30 January 1926.

35 *Shields Daily News* 9 and 12 October, 17 December 1925; *Newcastle Daily Journal* 26 March 1926; *Workers Weekly* 16 October 1925.

36 *Newcastle Daily Journal* 31 March, 1, 9 and 23 April 1926.

37 Kate Nicholas, *The Social Effects of Unemployment on Teesside 1919-1939* (Manchester: Manchester University Press 1986, pp. 151-3).

38 The historian concerned is Richard Croucher, *We Refuse to Starve in Silence: A History of the National Unemployed Workers' Movement 1920-1946* (London: Lawrence and Wishart 1987, p. 75); Home Office Report to Cabinet 19 April 1923 (NA: CAB 24/160/202); *Newcastle Daily Journal* 26 August 1925.

39 *Workers Weekly* 27 February and 24 July 1925; correspondence to Chief Constable of Durham (TWAS: T148-7) 3 December 1922.

40 *Blaydon Courier* 30 January 1926; *Workers Weekly* 5 June and 11 September 1925.

41 *Newcastle Daily Journal* 26 August 1925; *Workers Weekly* 11 September 1925.

42 *Newcastle Daily Journal* 8, 9 and 13 February 1926.

43 *Sunderland Echo* 7 and 28 July 1925.

Chapter Four

THE 1926 MINERS' LOCK-OUT AND ITS AFTERMATH

If the British General Strike of 1926 was short the struggle of the miners was not. After only nine days, and despite clear and growing support for General Strike action by ordinary workers, the General Council of the Trades Union Congress called it off. The TUC did not want the constitutional confrontation with the government that a protracted strike might involve, and so they were prepared to sanction a return to work with no guarantees against the victimisation of those who had taken part or the security of their negotiating rights in the workplace. Nor had they secured any terms for the miners.

In the coalfields this was just the beginning. The 1926 miners' lockout lasted for seven months after the nine days of the national strike, and in County Durham fewer miners returned to work before the end of the lockout than anywhere else.[1] The first part of this chapter draws out the role the NUWCM played during the dispute, and then later how the political repercussions of the lockout affected the unemployed movement.

Trades Union Principles

As we have seen, the NUWCM had been clear from its foundation that under no circumstances were its members to act as strike breakers. This held good during the General Strike and, more to the point, during the miners' lockout that followed.

During the 1926 General Strike the unemployed movement played a remarkable part and tributes were subsequently paid to it by the official movement. They gave full credit to the unemployed for respecting the principles of trades unionism and what the strike stood for. There was at no stage any serious blacklegging despite the mass unemployment. The unemployed refused to allow themselves to be used to undercut the employed workers, they understood their position.[2]

There are examples of how the politicised elements of the unemployed movement reacted. In early November 1926, as the lockout was drawing to an end, the Gateshead NUWCM organiser Alex McFarlane ('a well-known local Communist') chaired a meeting at Gateshead Town Hall; Jack Cogan, 'who takes a prominent part in the Gateshead branch of the NUWCM', was in support. The principal speaker, Sid Elias, apparently urged the local unemployed to join the miners' mass pickets because they 'were fighting a mass attack by the capitalist class against the working class'.

The police detective who was there reported that 'there is no doubt that this meeting was organised by the Communist Party under the cloak of the NUWCM'. Indeed, and given that public meetings openly organised by the Communists were being banned under the Emergency Powers Act this cloak must have been a convenient one. There is some evidence that the CP was consolidating its leadership of the local NUWCM during the lockout.[3]

Early on a Conservative on Newcastle Council described the NUWCM as 'a political organisation of a dangerous character' and demanded an enquiry into why the Council had provided it with the free use of premises in Pilgrim Street. Clearly, despite the politically-driven split that had occurred earlier, the 'Bolshevik' element was still active. In Blyth the NUWCM branch was affiliated to the Trades Council, and won praise for its efforts during the lockout. Delegate and NUWCM chairman, Communist Henry Crutchley, urged support for the miners' pickets; he fended off complaints in the press about the hut granted to his group by the Council being used for 'political' purposes.[4]

Nevertheless by the autumn of 1926 there are signs that morale was breaking up, amid recrimination and the pressures of survival. For example Birtley NUWCM circulated an appeal to lodge secretaries in the Chester le Street Guardians' area complaining that miners in dispute had been employed on the Fatfield Estate, a council building scheme near Washington. The NUWCM, whose members had obviously been denied these jobs, believed that this was 'a form of blacklegging against all unemployed workers'. It was the equivalent, they said, of the unemployed offering their services to the mine owners, which of course they had no intention of doing. They urged lodges to put pressure on the Council to withdraw these men: 'we ask you to stand behind the unemployed as firmly as the unemployed have stood behind the miners these last twenty weeks'.

In November desperate circumstances must have prompted G.R. Mowbray, on behalf of the Chester le Street District NUWCM, to urge a community effort to appeal to the government 'to achieve a resolution to this dispute because of the suffering being caused'. This was no call for a return to work but for a committee of all local bodies, including the churches and the chamber of commerce, to press the government to 'take steps to bring this appalling dispute to a conclusion'.[5] These appeals by the

NUWCM illustrate that the organised unemployed had stayed loyal to the miners' cause but also just how bad conditions had become by the time of the return to work.

School Meals and Child Health

The legal position regarding relief was the same as in 1921 since once more the lockout was judged to be a trade dispute. Once more Durham County Council implemented the Necessitous Schoolchildren Act, with up to three meals a day provided through the schools and funded by the rates. The Council spent more on feeding and provided more meals on this basis than any other authority in England and Wales, and by a very wide margin. The feeding centres also catered for expectant and nursing mothers and, crucially, single miners who were not eligible for relief.[6]

George Short, a Chopwell miner and Communist active during the lock-out wrote many years later that his Party and those on the left of Labour:

> …were the spearhead of the movement for free meals for schoolchildren. They were in the forefront of those who poured scorn on the old ideas that it was a 'disgrace' to apply for Poor Law Relief. Instead, in their public meetings, they endeavoured to show their colleagues what they could claim for and what they should apply for. A favourite method in the campaign was to cover a village with street meetings, street by street. This was a hard and painstaking job, but it effectively combated Tory propaganda in both press and wireless, and won wide support, particularly among miners' wives, and not only on school meals, but also on a whole variety of questions.

Applying for assistance for families should not be seen as a stigma, argued both the Communists and Labour left, but as part of the fight against the 'starvation weapon'. In a sense this was continuing the agitation for relief that the unemployed movement had pursued since the end of the world war seven years earlier.[7]

If Short is accurate this may help to explain the upsurge in membership of the Communist Party in the Durham coalfield during the lock-out. This included the recruitment of miners' wives, so that by November 1926 a Tyneside District Women's Department of the CP had been formed. Charlie Woods has confirmed the influence of the unemployed movement here:

> The NUWCM networks helped to provide the solidarity that was evident in 1926 and provided the machinery for the struggle of the miners to

be carried on. You've got to appreciate that we'd established a Labour County Council in the 1920s. I was in a lock-out in 1925, and application was made to the Education Committee of the County Council for the right to feed the schoolchildren from the rates. The Act for the feeding of Necessitous Schoolchildren was invoked. Before 1926 we had in quite a number of mining centres the machinery for the feeding of necessitous children of unemployed men and locked-out miners. This turned out to be an invaluable tool in the war that followed. For instance why I say this is because we had a different situation in Durham County than you had in Northumberland. There you had a Tory Council that didn't invoke the Act although there was agitation to get them to, they refused to do that but Durham did. As a consequence Northumberland mining families had to subsist on the old style of soup kitchen, where they collected food from the business people of the towns. Believe me they fared considerably worse than we did on the other side of the river. It shouldn't be forgotten that working-class representation on local authorities was an important basis for providing the sinews of war for the lock-out of 1926.

Woods had taken on the responsibility for organising the meals for schoolchildren in Blaydon and therefore he was in a position to understand the importance of this effort. What he describes as 'working-class representation' on Blaydon Council included valuable individuals such as its chairman, Harry Bolton, who had dual membership of the Labour and Communist Parties. He had secured the use of local authority facilities to produce the miners' newsletter *Northern Light,* which had been declared illegal under the Emergency Powers Act.[8]

Maggie Airey, also from Blaydon, reported in October that Blaydon Council was serving 13,000 meals a week to schoolchildren, nursing mothers, and expectant mothers. Shoes and clothing had been received through 'comrades in the women's co-operative guilds' in different parts of the country. Locally they had made up 'maternity bundles' for wives who could not claim from the national Women's Relief Committee Fund, which only applied to locked-out miners. 'The women are working splendidly in Blaydon, and I would urge women all over the country to get into this work of agitating for the feeding of the children'.[9]

There was a contrast in attitudes here between the mainstream Labour councillors on Durham County Council and the left. Councillor Tucker for example, defending the decision to approve £300,000 until the end of December 1926 for school feeding, stated that 'it is an exorbitant figure but it is money that is well spent because these little innocent creatures have no part in the struggle'.[10] For the councillor and many of his colleagues, school feeding during the lock-out was a vital humanitarian action in keeping with the values of the movement. For the militants it was more than this, it was a response to the coal owners and government's attempts to starve men back to work by penalising their families. School meals were part of the miners' class struggle, a point that seems to have been overlooked by historians. The role of the NUWCM in resisting organised attempts to use the unemployed to break the strike have been noted and appreciated. Its role in helping to provide 'the sinews of war' to continue the struggle seem to have been less well acknowledged.

Certainly, unlike 1921, neither the press nor the local Medical Officers of Health commented on any reluctance to take up Poor Law relief or any of the other services available through Child Welfare Centres. The Gateshead Medical Officer reported a significant increase in attendances for free or subsidised baby milk in 1926 compared to 1925. The Durham Medical Officer stated that there was no evidence that the health or nutritional status of the children had suffered during the lockout; such had been the success of the feeding efforts. A year later he complained of the Centres in the County that 'many of them are overcrowded by people who look upon these centres as places merely for the purposes of relief'. Admittedly this dispute was markedly longer than that of 1921 and therefore desperation could have overcome pride, but the campaigns to ensure that what was available should be claimed seem to have been effective and should be given some credit. As has been shown the NUWCM had experience in lobbying Boards of Guardians and they too became a factor in the lockout.[11]

The Boards of Guardians

Alongside the Labour local authorities there were efforts to use the Poor Law against the 'starvation weapon'. As has been described in the previous chapter the unemployed movement and the left had foreseen this possibility. The Chester le Street Guardians had had a solid Labour majority – 47 members out of 59, most of them miners and miners' wives – since 1925. They came from across the Labour political spectrum and included the traditional moderate Methodists, the Labour right and the Labour left, at least one dual-membership Communist, Alec Henry, and the ILP activist Anthony Bolam. Their collective view was that the law in relation to the payment of relief during the lockout was wrong and should be ignored in the interests of justice. They saw Poor Relief was one of what Charlie Woods would have called the 'sinews of war' and so they adopted generous relief scales including payments to single miners. Ministry of Health guidelines such as deducting the cost of free school meals from relief payments were ignored.[12]

As we have seen the Birtley Unemployed Committee and the Chester le Street District NUWCM branch were active lobbyists and they continued to be so throughout the lockout. For example in June Communist Billy Hall of the Birtley Unemployed Committee led 'upwards of 200 men and youths' to a Guardians' meeting and established that single men and those living in lodgings would be paid relief. In mid-August, just before the Guardians were removed by the government, '1,000 persons...the majority single men' marched to the Guardians from Washington, Birtley and surrounding villages and successfully re-instated the payment of relief in the Washington area.[13] The actions in the Board room were supported by and in the context of a strong unemployed movement and mobilisation in the working-class organisations as a whole. This was shown again at the end of August when the government in the form of Minister of Health Neville Chamberlain took action against the Board.

Once again the Ratepayers' Associations were mobilised and this time the retaliation went beyond letter-writing campaigns. The government accepted their argument that, in the words of Chamberlain's friendly biographer, 'Chester le Street bore, rather, the character of a Soviet...it looked as if a trade union, masquerading as Guardians, were financing an industrial dispute out of public funds.' It moved to disband the Chester le Street Guardians and replace them with appointed Commissioners who could be trusted to follow the law to the letter and impose huge cuts in relief payments to do so. Defiant, the Guardians agreed that 'The world will remember August 1926 when Chester le Street took their stand on the side of humanity and justice'. Communist Guardian and Unemployed Committee chair Alec Henry locked the Commissioners' representative in the Board room and was subsequently imprisoned for three months for intimidation. The Commissioners drastically reduced scales of benefit to deal with the Guardians' over-spend, and this included an almost halving of the scales for married women and children, as well as the end of relief for men 'in a trades dispute' and for all single men. By September 1927 the Commissioners had reduced spending on out-relief by a half compared to the previous year.[14]

In response, during September and October 'the biggest demonstrations in Chester le Street's history' were held in protest, and to support the elected Guardians. An estimated fifteen thousand people, including 'a large number of women and girls, wheeling perambulators or carrying children in their arms' marched; the Lodge bands and the banners of the Lodges and Labour Party Women's Sections were in support. In the first week of October over a hundred women (the majority of whom were married, according to a reporter, who did not explain how he knew this) supported by a lodge band protested to the Commissioners. A deputation of three explained how the scales were causing extreme hunger and hardship, but the Commissioners stood by their role as 'the trustees of the ratepayers'; the deputation left, telling the Commissioners that 'your time will come'. A week later the Divisional Federation of Labour Women's Sections organised 'a monster demonstration of several thousand women, together with several hundred men', the ranks including 'scores of women with babes in arms or perambulators'. Mrs. Eddy, Mrs. Bishop and Mrs. Bailey made up the delegation to the Commissioners but apparently their response caused the delegation 'to withdraw, hurling unpleasant epithets …'[15] The demonstrators dispersed after they were assured that the Commissioners had agreed to a further meeting, but of course the massive cuts remained.

The government gave serious thought to prosecuting the Guardians for fraud but abandoned the idea. Although Chester le Street was referred to as Durham's 'Poplar' the government appears to have learnt from that episode and held back from adding to the ranks of working-class martyrs. The Commissioners and their scales remained until the Labour government of 1929 repealed Conservative legislation and restored elected Guardians in Chester le Street, including some of the original rebels.

As we have seen recipients of relief were legally barred from serving as Guardians; therefore the Chester le Street members who were involved in the lockout – a large number - did not claim it. According to the official report of the government-appointed Guardians they had relied on almost enforced 'collections' from those who were receiving it to get by. The elected Guardians maintained that this was false, that in fact their relief equivalent was provided by Chester le Street Labour Party and not the locked-out mining families. Nonetheless modern historians have repeated the 'collections' allegation without challenge.[16]

Government pressure on Labour Boards continued. The Audit (Local Authorities) Bill 1927 provided that amounts surcharged could be recovered as a civil debt, and that Guardians convicted of unreasonable, or deliberately illegal, extravagance should be disqualified from serving on any local authority for five years. The Lanchester Guardians were surcharged (or rather, those of them who had voted to ignore Ministry regulations were surcharged) following action by Ratepayers' Associations, local Collieries and the Consett Iron and Steel Company in 1927; the court agreed that they had 'financed a trade dispute at the expense of the Ratepayers' and surcharged a total of £1,524. During the next year Houghton-le-Spring Board members were surcharged, as were the Labour members of South Shields Board of Guardians, despite the cuts to scales they had made. Gateshead Guardians had faced a legal challenge from the Ratepayers' Association since they had raised their scales in 1925; the Labour members were subsequently surcharged and had had to reduce scales further during the lockout to ensure that their overdraft from the Ministry of Health continued.[17]

As we will see the NUWCM in the region continued to lobby the Guardians and the Councils but knowledge of the fate of the Chester le Street representatives and the prospect of surcharging seem to have been effective arguments against defying the government.

Evictions

Where the local NUWCM was large and active there had been examples of successful support for unemployed households faced with eviction. This issue became more serious after 1926 when more and more unemployed miners struggled to pay their rents. In the 1920s George Short was active in the NUWCM and remembered how organising the unemployed could mean resisting evictions:

> Both here and in Newcastle this was a bitter thing, evictions taking place. I remember a case particularly, I was speaking at a meeting on the Windmill Hills in Gateshead, and someone came along and said they were putting somebody out on the streets. Then, if you could hold the house until sunset, you could have it for a few days more. There were the bailiffs taking things, furniture, out. So the people from the meeting put them back. As fast as the bailiffs took things out, the unemployed went round the back of the house and put them back! We won, and then of course we had a meeting with the landlord and try to agree a compromise, pay instalments or wait.

Short had attended the Lenin School in the Soviet Union between 1930 and 1931, after which he was living in Stockton. Therefore if he was speaking at Windmill Hills in Gateshead it would probably be in the period between 1927 and 1930 when he was on the CP/NUWCM panel of open-air speakers.[18] Some other successful examples are available, including a particularly interesting one from Birtley in 1928. This concerned the legal process of 'distraint' whereby bailiffs entered a tenant's home and seized their property to pay for rent arrears:

… the first attempt to distrain on a tenant's family in Birtley was scotched by the NUWCM, who as soon as they heard of this visit to the tenant's house got out a chalking squad, advertised what the Labour Council intended doing, chalked it in front of every councillor's door, and called a public meeting near the councillors' houses to show our disgust at this treatment of an unemployed worker.

Sympathetic councillors supported the NUWCM and the case was dropped. In the same year the CP and NUWCM organised open-air meetings and deputations in protest after Blaydon Council issued notices to quit to 28 Council tenants. The threat of eviction was withdrawn and other ways of dealing with large rent arrears explored.[19]

Nevertheless although some successful and imaginative action against distraint and eviction took place this cannot have been the general picture. There were many reports of evictions and threats of evictions in County Durham in 1928 and 1929, principally of miners and families for whom no work had been available since the end of the lock-out. For example in May 1927 200 notices to quit were served in West Stanley and 60 in Leadgate, where it was also reported that unemployed people were not wanted in new Council housing. Later that year evictions were taking place in Whitton, Newburn, Throckley and particularly Wheatley Hill, where 50 evictions had led to emergency accommodation for families in the Miners' Hall. In 1928 Chester-le-Street Council was apparently 'unsympathetic' when the unemployed fell behind with the rent and 'didn't hesitate' to use bailiffs and possess furniture. A year later Easington Council was issuing notices to quit for rent arrears. The numbers are too high to indicate that the NUWCM could have responded with anything like regularity.[20]

Victimisation

The defeat of the general Strike and the miners' lockout left the employers firmly in control. In the coalfields the victimisation of those seen as militants was widespread. Charlie Hall, the son of Billy Hall of the Birtley Unemployed Committee, had seen the CPGB Birtley branch membership grow in 1926. After the lockout, though: 'every single one was victimised, and they went to Lancashire - and the women went to work - and they went to Yorkshire, they went to Kent, they went to Australia: they were dispersed. And we went to London. I think there was one miner stayed in Birtley, in the Communist Party, and he didn't work till the revival of '38 and the coming war years. He was like the only one that didn't move'.

It has been noted that at least until the revival of the coal trade in the late

1930s those miners who were active in the CP or close to it tended to be checkweighmen. They were comparatively safe from victimisation because they were essentially employed at the collieries by the workforce; there is some evidence that militants were seen as good checkweighmen by the miners and therefore supported by them.[21] The decline in Communist Party membership in the region, as in the other British coalfields, was as marked and sudden as its rise had been. One explanation had actually been provided before the lockout by John Tearney, onetime District Secretary of the Party. He explained why he thought that the Party's growing influence in the Labour Party, in the unemployed and Minority Movements in the North East was not being reflected in increased membership. He drew attention to how the Party frequently described the surveillance, victimisation by employers and politically motivated arrest and imprisonment to which its members were prone; this was off-putting, claimed Tearney, 'because the average worker is not prepared to be a hero'. The scale of the employers' offensive after 1926 would have reinforced their hesitancy.

A few years later George Short, who had been involved in the lockout at Chopwell, pointed out that mass recruitment was not likely to be sustainable anyway. In his experience personal contact and discussion with potential members yielded solid results whereas 'those coming forward at mass meetings often tend to be paper members'. Very likely this had been his experience during the sudden influx of recruits.[22] Nevertheless, although Communist membership soon returned to its previously low level in the North East, it was during this lockout that the Party recruited some individuals who were to become key leaders of the NUWM in the region during the 1930s. Examples are George and Phyllis Short in Chopwell, Wilf Jobling and Maggie Airey in Blaydon and Chopwell, Jim Ancrum in Felling and Bob Elliott in Blyth.

The victimisation of activists in the NUWCM seems to have become more common, or possibly the reporting of it became more common, after the lock-out too. For example in 1927 the chair of Gateshead NUWCM had to seek admission to the workhouse with his family; evicted for rent arrears he claimed he had been refused accommodation by private landlords because of his political activities. A South Shields speaker who had 'exposed the tactics of the Board of Guardians' at a public meeting there was summoned by them to answer questions. Soon afterwards his outdoor relief was stopped and he too was admitted to 'the house'. In the same year one of the NUWCM Communists involved in a demonstration to the South Shields Guardians had a day's money stopped; by attending the demonstration, it was stated, he couldn't have been seeking work. In 1929 an activist in the

Newburn branch was struck off the unemployment register on the grounds that he was so busy advising the unemployed over their claims that he could not be seeking work. A South Shields contributor to *Workers Life* argued that such examples proved the need to organise because if the NUWCM was bigger such attacks would be much less likely. This may have been true, but as it was such attacks illustrated the potential for victimisation of the workless activist as well as those still employed.[23]

NUWCM Activity

NUWCM branches continued to be active in the region and there is some evidence that the movement was actually lively, despite the demoralisation generated by the defeat of the miners. Boards of Guardians reduced relief scales to balance their books after the heavy expenditures incurred during the lockout, and to conform to increasingly tight Ministry of Health regulations. This provoked responses from the organised unemployed. In South Shields for example the Board imposed 'drastic cuts' in relief in September 1927 in order to maintain its overdraft with the Ministry of Health. The NUWCM led a protest march of about 700 from Hebburn and Jarrow, and when J. Wallace, a Labour member of the Board, told them that their march was 'ill-advised' the demonstrators 'expressed considerable resentment' to him. However the following month 'a practical lesson for the workless' was demonstrated when the 'NUWCM showed what the workers can do when organised' – at least temporarily. Meetings were organised in Jarrow, Hebburn and South Shields at which Labour Councillors, Guardians, CP and NUWCM speakers shared the platform condemning the cuts, and the Guardians narrowly voted to rescind the new scales. The following month though the 'baby starving' Guardians gave in to Ministry pressure and restored the cuts.

The Newcastle Guardians cut their scales two months later, despite the protests of Labour members McCutcheon and McLoughlin; outside the sound of the slogans and drum and fife band of the NUWCM demonstrators provided a background. At the same time the Gateshead branch lobbied their Guardians to seek an assurance that they would not give in to Ministry pressure and reduce their rates of relief.[24]

There were further NUWCM demonstrations in Gateshead the following year, including a rally of '2,000 unemployed with banners, fifes and drums' at the Town Hall to press for improved relief work. According to the police 52 members of the Labour League of Ex-Servicemen took part, and the leaders included Gateshead NUWCM Secretary William Barron, Alf Chater and George Wheeler. Inside the Town Hall the Mayor at first refused to hear the deputation that had invited itself into the meeting, but eventually did so and agreed to speak at an NUWCM meeting that evening. There he stressed the Council's commitment to securing work for the unemployed but also the national system that was frustrating its efforts. Outside the Town Hall there were reportedly angry scenes as the police broke up sections of the demonstration that would not move on and clear the roads; Barron later protested, unsuccessfully, both in writing and by deputation to Gateshead Council that NUWCM members 'had been severely handled by the police without justification'. He replied that his members were 'studying ways and means of combating the brutalities of the police' but without an apparent result.[25]

Minister of Health Neville Chamberlain visited Tynemouth at the end of April 1928 and this sparked a mobilisation by the organised unemployed. NUWCM contingents from Blyth, South Shields, Walker, Wallsend and Willington Quay were to assemble with the local group in North Shields for a march to Tynemouth Plaza and a meeting with the Minister. The focus was on his recent ministerial circular re-iterating the point that out-relief should not normally be granted to single men. They were frustrated by the police but still managed a procession through North Shields (where 'the streets were lined with people') to a rally outside the Plaza addressed by Sam Langley and George Wheeler.[26]

NUWCM activists were also standing in local authority and Boards of Guardians elections at this time. In 1927 South Shields William Shaw stood for the CP in Council elections, as did James Thompson in Jarrow; neither in opposition to Labour candidates. In Newcastle a year later unemployed leader Sam Langley stood for the Board of Guardians as a Communist, despite being 'stated to be disqualified from activity as a Guardian by being in receipt of poor relief'. At the count he pointed out that regardless of 'sabotage by the official Labour Party' he had polled more than the official Labour candidate at the last election. At the same time in South Shields John Richardson, John Dowel, Thomas Henham and Thomas Hyman stood for the NUWCM, again, and like Langley, not in opposition to Labour candidates. The fact that they were not standing against Labour suggests that an arrangement had been made or at least that the NUWCM were avoiding the formal breach that opposing Labour would have meant. In Jarrow, on the other hand, it seems that NUWCM activists in the CP were opposing Labour at Council elections. In Sunderland Lenagh continued on his somewhat maverick course as an 'independent socialist' against Labour as well as the Conservatives. He was gaoled in 1928 for falsifying his nomination papers for a Council election but such was his support in

Bridges ward that despite his enforced absence he only lost by 87 votes.[27]

In response to the expectations of the Communist International, or Comintern, to which they were affiliated, British Communists made several efforts in the early 1920s to establish a 'workers' defence force'. The purpose would be to steward workers' pickets, meetings and demonstrations and to defend them against strike-breakers, police attacks and threats from the emerging 'fascisti' supporters of Mussolini in Italy. The only one to take off in any way began in 1927, the Labour League of Ex-Servicemen, known as the LLX, which despite its title was a Communist initiative. In the North East this was closely tied with the NUWCM through the unemployed ex-servicemen who were involved.

The local organiser was Alf Chater in Gateshead and there are police reports of him carrying out drills with groups of unemployed men on Windmill Hills. The LLX claimed a membership of 200 around Tyneside and Sunderland in 1928 and acted as stewards at CP and NUWCM demonstrations in the region. They did carry out a least one 'alternative' Remembrance Day event in 1927, when, led by Alf Chater, James Henderson and Sam Langley of the NUWCM, they paraded and laid a wreath at the Gateshead Cenotaph. This was inscribed 'From the Labour League of Ex-Servicemen in memory of our comrades who fell in the capitalists' war of world plunder' and was accompanied by a letter in the local press. They do not appear to have been involved in any confrontations, apart from the close-run thing in Gateshead described earlier, but if nothing else their presence, complete with khaki jackets and 'LLX' armbands, clearly had a visual impact.[28]

Advice and representation work continued but the exact role of the NUWCM could be variable. In Gateshead in the summer of 1928 Barron led a deputation to the Board of Guardians protesting about their refusal to allow the NUWCM to represent cases. The Board believed that it treated all applicants fairly, and in any case it did not think that the NUWCM 'represented the whole of the unemployed'. The branch still picketed Guardians' meetings where cases were reviewed. In contrast success was being reported over appeals to the Court of Referees, the next stage up from the Guardians and the Employment Exchanges. Gateshead, Newcastle, Throckley, Newburn, Blyth, and Felling branches were all reporting success in representation and the NUWCM headquarters maintained its access to expert legal advice and efforts to pool the local advisors' experience.

Local issues, largely generated by the policies of Boards of Guardians, continued to draw responses from active NUWCM branches. In 1929 the South Shields Guardians again succumbed to Ministry pressure and imposed compulsory 'test work' on relief claimants, and this included labouring work on South Shields foreshore and in shipyards that had closed. The NUWCM failed to achieve united action with the Trades Council and Labour Party – the reasons will be discussed below – but still campaigned and demonstrated against test work. They organised work-gate collections to support those denied relief for refusing the compulsory test work and during this had members summonsed for obstruction.[29]

There is some evidence too that the active branches were, towards the end of the decade, concerned with any issues that were brought to them. In October 1929 Gateshead NUWCM took up a complaint from a woman that the police were not helping her over neighbour problems. In January of that year Blaydon NUWCM held a public meeting in a school, chaired by Communist Steve Cotterill. The meeting elected a Parents' Council for the school with the task of 'agitating for adequate food, footwear and clothing' for the children because of the 'deplorable conditions under which they attended school in Blaydon' and to and press Durham County Council to implement the 'Necessitous Schoolchildren's Feeding Act'. The Parents' Council undertook to report back on progress to open meetings at the school. Rent problems continued, as we have seen, and so NUWCM branches had some success lobbying Blaydon Council where sympathetic left Councillors tried to support them, Chairman Harry Bolton declaring that 'we will not evict the unemployed from Council housing'.[30]

Early in 1929 the NUWCM as a whole coalesced around the demands of the second national Hunger March to London.

The 1929 National Hunger March

This march was in protest at further attacks on the position of the unemployed which the NUWCM anticipated. Besides the general demands of the unemployed movement – unemployment relief to be a central government responsibility, public works at trade union rates, shorter working days and raised school leaving ages to reduce unemployment – there were new and specific issues. These were the result of the government's Unemployment Insurance Act of 1927. The Act reinforced the requirement for claimants to prove that they were 'genuinely seeking work' by producing forms signed by employers to certify that they had inquired at that workplace. In most cases in the North East this involved daily treks on what all concerned knew to be a fruitless task. There simply were no vacancies. The Act also meant that from April 1929 new eligibility criteria would remove hundreds of thousands from their current unemployment benefit and on to Poor Law relief.

The Tyneside District NUWCM convened a conference in Gateshead to organise their participation in the march. It was reported that fourteen branches had been involved; on the basis of press reports it can be estimated that these were in Gateshead, Newcastle, Sunderland, Felling, Throckley, Newburn, Birtley, Blaydon, Blyth, Chester le Street and the surrounding mining communities. Clearly the local movement was still active, if probably dependent on the efforts of a small number of determined people who were making it their primary political work. Sid Elias chaired the March Committee and each branch was responsible for recruiting and preparing a contingent of marchers. This would have been a major logistical task for them; boots, outdoor clothing and funds had to be raised from Co-operative Societies, trade union branches and trades councils and Labour Party branches. This represented a higher level of organisation than came together for the first march, but they faced political opposition from two quarters.[31]

Unlike the first National Hunger March organised by the NUWCM the march of 1929 was opposed by both the Labour Party and trades union leaderships. Indeed, their opposition was to continue for the four other national marches that were to be organised in the following decade. During the previous year the Labour Party had formalised its proscriptions on joint activities with Communists and therefore Communists were barred from participating in Labour affairs as trade union or other delegates. The rebuttal of joint activity was endorsed by the TUC and obviously this would include co-operation with the NUWCM. Therefore the policy of the DMA Executive was to 'strongly advise our people not to participate' in the march because it would be 'futile, and impose further unnecessary hardships' on the marchers. Instead they 'should concentrate on the election' that was due a few months later and return a government that would have something to offer the mining areas.[32]

The political opposition was also direct. In Newcastle the *Evening Chronicle* ran a campaign about the Communist Party's central role in the organisation of the march, clearly trying to deter participation and support. This prompted a reply from a prospective marcher who declared that 'We will achieve nothing if we sit down at home and silently starve. Therefore we are prepared to try to achieve something by marching to the doorstep of those responsible for unemployment'. Similarly Charlie Woods, speaking at the open-air meeting to send off two Blaydon men for the journey, argued that the previous Hunger March had thwarted an attempt to reduce benefits; this march would demonstrate 'that they were not asking for charity but for the right to live'. The *Chronicle* campaign was noted with approval by the

Chief Constable in his report to the Home Office. He had refused to co-operate with Sid Elias over accommodation arrangements 'while the Party had anything to do with them'. Although the March Committee mobilised the number of marchers that they were aiming for the opposition seems to have had an effect.[33]

The *Sunday Worker* had stated in early January that the start of the march would involve 'prominent Northumberland and Durham trade union leaders' but by the end of the month this was scaled back to 'several prominent DMA leaders are identified with the arrangements for the send-off'. Such was the official hostility though that in the event the sole DMA presence was the ILP's Jim Stephenson, who had actually just come off the DMA Executive. The North East Co-op was represented, however, and its secretary had written to the Prime Minister to support the march, to which the Co-op was offering practical assistance.

The Tyneside contingent of 100 men, consisting according to the police of 'mining, engineering and shipyard workers', assembled at a mass rally in the Bigg Market on January 30th with banner slogans such as 'Baldwin Must Go!' and 'We Will Not Starve At Home'. Some in the crowd donated their overcoats to a few marchers who were still not properly equipped. Local NUWCM leaders Jim Ancrum, William Barron and Tom Thurlbeck, as well as Jim Stephenson and George Short made speeches attacking the Labour and TUC leaderships for their lack of support before the Jarrow drum and fife band led off the march. The first stop was Durham where, in the absence of support from the DMA, the Conservative Mayor of the City Council had arranged accommodation through the Salvation Army.[34]

Along the route Thurlbeck lost no opportunity to contrast what he described as the support from ordinary workers with the 'boycott' by trade union and Labour Party organisations, stating that 'it is sad to relate that we have had more help from our political opponents, such as the Mayor of Durham, than from persons we of the working class regard usually as leaders'. A dispute over alleged statements by DMA President James Robson led to him threatening to sue the NUWCM during the course of the march.[35]

Wherever the marchers stopped for the night there was a need for accommodation and food. The organisers' first call was on the local trades council and Labour Party who had been informed of their arrival well in advance. The North East contingent, like the others from every part of the country, found that over half were prepared to help because they supported the march or just because they sympathised with the marchers themselves. The remainder, in line with the policy of the national leaderships, refused to be involved. In those situations the marchers had to rely on the workhouse just as in 1921. Again, conflict arose on several occasions where the workhouse management tried to treat the men as 'casuals', in other words tramps, and impose the rules that usually applied to them: only the most basic of food and accommodation and severe restrictions of movement. When the North East contingent found this to be the case at Thirsk, with the police backing the workhouse master, they chose instead to march on through pouring rain to a better reception at Ripon. At other workhouses they successfully demanded better food – earning the description from one master as 'not a nice crowd' or found that sympathisers had provided it.[36]

All the contingents were timed to converge on London at the end of February. Most of the North East group had completed the march but some had had to drop out due to foot problems, and the severe weather could not have helped with the rain, snow and slush on the roads south. The march concluded with a massive demonstration of welcome and a rally in Trafalgar Square, addressed by Tom Mann and miners' leader A.J. Cook. The more bohemian element of the left, as defined at least by the *North Mail*, was present in Trafalgar Square too: 'women with red berets and red ties, many of them smoking cigarettes'. Predictably the Prime Minister would not meet a delegation but the marchers' demonstrations were able to raise enough money to pay for their rail fares home.[37]

The NUWCM considered the March a success. Eight years after the first march the movement still had the organisational infrastructure to recruit and equip local contingents and to get most of them down to London, and then raise the money for their fares back. They had raised the profile of the organisation and, politically, had been able to draw a contrast between the attitudes of the leadership of the labour movement towards the march and that of the rank and file. It also had a result: three days after the marchers went home the government announced it would suspend the planned changes to unemployment benefit eligibility for twelve months. Given the forthcoming General Election it was likely that the suspension would be permanent.

However the isolation of the NUWCM from the mainstream labour movement, in the North East as elsewhere, had been demonstrated during this second National Hunger March. This isolation had been growing since 1926 and was to have important effects in the following years.

Relations with Labour and the Union Leaderships

During 1926 the Communist Party and the Minority Movement in the unions attacked the TUC and the Labour leaderships as traitors to the working class, accusing them of calling off a General Strike they could have won and then abandoning the miners.[38] A response in kind was inevitable: within five months of the end of the lock-out the Durham Miners Association Executive was issuing its own warnings about the Tyneside Communist Party. For example in May 1927 it stated that the Communists were, from their office in Newcastle, 'issuing circulars containing vile attacks upon your leaders, and the leaders of the trade union and labour movement generally...' Two months later James Robson, President of DMA, stated that 'No-one could conscientiously be a member of the DMA and a supporter of Communism and the Minority Movement'. The DMA was the first of the miners' unions to enforce the Labour and TUC proscription on Communists and this issue frequently emerged until the end of the decade.[39]

In Sunderland Councillors Thurlbeck (the supporter of NUWCM delegations at the Guardians) and Bowery were expelled from the Labour Party in April 1928; critics of the Labour leadership since the 1926 lockout they were claimed to be 'associating with the Communist Party' by speaking at their meetings. In Blaydon dual membership Councillor and Guardian Harry Bolton, out of work since the lockout, had his relief equivalent paid by Chopwell DMA Lodge so that he could continue as a Guardian in 1928; this despite pressure on the Lodge by the DMA Executive to stop this because he was a Communist. Whereas it was still apparently possible to stand for Blaydon Guardians on a joint CP-Labour ticket at this time in Chester le Street it was not – Alec Henry was required to stand against Labour as a Communist and lost his seat. At the Lanchester Board of Guardians Communist Ralph Jobling captured a seat from a colliery manager in 1927, only to find Labour members siding with the Conservatives to deny him the seat: they claimed that his criminal record (imprisonment during the lockout for 'inciting disaffection') precluded him. In response the CP, with trade union support, successfully fielded his wife, 'Comrade Mrs. Jobling', who was duly elected. Clearly where the left had a hinterland of support the rightwards pressure could be resisted.[40]

Nevertheless the proscription of Communists from Labour affairs must have had an impact on the unemployed movement. A number of NUWCM branches had been embedded in their local trades councils and Labour Parties up until now but they were now at risk of being marginalised from the mainstream labour movement. In 1929, for example, NUWCM delegates to Chopwell and High Spen Labour Party were asked to leave the meeting because of their Communist affiliations, refused to do so, the meeting was closed and the police called. George Short, a union delegate, was also refused admission for the same reason.

This tension with the DMA Executive probably reached a high point at the Durham Miners' gala in 1928. Towards the end of the proceedings 'men from Scotland and Sunderland' who had been 'hurling epithets' at DMA General Secretary Richardson and MP Jack Lawson, rushed the platform so that Communist and Miners' Minority Movement activist Willie Allan could speak. Members of the Labour League of Ex-Servicemen, 'wearing the Soviet uniform of the LLX' held the platform and prevented DMA and Durham County Council chair Peter Lee from mounting it until Allan had finished, despite the arrival of a police escort.[41]

The traditional May Day events could be another example of the growing divisions. In 1928 when Gateshead Labour Party completed its May Day procession at Windmill Hills, 'a smaller procession' was provided by the NUWCM, and this 'eventually organised an opposition meeting not far from the Labour platform'. Later the NUWCM branches from Tyneside and Blyth held their own May Day march from the Bigg Market to the Town Moor; headed by banners and the Jarrow drum and fife band, they claimed a turn-out of several thousand at the rally, addressed by George Wheeler, Jim Stephenson of the ILP and others.[42]

During 1928 and 1929 issues took a new turn due to developments in the Soviet Union and the Comintern. The international Communist movement entered a policy phase that came to be known as 'Class against Class'. This was to have profound implications too for the unemployed movement in the next few years.

Class against Class

Both during the miners' lockout and in the years immediately after it the Executive of the Comintern, influenced of course by the Soviet leader Joseph Stalin, increasingly adopted a more aggressive line towards the British Labour and trades union movements. The origins of this had as much to do with power struggles within the USSR as with political analysis, and by mid-1929 the consequences for world Communist Parties had become clear. It was asserted that world capitalism was in terminal decline but the prospects for revolutionary socialism faced a major obstacle in the form of the left-reformist social democratic parties, such as Labour in Britain, and the leaderships of the trade union movements. They had both been incorporated into the workings of the capitalist state, just as in Mussolini's Italy, to the extent that they should be similarly regarded as 'social fascist'. It followed therefore that any form of alliance or joint work, still less formal affiliation, with these parties was out of the question; the working class required political leadership that was independent of those structures and that was to be provided by the Communist Parties.[43]

This was a controversial change of approach that took almost a year to embed in the British Party, involving two National Congresses and an enforced change of leadership. It had also led to a significant drop in membership by 1929, although the threat of victimisation during mass unemployment must also have been a factor. Many CP members were unemployed at this time, a good many of them blacklisted as militants since 1926. The critique of Labour and the TUC would have echoed their frustrations. Further, in 1927 the government's Blanesburgh Committee had reported on the future of unemployment benefit, proposing, in effect, an attack on benefit levels and eligibility, and tighter proof of seeking work. Margaret Bondfield, Labour MP for Wallsend, had been the TUC representative on the Committee and she went along with the recommendations. Hannington was disgusted at the failure of Labour and the TUC to campaign against Blanesburgh, but despite this he was a critic of the new line; as was to be the pattern in the coming years though his criticism was confined within the four walls of the Party.[44]

At the General Election in May 1929 the CP advised against voting Labour because it was in fact the third capitalist party; its own candidates polled dismally. Wal Hannington stood as a Communist in Wallsend against Labour's Margaret Bondfield, intending to 'expose' her as the TUC representative who had signed off the Blanesburgh Report. Hannington lost his deposit; he was active in London for much of the campaign and the Party seems to have struggled to find speakers for his election meetings. Another weakness is indicated by the fact that Lily Webb was to have stood in her former NUWCM patch of Gateshead. Instead she was deployed to her native Lancashire for agitation during a major textile strike, and the CP could not raise the funds for a deposit in any case. In Seaham Party General Secretary Harry Pollitt also lost his deposit, although the Party saw his campaign against Prime Minister Ramsey MacDonald in terms of support for the Dawdon miners' dispute. In this action the Dawdon miners were opposed by both the colliery management and the DMA; Felling NUWCM leader Jimmy Ancrum won an international profile for his success in organising a 'Workers' International Relief' campaign to feed the strikers and their families.[45]

The new policy soon had consequences for the local NUWCM too. In August 1928 the Newcastle District Communist Party conference had resolved that it 'must work with all left types' provided that they were opposed to 'splitting tactics' and the 'reactionary policies of the leadership'. This seems to have meant a door was open for joint work with the Labour left. By October of the following year however William Barron had been replaced by Alf Chater as organiser of the Newcastle and Gateshead branch. According to Chater, who showed that he was a Comintern loyalist, his erstwhile NUWCM comrade Barron had been expelled for 'political unreliability' and exactly the sort of 'right-wing conciliationism' of which the old leadership had been accused. Earlier, in February 1929, Harry Bolton, the dual membership chairman of Blaydon Council, had been expelled from the Communist Party for 'indiscipline and political unreliability.' His offence had been to criticise a Communist leaflet containing attacks on the DMA leaders that he believed were misplaced.[46]

We have seen that a measure of unity in action between Labour, the CP and the NUWCM had been possible in South Shields in 1927, but during the campaign against test-work two years later it was a different story. The Labour Party and Trades Council apparently refused to work with the NUWCM because it was an 'outside body', not affiliated to the TUC. Jarrow Labour Party held a public meeting against test work but insisted that opposing it was a matter purely for the trade unions; the Labour Guardians who were trying to stop test work refused to organise a demonstration against it, a decision the NUWCM would long hold against them.[47] These examples illustrate two different causes of isolation. One was due to the hostility of the labour movement leadership towards the NUWCM, refusing it affiliation on political grounds and thus freezing it out of where once it had been embedded. The other was self-inflicted; implementing the 'class against class' line had meant to break with and potentially alienate socialists like Harry Bolton, an influential ally they could not afford to lose.

Therefore the second (and still minority) Labour government faced intransigent opposition from the CP and by extension the unemployed movement. After its national conference in 1929 that was now called the National Unemployed Workers Movement, possibly reflecting that the former 'Committee' had been a reference to the original federation of local trades council unemployed committees; no longer appropriate given the drive for revolutionary leadership. In the North East the experience of the unemployed movement since 1921 demonstrated the effectiveness of joint work with the Labour left on local authorities and the Guardians, as well as the unions but here, as elsewhere, the NUWM was to begin its organisational career in isolation. This was evident during the next National Hunger March.

The 1930 National Hunger March

During the first nine months of Ramsey MacDonald's term as Labour Prime Minister official unemployment rose from 400,000 to 1,520,000. Labour were dependent on Liberal support in parliament but the manifestoes of both parties at the election had had similar commitments about employment. Alongside the rise in unemployment was a perceived lack of action on public works schemes, benefit levels and conditions for claimants. This was the official reason for the decision to organise a national Hunger March to London only one year after the 1929 march, but in fact the decision was not taken by the NUWM but imposed on it. The Comintern, through the CPGB Central Committee, saw an opportunity to demonstrate its independent opposition to the Labour Government. The NUWM leadership, who of course were the ones with the logistical experience of these events, were critical of the decision on practical grounds; as good Communists they carried it out nevertheless.[48]

A march that was in effect against a Labour Government was even less likely to attract local support from trades councils and others than even in 1929, and so it proved. The *Newcastle Journal* reported with satisfaction that 'Labour headquarters are making strenuous efforts to restrain Labour parties from assisting' with the march although 'restraint' is probably too strong a word. As historians have noted, Labour activists would have been reluctant to support a protest against the government, which in any case had only held office for nine months. The marchers' demands were the familiar ones of public works schemes or full maintenance, but also the abolition of test work and the 'not genuinely seeking work' rule.

At the beginning of April 1930 50 marchers assembled in the Bigg Market for the march to London. Their number was half of the target the Tyneside NUWM had been set, but that was the case too with every other contingent in the country. The national total was only around 350 marchers but for the first time they included a women's march, a small group of Lancashire textile workers. In the North East the march leaders 'were prominent members of the Communist movement on Tyneside' such as Tom Thurlbeck from Sunderland, Jim Ancrum from Felling – both involved in the previous year's march - and Chris Flanagan from Newcastle. Earlier they had stated their intention to 'protest at the failure of the Labour Government to find employment or alleviate the conditions of the unemployed in Britain'. Their banners included slogans such as 'We Refuse to Starve at Home' and Flanagan announced their belief that there would be 'no justice without a struggle'.[49]

The Home Office was informed that 'The Chief Constable of Newcastle states that most of the men comprising the Tyneside contingent are of the lodging house type ...' This deserves a little expansion. The Chief Constable was suggesting that instead of being respectable family men these unemployed were young with no stake in society. Unmarried, they would have had to leave the family home if they had one to receive any relief payments in their own right and hence the lodging house. Under the circumstances this should not be taken as a comment on their character, although there was a problem at Thirsk, apparently, where the police reported that two young marchers from Sunderland had absconded with the collection boxes.[50]

The less the local labour movement support, of course, the more the marchers would have to make use of local workhouses. As before this involved the prospect of having to defy the workhouse management over being treated as 'casuals', a policy the Ministry of Health encouraged as a means of deterring Hunger Marches. As before again there were occasions on the route south when they did this successfully and occasions when they marched on rather than accept the normal workhouse regulations. There were occasions too when the local accommodation found for them (and here the Co-operative movement played its part) involved floors in schools or Boy Scout Halls.

On arrival in London the Marchers took part in the May Day demonstration and tried unsuccessfully to lobby parliament; MacDonald and his ministers, like Baldwin before him, refused to meet a deputation. They did have a notable success with their London accommodation. Having been assured that they would not be treated as 'casuals' by the City of Westminster workhouse, 'they marched through the main gates and took the place over ... ran up the red flag, and installed the march council in the board room where it could receive visitors, discuss reports, and plan activities ... Food was brought in; the marchers' cooks took over the cookhouse and store room ...'[51]

Appeals were made for the money for the fares home; Sid Elias recalled how the cash he brought to the booking office for the Yorkshire and Tyneside fares was later examined by the Special Branch. The historian of the Hunger Marches notes that the main achievement of the 1930 initiative was the rebuffal of the use of the Poor Law against them.[52] During the next month of June the Parliamentary and local Labour Parties were alive with debate about unemployment, but they could not have anticipated the dramatic reaction of their leadership to the economic crisis.

Notes

1   Anthony Mason, *The General Strike in the North East* (Hull: Hull University Press 1976); Hester Barron, *The 1926 Miners' Lockout: Meanings of Community in the Durham Coalfield* (Oxford: Oxford University Press 2010); see review of

the Barron book by Don Watson, *Twentieth Century British History* Vol 22 Issue 4 (December 2011).

2   Charlie Woods, interview with Peter Brabban 1979; See also James Klugmann, *History of the Communist Party of Great Britain Vol 2: 1925-1926, The General Strike* (London: Lawrence and Wishart 1980, p. 149).

3   Minutes of the County Borough of Gateshead Watch Committee 22 November 1926 (TWAS: CB GA/57/15).

4   *Newcastle Journal* 3 June 1926; *Blyth News* 6 April, 3 and 23 May and 15 November 1926; *The Miner* 28 August 1926.

5   *Chester le Street Chronicle* 15 October and 5 November 1926.

6   *House of Commons Written Answers* 24 March 1927 pp. 583-4.

7   George Short, 'The General Strike and Class Struggles in the North East 1925-28', *Marxism Today* Vol 14 (October 1970, p. 314).

8   Charlie Woods, interview with Peter Brabban 1979; see also Joe Clarke, 'The General Strike in the North East' *North East Labour History* No.10 (1976, pp. 4-8).

9   Letter in *The Woman Worker* 7 October 1926.

10   *Sunderland Echo* 27 October 1926.

11   *Annual Report of the Medical Officer of Health for the County Borough of Gateshead 1926* (Gateshead: County Borough of Gateshead 1927, p. 11); *Annual Report of the Medical Officer of Health for the County of Durham 1926* (Durham: Durham County Council 1927, p. 34, p. 39); *Annual Report of the Medical Officer of Health for the County of Durham 1927* (Durham: Durham County Council 1928, p. 33).

12   Christopher Thomson, 'The Chester le Street Union 1926: Creativity and Defiance in a Community Under Siege' B.A. Dissertation University of Manchester 1984.

13   *Blaydon Courier* 26 June and 14 August 1926.

14   Keith Feiling, *The Life of Neville Chamberlain* (London: MacMillan 1946, p. 140); *Durham Advertiser* 2 September 1926; Christopher Thomson, *The Chester le Street Union.*

15   *Chester le Street Chronicle* 3 September, 8 and 15 October 1926.

16   *North Mail* 23 July 1927; an example is Hester Barron, *Meanings of Community*, p. 100.

17   *North Mail* 21 and 25 July 1927; Sam Davies, 'Legal Challenges to Labour Rule: Gateshead Politics Between the Wars' *North East History* No. 41 (2010 pp. 10-37).

18   George Short, interview with Peter Brabban 1979; John McIlroy, Barry McLoughlin, Alan Campbell and John Halstead, 'Forging the Faithful: The British at the International Lenin School' *Labour History Review* Vol 68 No 1 (April 2003, p. 123).

19   *Workers' Life* 24 February and 27 July 1928; *Blaydon Courier* 21 July 1928.

20   *Workers' Life* 6 May, 30 September, 25 November 1927; 17 February 1928, and 31 May 1929.

21   Charlie Hall, interview with Kevin Morgan, Communist Party Biographical Project (BLSA); see also Joe Clarke, *The General Strike*; Matthew Worley, *Class*

Against Class: The Communist Party in Britain Between the Wars (London: I.B. Tauris 2002 p161).

22   *Workers' Weekly* 24 April 1925; Minutes of the Central Committee of the Communist Party of Great Britain November 19 1932 (LHASC). For CP membership figures in the region see Andrew Thorpe, 'The Membership of the Communist Party of Great Britain 1920-1945' *Historical Journal* Vol 3 No 43 (2000 pp. 777-800).

23   *Workers' Life* 28 January and 1 July 1927, 14 June 1929.

24   *Workers' Life* 9 and 16 September, 14 October and 11 November 1927; *North Mail* 9 September, 28 October and 2 November 1927.

25   *North Mail* 8 March 1928; Minutes of the County Borough of Gateshead Watch Committee 19 March and 16 April 1928 (TWAS: CB GA/57/16); County Borough of Gateshead Constabulary Report 12 March 1928 (NA: HO/144/13864); *North Mail* 5 April 1928.

26   *Workers' Life* 11 May 1928; *Shields Daily News* 28 April 1928.

27   *North Mail* 25 and 26 October 1927, and 3 April 1928; *Shields Daily News* 3 April 1928; Matt Perry, *The Jarrow Crusade: Protest and Legend* (Sunderland: Sunderland University Press 2005, p. 37); *North Mail* 29 February 1928.

28   County Borough of Gateshead Constabulary Reports 10 and 14 November 1927, 25 May 1928 (NA: HO/144/13864); *Newcastle Evening Chronicle* 10 November 1927.

29   *Newcastle Journal* 4 July 1928; *Workers' Life* 14 and 21 September, 12 October 1928; *Blyth News* 28 June 1928; *Workers' Life* 23 September 1927, 2 and 23 November 1928.

30   Minutes of the County Borough of Gateshead Watch Committee 14 October 1929 (TWAS: CB GA/57/16); *Blaydon Courier* 26 January 1929; 19 May and 21 July 1928.

31   Peter Kingsford, *The Hunger Marchers in Britain 1920-1940* (London: Lawrence and Wishart 1982); *Workers' Life* 21 December 1928; *Sunday Worker* 6 January 1929.

32   Kingsford, *The Hunger Marchers*; *Newcastle Journal* 28 January 1929.

33   *Newcastle Evening Chronicle* 14 January 1929; *Blaydon Courier* 2 February 1929; Report of the Chief Constable of Newcastle on Tyne 23, 28 and 29 January 1929 (NA: HO 144/12143).

34   *Sunday Worker* 6, 20 and 27 January 1929; Report of the Chief Constable of Newcastle on Tyne 23, 28 and 29 January 1929 (NA: HO 144/12143); *Newcastle Journal* 30 and 31 January 1929.

35   *Sunday Worker* 3 February 1929.

36   Kingsford *The Hunger Marchers*; also Wal Hannington, *The Story of the National Hunger March* (London: National Unemployed Workers' Committee Movement 1929).

37   *Newcastle Journal* 25 February 1929; *North Mail* 25 February 1929.

38   For a full account see John McIlroy, 'Revolutionaries' in John McIlroy, Alan Campbell and Keith Gildart (eds.), *Industrial Politics and the 1926 Mining Lockout: The Struggle for Dignity* (Cardiff: University of Wales Press 2009 pp. 269-99); also Willie Thompson, *The Good Old Cause: British Communism*

1920-1991 (London: Pluto Press1992).

39   Durham Miners' Association Executive Circular *Disruptive Organisations Operating in Durham County*, 25 May 1927 (GLS); *North Mail* 25 July 1927.

40   *North Mail* 23 April 1928; *Workers' Life* April 13 and 27 July 1928; 3 and 10 June 1927.

41   *North Mail* 20 and 23 February 1929; *Newcastle Journal* 30 and 31 July 1928.

42   *Newcastle Journal* 7 May 1928; *Workers' Life* 11 May 1928.

43   For a full account see Noreen Branson, *History of the Communist Party of Great Britain 1927-1941* (London: Lawrence and Wishart 1985); also Willie Thompson, *The Good Old Cause* and John McIlroy, *Revolutionaries.*

44   Richard Croucher, *We Refuse to Starve in Silence: A History of the National Unemployed Workers' Movement 1920-1946* (London: Lawrence and Wishart 1987 pp. 98-99).

45   *Sunday Worker* 5 and 26 May 1929; *North Mail* 7 and 20th May 1929. Richard Croucher (*We Refuse*, p. 98) states that Hannington's campaign must have been 'lively' but there is no evidence of this in the local press. Pollitt (*North Mail* 20 May) saw the Dawdon miners 'strengthening their ranks for the final struggle to overthrow the entire capitalist system'. See also Jim Ancrum, 'The W.I.R. and the Dawdon Lock-Out' *Labour Monthly* No 9 (1929 pp. 555-558); on the dispute itself see Stuart Howard, 'Dawdon in the Third Period: The Dawdon Dispute of 1929 and the Communist Party', *North East Labour History* No.21 (1987 pp. 3-17).

46   *Workers' Life* 24 August 1928 and 4 October 1929; *North Mail* 16 February 1929.

47   *Workers' Life* 5, 12 and 26 April 1929.

48   Minutes of the Central Committee of the Communist Party of Great Britain, 11 and 12 January 1931 (LHASC.)

49   Minutes of the Central Committee 11 and 12 January 1931; *Newcastle Journal* 26 March 1930; *Northern Echo* 3 April 1930.

50   Report of Assistant Commissioner Metropolitan Police to Home Office April 1930 (NA: HO 144/20697).

51   Peter Kingsford, *The Hunger Marchers in Britain*, p. 125.

52   John Halstead, 'The Reminiscences of Sid Elias', *Bulletin of the Society for the Study of Labour History* No 38 (spring 1979, p. 47); Peter Kingsford, *The Hunger Marchers in Britain*, p. 127.

Chapter Five

MEANS TEST PROTEST 1930 –1933

The Coming of the Means Test

The Wall Street stockmarket crash and trade recession of 1929 caused British unemployment to reach 20% of the insured workforce by the end of 1931. The Labour government could neither agree on how to tackle this crisis nor how to meet the accelerating costs of unemployment benefit. In August 1931 Prime Minister James Ramsay MacDonald made a unique response to the economic crisis: he and some Cabinet colleagues formed a 'National Government' coalition with the Tories. As a result, at the General Election of October 1931 the Labour vote collapsed to the extent that MacDonald's 'National Government' was returned with a massive majority. The parliamentary wing of the labour movement was too small for effective opposition as the new government embarked on a series of crisis measures to reduce public spending, with the worst consequences being felt by unemployed workers and their families.

In December 1931 unemployment benefit for adults was reduced by 10%. As George Short remembered:

At this period the 10% cut amongst the unemployed meant deep inroads into standards of life that were already very low. We were a man, wife and two children getting 28s a week and out of that we had to pay 12s rent. So a 10% cut in that meant the difference between a meal and going hungry in those days …

The Anomalies Act removed large numbers of married women from the unemployment register even when they had paid National Insurance contributions. In Sunderland and Newcastle up to 80% of married women claimants were removed from the register almost overnight. Unemployment benefit would expire after six months; any further claims were classed as 'transitional payments' and the responsibility of local Public Assistance Committees who replaced the old Boards of Guardians. These PACs were composed of local councillors but did not, in the eyes of the unemployed, represent any real change. They met in the same buildings, employed the same Relieving Officers and took the same decisions about relief in cash or in kind as the old Guardians.

The government was determined to reduce spending on benefits and to eliminate what it saw as 'waste' and inappropriate payments. Claimants whose unemployment benefit was exhausted were referred by the Employment Exchange to the PAC; they sent an inspector to their homes to assess every aspect of their incomes and resources under the Means Test. All savings were taken into account, including any due dividend payments from the Co-op. The PACs then decided whether any benefit was to be paid, in line with their existing, often lower, scales for uninsured people. Any cash was paid through the Employment Exchange and payments could also be 'in kind'. Phyllis Short recalled:

> … we were living on 28s a week. I got a little job at the fever hospital in Stockton as a cleaner, I got £1 a week and so they stopped 9s a week off his money. That was how the Means Test worked, any money coming in from a son or daughter working was counted in and taken off your dole.[1]

The type of 'inquisitorial methods' complained about by the unemployed in the region ten years previously paled into insignificance by comparison. The Means Test was being applied to 900,000 people by the autumn of 1931 and it was the target for the campaigns of the unemployed for the rest of the decade. This chapter examines how the official labour and the militant unemployed movements in the North East responded in the early 1930s.

Protest

Some protest was purely individual, as Bobbie Qualie, an NUWM activist in Sunderland recalled:

> It was tough, very tough. That was the reason why, if you go in the labour exchange now, you see a grill across that thing, because many men used to jump over the top of that thing, jump over the counter, and slug the clerk, because the clerk used to say, "No money for you!" "No money for you!" he'd say, and you'd end up with the police being called.[2]

Protest was also political, and the NUWM and the official labour movement began the decade as rivals for its leadership. At the end of November 1931 Wallsend Labour Party agreed to organise a series of meetings to 'protest against the brutal manner in which the Means Test was being applied by the local PAC'. This had been prompted by 'appeals from the genuine unemployed who would not associate with the Unemployed Workers Committee, which is a Communist organisation'. In the first week of December 1931 thousands demonstrated outside Wallsend Town Hall, where there were angry scenes in the public gallery. In the second week Labour councillors led a march of 5,000 to the south area PAC office in Newcastle, 'led by the huge banner of the Wallsend branch of the Municipal and General Workers' Union', the Boilermakers' Society and the Labour Party. The same leadership was evident when 2,000 marched in Wallsend four days later. During this time there had also been demonstrations outside the home of the Mayor of Wallsend, which had been driven back by baton-wielding police; this may have been an NUWM initiative, repeating some actions of the 1920s. In Blyth, when the same thing happened, it was certainly appeared so when the Mayor of the town announced that he 'would not be intimidated by Communists'. Wallsend Labour Party and Trades Council had formed a 'Council of Action' by mid-December to advise the unemployed and asserted that they 'would only give assistance to trade unionists'.

In the Wallsend area it was the mainstream movement that continued the initiative into early 1932, so that in the eyes of the local press it was the 'centre of the agitation against the operation of the Means Test'. A Joint Action Committee was formed in Willington Quay, made up of trade unions, Co-op Women's Guilds, churches and the British Legion to press for 'workers' representation' on the PAC Sub-Committee to 'secure fair treatment', as was the case with the Courts of Referees. In January 1932 Wallsend Council of Action sent a deputation accompanied by a demonstration 'of several hundred' to draw attention to specific cases, and press for trades council representation on the PAC. Assured that the matter would be looked into, the deputation reported back to the open-air public meeting.[3]

At the end of 1931 a deputation from South Shields Labour Party and Trades Council, all 'respectable trade unionists, and members of the Labour Party, which is a respectable organisation' had sought a meeting with the Council's PAC to press them on Means Test issues. This had been refused, and referred to a lower level sub-committee. The furious delegation had interrupted the meeting and eventually been escorted out by the police. In mid-January 1932 a large demonstration accompanied a deputation to South Shields Town Hall to support the right of the deputation to be heard by the full PAC; in this they were successful. There were an estimated 15,000 on the march, headed by six miners' lodges with bands and banners, contingents from trades unions, Labour Party branches and Women's Sections. According to the press 'members of the Minority Movement' had attempted to 'squeeze in to the ranks' but had been frustrated by the police, who also took down their red banner. They had to join in at the end of the march and the police later thwarted their efforts to hold another one.[4]

NUWM and the Minority Movement

Dave Springhall, acting District Secretary for the North East, gave a damning account of the state of the Party in the area at the Communist Party Central Committee in January 1932. He reported that there were less than 200 members in the district, 'only a handful are employed' and only 18 were women. They certainly hadn't impressed him; 'bums and stiffs' and 'lumpen proletariat elements' also featured in his description. He stated that the Labour Party had been far more active in organising meetings and demonstrations against the Means Test, and he included the Wallsend marches described earlier in his catalogue of the Tyneside District's failings. According to him, 'In the face of this Labour Party campaign our comrades in Wallsend are tending to retreat, and think that the only thing they can do in this situation is through the groups of NUWM comprising only a few score, to push the Labour Party to do things, and this clearly is a complete negation of our line of independent leadership'. It is understandable then that Springhall should conclude that the Party on Tyneside was in a 'state of chronic isolation from the masses'.[5]

This reflected Springhall's recent and bruising encounter with the realities of operating as a small and sectarian organisation in Tyneside politics. He had led an unsuccessful Minority Movement attempt to stimulate a strike at Tyne Dock in response to a wage cut that had been accepted by the union leadership. He may also have been present at the 15,000-strong Labour Party march in South Shields described above. Inevitably, there was no recorded discussion of how far the Party (through the Communist International) had itself contributed to its 'chronic isolation from the masses'.

Although clearly the Labour Party was leading anti-Means Test activity in some areas there were parts of the North East where the Minority Movement and the NUWM undoubtedly had a presence and an impact. Springhall's report should not necessarily be accepted as an accurate assessment.

One example is the major role it played with the Arab merchant seamen in North and South Shields in 1930 and 1931, where the sailors were on strike against both the shipping companies and the attitude of the National Union of Seamen. During the summer of 1930 Minority Movement speakers appeared regularly at the New Quay in North Shields and Mill Dam in

South Shields in support of the Arab sailors. They also condemned what they saw as attempts at divide and rule, accusing management and the NUS of '… stirring up racial feelings for the purpose of creating conditions where seamen will be fighting for jobs, so as to pave the way for ship owners to force a further reduction of wages on the seamen and to keep them divided …' On August 2 though there were clashes between the Arab pickets and the white sailors who were crossing their lines at the shipping office; the police responded with a baton charge and street fighting broke out. The police action seems to have been aimed at the strikers because of the 27 men who later appeared in court 21 were Arabs and 3 were Minority Movement activists. One of them, Walter Harrison, was charged with incitement to riot and was gaoled in November. Harrison was also active in the NUWM in North and South Shields.

The Arab sailors tried to continue their strike, obviously without any support from the NUS and as was usual at the time the South Shields Board of Guardians refused the men outdoor relief because they were engaged in a trades dispute. Therefore at the end of September they adopted the tactic of the mass entry to the workhouse, which suggests that they were in contact with NUWCM veterans who had tried this in the past. Unfortunately this time it failed. Those who were not British nationals were deported and the others too had to leave.[6]

The Minority Movement though was influential in preventing inter-racial trouble in North Shields the following year, through the speaking efforts of Alec Robson. Alec 'Spike' Robson was a boxing champion and First World War veteran who had joined the Communist Party during the unemployed agitations of 1921. He was active in the Seamen's' Minority Movement and, when between ships, North Shields NUWM. '500 to 600 men gathered in dense crowds at the New Quay' at the end of July 1931 when white sailors attempted to get work that had been assigned to Arabs. Robson and other speakers 'deprecated the attitude taken up towards Arabs by North Shields seamen' and insisted that the Arabs were union members and therefore just as entitled to sign on a ship as they were. A reputation as a boxing champion must have been an asset in such situations.[7]

Both Robson and Harrison had leadership roles in the NUWM too. In October 1931, whilst he was free on bail, Harrison was part of a deputation 'from unemployed seamen and other workers' at South Shields Council. They had been elected at a Market Place rally to ask for a town meeting to condemn the National Government for the cuts and the Means Test. Although they had support from some councillors the matter was referred to another committee on procedural grounds. Later that month Harrison and a comrade from this deputation also pursued the issue of access to South Shields Market Place for public meetings. They questioned the constitutional right of the Chief Constable to place time limits on meetings, and his far from impartial approach to granting permits for demonstrations. The Council supported its Chief Constable.[8]

Across the river in North Shields the following month a bitter dispute flared up between unemployed merchant sailors and officials of their own National Union of Seamen. These men, unemployed for some time, had fallen behind with their subscriptions because they could not afford to pay them. This was surely understandable in view of the level of relief they would have had to live on. But when they were offered work on a Tyne ship the local NUS full-time official refused to allow them to sign on because they were not up-to-date members; they claimed that the backdated subscriptions being demanded were unaffordable.

In response a Minority Movement-led demonstration occupied the NUS office to press a case to the North East Area Secretary: union rules were being enforced too strictly and the official responsible should be transferred elsewhere. Later a demonstration of 500, 'following the red banner of the Seamen's Minority Movement ... attracted a dense crowd of spectators' when they held a mass meeting at Harbour View. This agreed a deputation led by Alec Robson to meet the local Police Inspector to put the case for the official's removal, which suggests that feeling was so high that the man was in danger. What followed was a success indeed for the movement – two days later the NUS official had been transferred and 40 North Shields men had signed on board an oil tanker.[9]

The NUWM came to the fore over the operation of the Means Test in North Shields. At the beginning of 1932 an NUWM deputation met a Tynemouth PAC official to discuss what they called 'harsh anomalies' in the payment of relief and the imposition of task work, and were referred to the PAC meeting. Later, following a mass meeting at Harbour View, Walter Harrison led a deputation 'from the National Unemployed Workers Movement of the Communist Party' into the PAC meeting while a crowd of supporters demonstrated outside. North Shields NUWM wanted, as had the Trades Council in Wallsend the previous year, to be represented on the PAC. They also wanted to be recognised as advocates for claimants, and for the PAC to pay relief scales at the same rate as unemployment benefits and to include a coal allowance.

PAC chairman Councillor Stanley Holmes dismissed the idea of NUWM representation on the grounds that it was 'only a very small section of the unemployed, led by what I consider to be agitators ... who get their instructions from outside'. On the other hand they were prepared to discuss cases 'with the trade unions, who look after their members' but the Committee 'would not permit such cases to be represented by other individuals' and nor would it 'receive a deputation if it was accompanied by a demonstration'. Although the Ministry of Labour recognised the NUWM when it came to employment benefit claims local authority PACs were not obliged to do so for transitional payments claims. Clearly Tynemouth was one that would only recognise the official movement as advocates.[10]

Action on Teesside

In June 1932 George Short explained to the Communist Party Central Committee how, in his experience, the NUWM could take up the leadership of the unemployed. At an open-air meeting in Stockton of about 600 unemployed nearly fifty had come forward to join the NUWM against the wishes of the Labour Party. This was because the NUWM had offered to 'picket every worker's house for a worker who was refused by the PAC. This had a tremendous effect on the unemployed'. Short was not clear in his report about the objective of the picket, whether it was to resist distraint or for some other purpose, but he claimed that 'the main thing was the question of action'. In making this kind of commitment the NUWM in Stockton had 'shown by deed the difference between a revolutionary organisation and one based on constitutional methods'. Indeed, during the 1920s the movement's willingness to use 'non-constitutional' methods had stood it in good stead.

It has been recalled that the NUWM started in a very small way in Middlesbrough, with only about six men, and that people were put off by its well-known Communist connections. It had certainly had established itself in nearby Stockton at this time. In October 1931 a meeting at Stockton Cross had proceeded into a demonstration and two deputations to the Council. One was from Stockton and Thornaby Unemployed Workers Association (affiliated to the trades council and so therefore 'official') and led by MP Frank Riley. The other was from the NUWM and led by George Short. This may have been the meeting Short was referring to in his report to the CP Central Committee.[11]

Further demonstrations followed. Short recalled a success:

We had the problem that unemployed worker's children in Stockton were getting 3s a head from the PAC whereas those in Thornaby, Middlesbrough, places that came under the North Riding Council; they were getting two bob a head. At that time Stockton came under Durham

County Council and that was Labour, paying more for children. But the boundaries meant we had the peculiar position that you could be standing in the same dole queue in Stockton but the man signing on behind you would be getting more for his kids. The NUWM raised a big campaign about this. We organised a march from Stockton, Thornaby, South Bank and elsewhere to Middlesbrough Town Hall. The people from South Bank had a drum and fife band. We'd had an agreement beforehand that the head official of the PAC would meet us. We extracted a promise from him that if the Middlesbrough Council publicly agreed the PAC would pay the extra bob. We went out and told the crowd that the target was now Middlesbrough Council. So later we organised a demonstration to the Council and eventually they accepted the argument. We won the three bob![12]

During the summer and autumn of 1932 Teesside witnessed a number of NUWM rallies and demonstrations. In the first week of August Middlesbrough Council did increase some relief scales, but made largely negative responses to the movement's demands. It stated that there was no evidence of widespread malnutrition amongst schoolchildren, they had no statutory duty to provide footwear, and denied that applicants were being rejected for Council housing because of unemployment. The NUWM spectators in the gallery were refused leave to speak, and were ejected by the police following 'disorder': an unemployed man held up his shoe, 'worn to the upper', threw it at the councillors and shouted 'what we have to wear. No sole, like you have no soul'. Outside in Victoria Square the crowd, 'an angry demonstration of the unemployed accompanied by their wives and children' were addressed by a speaker standing on a wall until again the police dispersed them.

After a meeting at Stockton Cross at the end of October George Short led a protest march and small deputation to the home of the councillor who chaired the Stockton PAC. There he secured an agreement to a series of regular meetings to discuss cases and issues. Early the next month Short and two women formed the deputation sent by a march to the Stockton PAC, only to find the road closed off by the police. They wanted the PAC to press Durham County Council for higher relief scales and a coal allowance for the unemployed along with free school meals.

There was what seems to have been a rare example of co-operation when, in October 1932, 1,000 people took part in a rally organised by Darlington NUWM and the Darlington Trades Council Unemployed Association. A month later 'hundreds of unemployed men associated with the NUWM' marched on Middlesbrough Town Hall to query why relief payments were being refused to two of their members; around 250 from South Bank with their drum and fife band returned to demonstrate on the following day, only to find that 100 of them were refused when they went to sign on that afternoon. They should have signed that morning but had not because they were on the demonstration. This sparked off a disturbance when they rushed the labour exchange and were dispersed by the police. Eventually they were allowed to sign on and further trouble was averted by 'tactful handling on the part of the labour exchange staff, the police, and the leaders of the unemployed'.[13]

The 1932 Labour and TUC Conferences

In September 1932 the TUC Conference was held in Newcastle City Hall and the regional NUWM demonstrated outside the building in significant numbers. 'More than 1,000 Communists and members of the unemployed organisation, men, women and children' marched from a rally on the Town Moor to City Hall, then to another rally at the Bigg Market addressed by Wal Hannington and Willie Allan from the Miners' Minority Movement.

TUC chairman Walter Citrine successfully blocked a request to hear an NUWM deputation led by Bob Smith, a Communist who had been gaoled following an unemployed demonstration in Stanley a year previously. The deputation wanted to put 'proposals for united action by the employed and unemployed to smash the Means Test and further cuts', but Citrine, despite protests from some delegates including one from Tyneside, ruled that the deputation would not represent the local unemployed but the NUWM, a Communist front. Delegates voted by 1,577,000 to 963,000 to refuse the deputation a hearing; such support as there was could more than likely be the result of sympathy for the unemployed rather than politics; a later motion from the floor in favour of joint working with the NUWM could not find a seconder.[14]

At the Labour Party Conference the following month delegates debated a national campaign of protest against the Means Test. The prospective parliamentary candidate for Seaham, Manny Shinwell, led the attack, having first warned Conference against allowing 'external organisations' (i.e. the CP and the NUWM) to organise the unemployed to deal with the Means Test; that should be undertaken by the Divisional Labour Parties and the trades unions. The point was how to do this. Shinwell argued that it was impossible to ask 'our people to exercise patience until a Labour Government is returned to power,' and the Parliamentary Labour Party was too weak in numbers to trouble the Government. Instead he asked 'whether the time has not arrived when the movement as a whole should refuse to undertake any longer the administration of the Means Test'. This of course would mean that Government-appointed commissioners would do it, 'but they will find it a little bit too much for them ... and there is nothing to stop our local authority members giving the commissioners as much trouble as they possibly can'. He argued that this to be effective it would have to be a country-wide policy led by the Labour Party National Executive.

As we shall see, Shinwell was articulating the anger felt by Labour councillors in the North East and of course elsewhere about what was going on. It seems likely that this policy would have been popular with them. Instead the National Executive fielded George Lansbury, who drew on his credentials as the one-time imprisoned leader of Poplar Council to argue against the idea. His main point was 'I do not believe that this Conference is in a position to determine that for the whole of the country'. In other words it was not the role of the Conference to mandate non-co-operation with the working of the Means Test across the party and its councillors. Labour was just not that kind of organisation. Conference voted down Shinwell's proposals in favour of work for the return of a Labour Government and thus the abolition of the Means Test.[15]

It is worth speculating about what might have happened if Labour had accepted Shinwell's argument. If Commissioners had had to be appointed across all the areas of high unemployment and if Labour councillors had been supported to follow their decent instincts, then the Government could have found it very difficult to operate the system. Concessions at least might have been forthcoming. The anger certainly seems to have been there in the Labour ranks in this region and elsewhere. In 1931 Labour members of Gateshead Council had unsuccessfully moved against implementing the Means Test; the following year Sunderland Labour councillors withdrew from the PAC in protest, as did their colleagues in Wallsend and Hartlepool; the Labour group at Newburn Council boycotted the Hexham PAC because 'they refused to carry out the despicable work of the Means Test'. A week after the Party Conference Durham County Council, or rather its ruling Labour Group, famously did vote to cease co-operation with the Means Test. They knew this would mean appointed Commissioners, but because of the Council's 'generosity' with relief payments they were being threatened with this anyway. They had been told officially in September that they were not carrying out their statutory duty in regard to the Means Test. Their mood could be summed up by the Councillor who declared that 'I will not be a party to the still further degradation of my own class ... let the so-called National Government take the responsibility and be seen to do so ...'

By their Means Test protest they were 'hoping we have given a lead to the whole of the country which will eventually be the means of smashing this infamous Act'.

In terms of Labour Councils though, this was not to be. The co-ordinated action set out by Shinwell did not happen. Such a potential conflict with the elected legislature was not the course the national leadership was prepared to take. These two major conferences of the labour movement condemned the Means Test and the Anomalies Act and re-affirmed the principle of work or full maintenance; but they had clearly shunned the NUWM, and their own occasional demonstrations were the only extra-parliamentary action they were likely to support.[16]

Attempts to get the Durham Miners Association to commit to a more militant approach were not successful at this time. At the end of December 1931 a conference of 46 lodges at Chester le Street called on their Executive to lobby for the abolition of the Means Test, but Communist checkweighman George Lumley's amendment to mandate DMA members serving on PACs to 'refuse orders meaning a reduction in the standards of life for our people' was lost. This would have meant non-co-operation with the Means Test as distinct from leaving the field to the Commissioners as Durham County Council did the next year. In April 1933, just before the trial of the county Hunger March leaders, as we shall see, the DMA Executive rejected 'by a substantial majority' motions by some lodges for a forty-eight hour strike in the mining industry against the Means Test. There were other radical voices. Shortly after the Chester le Street DMA conference the Tyneside Federation of Trades Councils attracted 200 delegates from the unions and the Labour Party who were members of PACs to their own conference in Newcastle. This meeting also called on the TUC to demand the abolition of the Means Test, but once again a motion in favour of calling for industrial action if this failed was not carried. The confrontations over the Means Test in the next two years were led by the NUWM.[17]

The North Shields Clash

The sour relations between North Shields NUWM and the Tynemouth PAC had deteriorated further by the autumn of 1932. During August and September the NUWM held public meetings to expose the comparatively low rates of outdoor relief in Tynemouth Borough as well as the fact that claimants were not actually receiving what they were supposed to. At the end of September the NUWM held a meeting at Harbour View and then marched to the nearby PAC offices and the Town Hall to protest at the arrangement to send a woman with three children to the workhouse. The branch subsequently claimed that it was this intervention that had ensured that her case was successfully considered for outdoor relief. However the Council also re-iterated its position that no deputation would be met if it was accompanied by a demonstration, and nor would it meet a deputation from the NUWM, only from 'unions representing organised labour in the borough'.

The NUWM challenged this on in early October after a mass meeting of several thousand people at Harbour View. They were addressed by Spike Robson, who had also arranged for the PAC chairman Councillor Stanley Holmes to speak and answer questions. The reception given to Holmes was rough; he was 'persistently howled down, women armed with tin megaphones were amongst the most boisterous of the shouters'. Nor did a Labour councillor fare much better, being an obvious target for Communist supporters. When Robson resumed the rally agreed on a demonstration to the PAC meeting later that day to press for higher relief scales.[18]

The police were obviously expecting to tackle a large demonstration because they had arranged for reinforcements from Newcastle. When the marchers, headed by a band and NUWM banners, men and women, 'some with babes in arms' arrived from Harbour View they found the road to the PAC offices in Northumberland Square cordoned off and the deputation refused entry. The marchers resumed their route but again they were blocked, and then once more; Spike Robson began to address the crowd, according to the NUWM to tell them to re-assemble at Harbour View, but then the police made their first baton charge. The march was broken up, the banners struck down, the crowd moved back to Harbour View but then returned, to be met by another charge. According to the press 'men and women were knocked down and trampled upon in the rush and the scenes were very ugly'. Arrests were being made and the crowd tried to rescue those arrested; shop windows were broken and sections of the crowd fought with the police at times during the afternoon, and another baton charge was made. According to Charlie Woods' report in the *Daily Worker* the women in particular were 'conspicuous by the determination with which they resisted the charge of the police, slogan boards and sticks being used to defend themselves'. There was clearly some fierce brawling going on and a mass meeting later lobbied the Chief Constable for the release of those arrested. The next day three North Shields NUWM leaders including Robson and Harrison were arrested at their homes.[19]

The arrested men were remanded from the magistrates' court – Harrison declaring that it was the PAC who should be in the dock, for they were starving women and children – to Newcastle Crown Court amid a heavy police presence to hold back a sympathetic crowd. The men were charged, variously, with common law riot, assaulting the police, and criminal damage. Lord Justice Goddard presided and threatened contempt of court proceedings against those at a Newcastle meeting who had sent him a telegram demanding their release. Robson and Harrison could have avoided their four months gaol sentence and been bound over if they had agreed 'not to give political speeches likely to cause agitation'. This they refused to do.

There were some interesting consequences to this clash. NUWM branches and some sympathisers protested to the Council over the actions of the police, but that was predictable. A significant reaction was that of Tynemouth Labour Party, who, to the surprise of some in the town, protested to the Council and submitted an emergency resolution to the Labour Party Conference. Delegates there agreed to condemn 'the batoning by police of workers taking part in unemployed demonstrations in North Shields and elsewhere' and called for the Home Office to ensure that unemployed demonstrators were given full facilities by the police and not 'looked on as enemies'. The reaction was significant because Labour had never shown sympathy for the NUWM in the town; neither had Tynemouth Trades Council, who now joined with the NUWM branch in a deputation to the PAC at the end of October. Here too, for the first time, Tynemouth PAC agreed to meet a deputation that included the NUWM.

This deputation pressed for relief scales to match the minimum subsistence level put forward in recent social survey reports, and only a quarter of it at most to be paid 'in kind'; better employment terms for those on relief work, Trades Council participation on the PAC and representation rights for the NUWM there. They were unsuccessful and this joint exercise does not appear to have been repeated; it was probably local anger at the action of the police that had prompted it. Finally, Harrison was one of the Communist candidates for the Tynemouth Council elections at this time, his campaign obviously hampered by his arrest and remand in custody. Nevertheless he came second in Central Ward, some 40 votes ahead of Labour. Besides public sympathy this vote was probably also a reflection of the community and advocacy work the NUWM was putting into the area, a point which will be discussed in detail in another chapter.[20]

Representation and Building the NUWM

The introduction of the Means Test created more demand for the advice, advocacy and representation roles of the unemployed movement. George Short recalled how representing a claimant, and especially one who had been turned down, could be combined with publicity, politics and participation through the regular public meetings his branch held at Stockton Cross:

When a person went before a tribunal he was entitled to have a lawyer or a friend. The unemployed couldn't afford lawyers so the NUWM took on the role of friend. But the importance was not just the ability to argue a case, although you made yourself absolutely well acquainted with all the regulations and what you could get and what you couldn't get and we put out in cyclostyle form all the things people were entitled to, it wasn't just the ability to argue a case it was the knowledge that if an injustice was inflicted on an unemployed man then the whole town would know on the Wednesday night, the Friday night or the Sunday night. And these meetings, these meetings in Stockton for example, were not just frothy propaganda they were report back meetings where you gave the details of cases taken up and gave people encouragement not to accept things.

At the same time:

If you got someone pulling a fast one, you're negotiating about his case with the labour exchange but the clerk says, 'but he hasn't told you the whole story', and then he began to list one or two big loopholes, things that weren't part of the case you'd been primed with, well me, for myself, I just washed my hands of it then and there on the spot. And reported that case back to the next meeting at Stockton Cross. And that encouraged the unemployed to be straight about their real circumstances. You had to have absolute honesty from them. If you could bend the rules, get away with something, you did it without shame, because you were dealing with people who were near starvation level.[21]

The TUC General Council of 1932 did, in response to rising unemployment, recommend to Conference that local trades councils form unemployed associations under their auspices. This of course had been the practice in the previous decade; now a model constitution was issued, and for the associations to be affiliated they would not be involved with the Communists. According to the General Council this was a way to link, through advice and representation, unemployed trade unionists and unemployed non-unionists; the later could join and receive assistance if they undertook to join a union when they found work. In 1932 58 trades council unemployed associations were currently functioning with memberships ranging from 50 to 1,000. This was obviously a response to the NUWM as well. Gateshead Trades Council, for example, established an Unemployed Association in March 1934, 'under T.U.C. rules' asking 'are the unemployed to be left to Communist depredation?' The TUC must have hoped that it could head off the NUWM by offering the same services and at the same time work on union recruitment. These centres in the North East will be discussed in the next chapter.[22]

As in the 1920s, therefore, the NUWM did not have a monopoly over advice and representation work. There were however some crucial differences between NUWM activity here and that of the trades unions and Trades Council Unemployed Associations. To require clients to be trades unionists in a region with traditionally low levels of female employment effectively excluded women, and others, from assistance and representation. In contrast the successful cases publicised by branches of the NUWM in the area included single mothers facing the workhouse, young teenagers, elderly people and people with disabilities, none of whom were likely to have been trades union members.[23]

There could also have been issues of visibility. The NUWM branches held meetings in their local 'speaker's corners': the Market Places in Blyth and South Shields, Windmill Hills in Gateshead, Harbour View in North Shields, Stockton Cross, and Felling Square for example. These venues were also near the Labour Exchanges and PAC offices, and in Blyth at least NUWM leader Bob Elliott held advice sessions outside both places.[24] Therefore it should have been easy for people who did not have access to a trade union network to know where to go and who to speak to as regards help from the NUWM.

The reports the branches sent to NUWM headquarters, and occasionally to the *Daily Worker*, between 1930 and 1931 show a spread of activity and problems around the region. Morpeth were holding regular political education meetings, a Christmas draw, and the young workers had a football team; they had also had outdoor public meetings and won some benefits appeal cases. But despite some 180 members it was reported that 'the members do not seem to realise their responsibilities, they will not attend meetings and demonstrations'. Functioning branches of over fifty were reported in Ashington, Seaton Deleval and Bedlington in south Northumberland too. Although Scotswood branch had their own hut for meetings 'the members of this branch are exceedingly slack' and all work was left to a small committee. Sunderland claimed 125 male and 85 female members at this time, and had won 15 out of 56 appeals at the Court of Referees.[25]

In Blyth both unemployed women workers and housewives were being recruited into the branch women's section, 'so that 'owing to the women responding to the call of the NUWM the men are beginning to sit up and take notice'. At their instigation a meeting was held with the Labour Exchange manager where the women raised issues about their treatment by officials as well as the withholding of benefit without explanation. 'Satisfaction, as far as the manager could go, was achieved ... better treatment is expected in the future'. The Blyth branch was becoming particularly active at this time. In September 1931 Ned Breadin addressed a large public meeting in the miners' welfare hall to protest at the 10% cuts, and two weeks later the NUWM organised 'one of the largest public demonstrations of protest held at Blyth in modern times' and in which 'women formed a large part of the audience'. The meeting marched to the Town Hall where a deputation including Breadin and Bob Elliott put the views of the meeting to the full Council; it actually agreed with their opposition to the Means Test, although that did not prevent the Council from co-operating with implementation three months later. Blyth NUWM took part in an anti-Means Test rally organised by the Labour Party and succeeded, through the support of the audience, to have Ned Breadin speak; it also tried with less success to bring political discussion into meetings of the Mayor's welfare schemes for the unemployed.[26]

An NUWM branch and committee was re-formed in Birtley in September 1931after an open-air rally of 400. In line with national policy, between December 1931 and January 1932 the branch held a meeting aimed at union branches and lodges – although their particular participation in this effort to unite the employed and unemployed was not reported – to formulate demands for the PAC. These included extra coal and relief payments during the winter, non-co-operation with the Means Test and payments to the unemployed equivalent to the 10% cut. Similarly Gateshead branch claimed an attendance of 600 at the Ravenworth Picture Hall in February 1931.[27]

At least one of the North East demonstrations broke the mould of what was usually done by the left. In Felling the NUWM, led by Jim Ancrum, organised a march headed by 1,000 schoolchildren to the PAC to campaign for free school meals and footwear, as well as public works schemes at union rates and non-co-operation with the Means Test. Although a deputation was admitted to talk to the PAC the demands could not be met. The Felling NUWM also negotiated more frequent meetings of the PAC to expedite claims; successfully got people rehoused and presented a 6,000 name petition for additional winter fuel allowances.[28]

Reports to meetings of the NUWM National Administrative Committee (NAC), where Tyneside and Northumberland were represented, also give a picture of activity. A pooled fares system enabled representatives to attend these meetings in London, but one-time national chairman (and secretary of the Newburn branch) Sid Elias recalled another method:

… we had a little feller who always used to bicycle all the way down from Tyneside. I can't remember his name. He came from Birtley in County Durham. He bicycled all the way down and then bicycled all the way back, aye …

According to the NAC reports by January 1932 Sunderland NUWM were claiming 100 women members, with 20 of them attending section meetings. They had formed the 'Red Magnets', a branch of the national Workers' Theatre Movement, not just to propagandise but as training in public speaking and to encourage self-confidence. Chris Flanagan and Sam Langley from the North East now had national, if unpaid, roles as speakers on propaganda tours for the expanding unemployed movement: by September 1932 it reported 387 active branches reporting to 32 District Committees, including Tyneside, Northumberland and Teesside. This number of NUWM branches came to more than six times as many as the 'official' trades council unemployed committees reported by the TUC at the same time. There is no doubt that the introduction of the Means Test rejuvenated the NUWM although it acknowledged that several of the new branches were in fact the revival of old ones.[29]

Nevertheless there were constant organisational issues predictable with an organisation by and for the unemployed. For example it was reported in 1931 that 'the re-opening of a local colliery has caused a decline in the membership of the Wrekenton Branch'; obviously such occasional good news would reduce membership and activity. Another issue was the consequences of poverty; in the Morpeth branch political literature was lent, not sold, to the members because they had no money to buy it; in North Shields, where the NUWM tried to build a Minority Movement among the women workers on the fish quay, Daily Worker sales could never get beyond one a week, shared, for the same reason. Poverty too is recalled by Phyllis Short's account of the women in Stockton NUWM:

We had the women's section and we used to have little social evenings, but if there was a meeting at the Cross we all went to that or over to Middlesbrough for a meeting. And we used to run jumble sales but in those days it was hard to get old clothes. Also we joined together to help somebody who was really poor and having a baby, say, we'd have a street collection round the doors, even if they could just gave you a piece of bread.[30]

Therefore it was not surprising that the NUWM paper the *Unemployed Special* folded after a year in 1933. Headquarters stated that this collapse and the large amounts always owed by the branches for pamphlets, 'represented extreme neglect throughout the movement'. Nor did the successor paper the *Unemployed Leader* fare any better. This folded in 1934, headquarters complaining that 'nearly half the branches never attempt to take a single copy of the paper'. The fact of the matter was that trying to sell the *Unemployed Special* and presumably the *Daily Worker* regularly to people on the breadline was over-ambitious.[31]

This was in the context of the comparatively low level of Communist Party membership in the North East, even allowing for a rise associated with increased activity by the unemployed movement. A continuous theme for both the CP and the NUWM leaderships was unity in action of both employed and unemployed workers, which for them in the early 1930s meant joint work between the NUWM and the Minority Movement. On Tyneside at least the issue was that these activists were more often than not one and the same, as was the case with Harrison and Robson of the NUWM and the Seamen's MM. It was reported to the NAC in 1932 for example that in South Shields 'the dockers' Minority Movement decided to form a women's section of their own which meant the temporary collapse of the NUWM section'. There were not enough activists for both at the same time. In the country as a whole the Minority Movement had, through unemployment, collapsed and been absorbed into the NUWM by 1933. Nevertheless they continued with their cardinal principle of supporting employed workers in struggle such as during the dispute at Ryhope colliery near Sunderland in autumn 1932. NUWM members collected for the strikers, supported their pickets and encouraged them to join NUWM events.[32]

Members paid 1d a week in subscriptions and branches in turn paid a levy for the headquarters legal department to represent appeals at the Umpire's hearings. Here money was vital, to support the legal department and to ensure that individual members could be represented. The Ministry of Labour had recognised the NUWM as a bone fide organisation to represent claimants and appellants in 1930 but it increasingly insisted that membership be proved, the appellant being required to show a paid-up membership card before the NUWM could take part. National Administrative Council reports between September 1932 and May 1933 suggest that in each quarter of the year the NUWM was taking nearly 250 appeals to the Umpire of which they were winning over 90. By April 1934 the movement was claiming that it was supporting one third of all the appeals referred to the Umpire and that it was winning just under half of them. An appeal was always worthwhile but the legal department had to remind branches that the input of their local knowledge of cases was essential.[33]

The 1932 National Hunger March

The national protests against the Means Test were the context for the National Hunger March of 1932. It was bigger and better organised than 1930 and of all the Hunger Marches it generated the most conflict with the state and the police. The principal demand was the abolition of the Means Test and the Anomalies Act, and to this end they intended to present parliament with a petition that had exceeded a million signatures when they arrived in London.

Around 150 marchers from the North East left the Bigg Market at the end of September, led by Bob Smith and Sam Langley. The Teesside contingent joined them at Darlington; the ages ranged from 14 to 65 and 'most trades were represented'. Once more the march was not supported by the official trade union and Labour Party leaderships, with the *Newcastle Journal* dutifully reporting how appeals for help were being declined by 'local trade union officials'; Durham County Council similarly declined to supply the marchers with food and equipment, which to the Communists simply confirmed that its talk of fighting the Means Test was empty. Nevertheless public feeling against the Means Test was such that there were numerous examples along the route of local union branches, Co-op societies and Labour branches or individuals providing food or some sort of accommodation.[34]

The 1932 initiative included another women's march, a contingent of around 40 who marched from Barnsley to London. As one historian has noted, women with children who intended to march would need to have childcare organised for about five weeks, and this in itself would require a politically sympathetic family network. In the North East the available names of the women marchers in 1932 show they were from a Communist milieu and hence such a network: Mrs Chater, Maggie Airey, and Phyllis Short. All were Communists, two as we have seen married to the Communist NUWM activists Alf Chater and George Short, and Maggie Airey was a niece of Charlie Woods. Phyllis Short recalled that the plan for a separate women's march was because of the potential for bad publicity:

> It was decided that the women shouldn't march with the men. So that there wouldn't be the talk in the country that they were, you know, linking up with the men. And then there were the stories that we'd gone on the march leaving the families for someone else to look after, that it

was a damned good time that we were out for, which we proved to them that we weren't. The discipline was very strong. You weren't allowed to have contact, you know, with men, you didn't go off for an evening with somebody and have a feed on the sly, there was none of that, and we weren't allowed to go into a pub at all.[35]

After the assembly and enthusiastic send-off in Burnley the trek began:

That first day we walked about fifteen miles, and we slept in a church hall. Next morning when you got to your feet you fell back on your bottom what with the strain of the walking, and not being properly fed, because we just sat at the roadside and had a bit of bread and a bit of cheese, or had to do without until we got to some town or village where they would help us, give us a meal. We had two people who used to go on ahead to the place, we called them the advance guard, they'd meet Labour Party officials and sort of help prepare for us coming. About a mile outside we'd be told, "Straighten yourselves up, don't let them see your heads down", you know, and march as if you really mean it...We had no band with us, just walking sticks, and we sang along the roads of Britain. It was no joy ride; the only encouragement was that you were interesting people in what was happening in the country and what was happening to the people in the country.

As with all of the Hunger Marches every stop was an opportunity for an open meeting to explain the issues around which they were marching. Again this was an opportunity to bring the women forward as public speakers, as she remembered: 'Every place we passed through we had a small meeting. We even stopped in a small village and had a meeting. And I mean I never did any speaking before and they said it's only you that's free this time'. Years later what she recalled of those meetings was:

… the support we got from the working- class women who came to help out and encourage us to go on. The women who came to our meetings were marvellous, they couldn't go themselves but they knew we were trying to improve conditions for them too. You'd spread the idea that if we all got together we could do something. Large numbers of women came to our meetings because it was a women's march.

As with the other marches again there were occasions when the women were thrown back on the workhouse:

We slept in workhouses and if a village heard that you were coming they arranged a meal for you before you went in to the workhouse at night to sleep but you just had to live on workhouse fare. In the workhouses they deliberately tried to discourage you from marching. In one we went into this big room, they just pushed us in, they didn't give us anything to eat that night, just threw all these blankets at us and this was done on purpose. We caught on straight away. And many times when we went into a workhouse they would strip us and put us in a bath, and have two attendants stand, watching you get a bath. Then we had to put on these white nighties they gave us. And more often than not we had to sleep on the floor, even in the workhouses. And they would give you this hot skilly in the morning and we used to call it a doorstep of bread and a bit of cheese, and until you went into your next stopping place that was all you got to eat.

Fortunately it was not always like that. There were some successful efforts to defy workhouse rules, as well as practical local support:

On the other hand in some places you had the workers really supporting you, by organising massive meals and they wouldn't send us to the workhouses, they used to say, you'll stay in the church hall, the Co-op Hall, or the Labour Party rooms, and the men used to take our shoes away and mend our shoes for the next morning. And the women used to take our underclothes away and wash them; they were really good to you. We marched through Nottingham, past a shoe factory there and they didn't just throw money out to us they threw new shoes out as well, which meant that some of us got new shoes to walk in.[36]

Historians have recognised that whereas Hunger March women from the textile industry areas in Yorkshire and Lancashire had a background in the mills and were unemployed workers in their own right, for the coalfield women of South Wales, Scotland and the North East it was different. They had little background of paid work and so their campaign was on behalf of the men; as Phyllis Short explained, 'But the biggest thing was that we brought it to the notice of the country that we were fighting just as hard for the men to have a job. The greatest contribution of the women's section was standing by our men and demanding their right to work, not our right to work, our men'. Although the official Communist position was that these were unemployed women marching against the Anomalies Act, for women like Phyllis Short the campaign against the Means Test was a continuation of the mining lockouts, where the solidarity of the women with the miners in their dispute was such a noticeable feature of the struggle in the North East.[37]

In London Sam Langley was one of a number of activists who gave short speeches from the plinths in Trafalgar Square. They were all noted by the Special Branch and used in the subsequent trials. Langley stated:

I want to talk this afternoon about the experiences of the North East contingent of the Hunger Marchers from leaving Newcastle to until reaching London. Comrade Elias has pointed out that we have met with very much opposition. I want to tell you here this afternoon this opposition has not only come from the conservative and liberal councils but it has also come in a more forcible way from all the labour parties and trades councils from Newcastle to London.

Despite this and the foul weather though, they had attracted important support:

… in every town, without exception, we've mobilised the workers, employed and unemployed, in support of the demands of the national hunger marchers. In every place we've visited, without exception, workers have come out on the streets. They've marched more than 5 or 7 miles out to meet us. In cases where the trades councils and the labour party have repudiated the march this has happened. Just outside Doncaster for 2 1/2 miles the miners lined the streets, welcoming the marchers …

Langley made reference to the demonstrations in North Shields, Birkenhead and elsewhere and stated that it was this mass action that would drive down the National Government. Labour Councils on the other hand were implementing the Means Test and using the police against the unemployed. In 1932 the ILP had disaffiliated from Labour and adopted a revolutionary position, thereby becoming a rival to the politics of the CP and thus a target for the NUWM. According to Langley ILP representatives were of the same stripe as Labour, including their MP John McGovern who had wanted to present the Marchers' case to parliament:

And we have in this country an organisation that is known as the Independent Labour Party. The Independent Labour Party has played its role in this game of assisting the present ruling class. ..It is not only the question of the Labour Party; it is also the question of the ILP, united in their efforts to assist the present ruling class. In London we recently had another experience, the experience where the ILP, in the form of McGovern, has attempted to lead the unemployed marchers into constitutional terms. I want to tell the workers here this afternoon that we must not, as workers, rely on any kind of fakir, no matter which, ILP-er, Labour, socialist or any other body.

Referring to the forthcoming demonstration Langley uttered the words that were to land him in court, as we shall see:

… and it is to be hoped that the London unemployed and employed worker who comes on that demonstration on Tuesday comes prepared to meet the batons of the police and all the forces that are to be put against them. I want to ask you to come into the struggle on Tuesday night to bring this fight to its logical conclusion and force this government to its knees.[38]

Another speaker at Trafalgar Square was Mrs. Chater from Gateshead, who, like Phyllis Short, had been encouraged to address meetings on the route down. According to the Special Branch, 'Mrs Chater from Tyneside said she was the mother of five children, and added that she had never before spoken from such a public platform. She told one or two emotional stories about the condition of children in the unemployed areas of Tyneside and said nothing of interest to this Department'.[39]

Mrs Chater clearly developed as an NUWM speaker because she continued in that role on her return from the march. Along with fellow marcher 'Comrade Maggie Airey' she was busy speaking at Co-op Women's Guild meetings in the North East at the end of 1932, encouraging the Guilds to 'present special women's demands to the local authorities'. These would have concerned maternity care, free school meals, and improved child health facilities. Mrs. Chater was also the speaker at the Winlaton and High Spen Labour Party May Day rally in 1933; this gesture towards the NUWM by the official movement was probably the individual work of the Winlaton Labour Party chairman, Steve Lawther, long a sympathiser with the CP. Not all local outcomes were so positive, though; West Hartlepool activists returned from the Hunger March to find that the rest of the branch had disassociated itself from the NUWM, which they believed 'was too associated with the Communist Party'. They were not interested in advocacy at the PAC and were content to have an unemployed social club, 'not a real NUWM at all' as the disgusted Communist secretary put it.[40]

The NUWM never presented the petition in London because the police confiscated it, and several of their meetings and the demonstration to parliament were attacked by mounted police and broken up, but not without mass fighting. The NUWM headquarters building was raided, and key leaders like Hannington, Elias and Tom Mann were arrested and subsequently gaoled for sedition or incitement. Sam Langley was in court after them, accused of 'incitement to resist the police': under the circumstances his words, quoted above, were said to be inflammatory. The judge complimented him on how he conducted his own defence but gaoled him nevertheless.

What did the Hunger March achieve? A three-day parliamentary debate on unemployment, during which the behaviour of the police was severely criticised, a theme taken up by a number of magazines. The National Council for Civil Liberties (now called Liberty) was established as a direct result. A small concession was made in the transitional payments legislation which meant a Means Test would not count half of a disability pension or savings up to £25; small, but probably important for a number of claimants. Politically the NUWM was encouraged by the extent of grass roots support that had been shown for the marchers despite the press and the labour movement leadership.[41]

The 'Commissioners Marches': Protest and Reaction

As with Chester le Street in 1926, when the Commissioners took over the administration of the Means Test in County Durham the effects were immediate. It was reported that 25% of claimants had had their benefits reduced and 5% struck off without appeal; certainly the Commissioners were estimated by the Ministry of Labour to have saved £300,000 on transitional payments during their first year in County Durham. The Commissioners' new scales, as Councillor Clough at Lanchester declared, amounted to 'a wholesale slaughter of the innocents'.[42] Therefore in January 1933, during a severe winter, the NUWM organised a county-wide Hunger March to Durham, with contingents linking up from all over the county, as far as Stockton and South Bank. They intended to lobby both the Commissioners and the County Council with demands such as the recall of the Commissioners, the abolition of the Means Test and the restoration of the cuts of 1931. The more immediate demands included extra winter payments, free school meals and clothing for the children of the unemployed. At this stage too the NUWM was organising local Hunger Marches in several other regions.

The official labour movement, as represented by Labour councils and most of the trade unions, recognised the Durham march as a Communist-NUWM initiative and were as negative as they had been for the national Hunger Marches. Nor were the local authorities along the route any more helpful. A march on this scale would need, as the District NUWM appeal put it, 'accommodation such as halls, and the use of boilers, and other requirements to be put at their disposal' but Lanchester and Stockton Councils for example replied that this was not in their remit; marchers requiring food and accommodation should apply to the Poor Law institutions. Nevertheless after the march the 'Felling Anti-Means Test Committee' thanked a long list of local businesses in the town for their 'magnificent donations' of food and money to support the Felling contingent in their protest against 'the vicious operation of the Means Test'. There was clearly local sympathy for the position of the marchers, understandably from local shopkeepers who faced both high rates to pay for relief and the loss of trade from unemployed customers.[43]

In the event the 200 marchers from the Teesside area, who had the furthest to travel, arrived at Ferryhill the night before with their drum and fife band. They were accommodated by the charity the I.O.G.T. They explained to reporters that their band was associated with their successful deputations to have an individual's benefits restored, and that they were determined to meet the Commissioners. On arrival in Durham the next day they were joined by contingents from all over the county; one press report judged the march to have 'fallen far short of expectations' but even so another report described 'several thousand people from all parts of County Durham, including many women', attending. Ex-servicemen still seem to have been involved in the movement because alongside the usual 'Smash the Means Test' banners another read 'Life and limb we gave for you, bread and butter we ask of you'. Mrs. Grainger from Gateshead ('a conspicuous figure in her small red hat') was one of the leaders of the demonstration and speakers included Communist checkweighman George Cole and Sam Langley, both of whom 'made many harsh references to so-called working-class leaders on the County Council'.[44]

There was a problem, though; years later George Short recalled that although the march was a partial success in that they had 'an enormous rally of the unemployed', they had also 'made a stupid mistake, we got there too late and there was hardly anybody from the Council there'. Either through revolutionary disdain or simple inefficiency, NUWM secretary Alf Chater had neglected to arrange a meeting with the Council or even to ascertain when the relevant people would be present. The Commissioners too had only received his letter at short notice and so he had not received their reply that they would not receive deputations. The marchers found their route blocked by police who would not allow them near the Council offices; Labour Councillor Stewart tried to address them, only to be heckled and jeered at. Once the collections for their fares home had been made the march dispersed, Sam Langley declaring that 'it won't be long before we're back again'.[45]

In fact it was only two months before a second march was held in April. This apparently was smaller, around 1,000, and more aggressive in atmosphere, but once more no arrangements had been made to meet deputations. Mrs Chater from Gateshead – another, apparently, 'conspicuous figure in a red tam o'shanter' – stood on a lorry to address the crowd who had assembled with banners and a band. Clearly she had grown in confidence since her first performance in Trafalgar Square. She was part of the deputation that tried to negotiate a meeting with the County Council; they were absent for a long time and left the crowd leaderless and unoccupied. While this was going on confrontations took place with the police cordon around the Commissioners' office and baton charges led to serious clashes for several hours. There are reports of broken windows; from anywhere up to 30 demonstrators and 16 police injured, Alf Chater and Communist miner Billy Todd were taken to hospital after being struck unconscious by batons. Eighteen demonstrators appeared in court that month charged with anything from obstruction to riotous behaviour. The prosecution demanded exemplary sentences as a deterrent, and produced weapons which the defendants claimed were 'planted'; rather than inciting the crowd to break the police lines the NUWM leaders claimed that they had been trying to control them. Seven of them, including Wilf Jobling and Alf Chater went to gaol, their supporters 'giving cheers for the class war prisoners'.

This was the last attempt at a county-wide Hunger March in Durham, although by no means the end of activity. On the positive side members of the County Council and the Durham PAC did ensure after this that they received deputations from the unemployed and even cited the 1933 disturbances as among their reasons for doing so.[46]

The 'Battle of Stockton Cross'

In the week before the April clash in Durham George Short and David Catterick were gaoled in Stockton after a disturbance at the Cross. The police had banned gatherings by the CP and the NUWM at this traditional meeting place although other parties such as the ILP were still allowed to meet there. The NUWM tried to assert 'the freedom of the Cross' by organising a rally there but the police dispersed them, as George and Phyllis Short recall:

> I was arrested at the protest demonstration, handcuffed and frog-marched down the High Street. She raced through the cordon and grabbed my wrist, so they took her in as well. I was charged with obstructing the police and disturbing the peace. She was charged with assaulting the police, she, seven stone then and a TB case, she was supposed to have assaulted this bloody big fella about eighteen stone.

Phyllis:

> Mind, I did bite his fingers … They dropped the charges against me, that was usual then if there were bairns in the house, otherwise they'd have had to put them in care if I was in gaol.

George Short and Catterick conducted their own defence:

> I defended myself and spoke for an hour. I said that it was the Means Test and the cuts that were disturbing the peace. In order to prove this I cited umpteen cases, they couldn't stop me because I was entitled. I refused to be bound over because it would have been an admission of guilt. I got four months. It was already decided that I was going down; it was just a question of how long for. You didn't have any illusions about their freedom and democracy, how far it went for the unemployed.

At the end of the case around 500 local supporters, 'mainly young men but with a considerable number of women' held a protest march to the Cross with a drum and fife band but were thwarted by a police cordon.[47]

Between autumn 1931 and spring 1933 then several of the leaders of the regional NUWM – Harrison, Robson, Chater, Flanagan, Smith, Langley, Jobling and Short – had spent time in prison following demonstrations. After the widespread protests and disorders of autumn 1932 the NUWM national committee had stressed to branches 'the importance and absolute need for effective marshalling of demonstrations and steps should be taken on all future occasions to improve our work in this respect'. Clearly this was not always easy, but in Durham it seems that the deputation had left the restless demonstrators unoccupied and unaware of what was happening. As we shall see this mistake was not repeated during future mass demonstrations.[48]

Political Change

There were clear signs of a changing and less sectarian political attitude becoming visible. There was still consistency in some respects of course: when Ned Breadin and Bob Elliott stood for the CP in the Blyth Council elections in October 1933 it was on a 'class against class' basis; their objectives included 'exposing the role of the Labour Party with its policy of collaboration with the capitalist class'. However in April 1933, before the second Commissioners March, a full Gateshead Council meeting received a deputation from the 'Workers Rights Committee' about the Means Test. This consisted of Jack Cogan, the local ILP's campaigner for the unemployed for a decade, together with Richard Hearn and Alf Chater of the NUWM. When Jobling, Chater and the others were released from prison in September 1933 the guests at the 'welcome home' social included 'Comrade Charles of the ILP Divisional Council' who expressed pleasure at 'being able to be present in an official capacity'. These examples are in significant contrast to the anti-ILP rhetoric of Langley's Trafalgar Square speech. The welcome party agreed on 'the urgent need for a united front in the struggles that lie ahead', as did a joint CP and ILP meeting in Felling's Imperial Cinema that April.[49] The next chapter begins by examining this change and its consequences, which must be understood in the context of the relations between the NUWM, the Communist Party and the Comintern between 1930 and 1935.

Notes

1   George Short, interview with Peter Brabban 1979; Phyllis Short, interview with Peter Brabban 1979; on the Means Test see Stephanie Ward, 'The Means Test and the Unemployed in South Wales and the North East of England 1931-1939' *Labour History Review* Vol 73 No1 (April 2008, pp. 113-133) and Noreen Branson and Margot Heinemann, *Britain in the Nineteen Thirties* (London: Granada Publishing 1973); on the local effect of the Anomalies Act see *Newcastle Journal* 21 November 1931.

2   Bobbie Qualie, interview with Peter Brabban 1979.

3   *Sunday Sun* 29 November 1931; *Newcastle Journal* 2, 11 and 15 December 1931; *Shields Daily News* 10, 11 and 17 December 1931; *Sunday Sun* 10 January 1932.

4   *Shields Daily Gazette* 31 December 1931, 7 and 15 January 1932.

5   Minutes of the Central Committee of the Communist Party of Great Britain 16 January 1932 (LHASC).

6   See David Byrne, 'The 1930 "Arab Riot" in South Shields: a Race Riot That Never Was', *Race and Class* No 18 Vol 3 (1977, pp. 261-277); *Shields Daily Gazette* 13 May 1930.

7   *Shields Daily News* 28 July 1931.

8   *Shields Daily Gazette* 1 and 24 October 1931.

9   *Shields Daily News* 16 and 17 September 1931.

10   *Shields Daily News* 14 and 16 January 1932.

11   Kate Nicholas: *The Social Effects of Unemployment on Teesside 1919-1939* (Manchester: Manchester University Press 1986, p. 151); Minutes of the Central Committee of the Communist Party of Great Britain 4 June 1932 (LHASC); *Northern Echo* 7 October 1931.

12   George Short, interview with Peter Brabban 1979.

13   *Newcastle Journal* 9 August 1932; *Northern Echo* 6 and 9 August, 28 October, 3, 9, 10 and 12 November 1932.

14   *Newcastle Journal* 7 September 1932; *Report of the 64th Annual Trades Union Congress* (London: Trades Union Congress 1932, pp. 279, 298-301).

15   *Report of the 32nd Annual Conference of the Labour Party* (London: The Labour Party 1932, pp. 175-7).

16   *Gateshead Labour Herald* November 1931 (GLS); *Newcastle Journal* 1 September, 12 and 14 October, 15 November 1932; *Blaydon Courier* 8 April 1932.

17   *Newcastle Journal* 21 December 1931; *Northern Echo* 24 April 1933.

18   On the North Shields CP and NUWM at this time see North Tyneside Community Development Project Final report Vol.1: *North Shields: Working Class Politics and Housing 1900-1977* (Newcastle on Tyne: Benwell Community Project 1978, pp. 26-33); *Shields Daily News* 1 and 5 October 1932.

19   Minutes of the Tynemouth County Borough Watch Committee 9 November 1932 (TWAS: CB.TY/A/42/14); *Shields Daily News* 5 and 10 October 1932; *Daily Worker* 7 October 1932.

20   *Shields Daily News* 5 November and 10 October 1932; *Report of the 32nd Annual Conference of the Labour Party* (1932, pp. 245-6); *North Shields: Working Class Politics and Housing 1900-1977*, p. 31; *Shields Daily News* 2 November 1932.

21   George Short, interview with Peter Brabban 1979.

22   *Report of the 64th Annual Trades Union Congress* (1932, pp. 121-3); *Gateshead Labour Herald* February and May 1934 (GLS).

23   *Heslop's Local Advertiser* 15 December 1933 and 12 January 1934 (GLS); *North Shields: Working Class Politics and Housing 1900-1977*, p. 33.

24   *Unemployed Leader* vol 3 no 5 September 1934.

25   NUWM Branch Activities Monthly Reports October and December 1930, February, May, September 1931 (MML: Hannington and Brown Papers A1 and A2).

26   *Daily Worker* 6 and 8 March 1930; *Blyth News* 28 September, 8 October 1931; 22 May 1933; *Newcastle Journal* 3 December 1932.

27   *Daily Worker* 19 September, 5 December 1931, 9 January 1932.

28   *Unemployed Special* No 9 January 1933; *Heslop's Local Advertiser* 15 December 1933 (GLS).

29   John Halstead, 'The Reminiscences of Sid Elias', *Bulletin of the Society for the Study of Labour History* No 38 (spring 1979, p. 43); Minutes of the NAC Meetings January, May and September 1932 (WCML). On the Workers' Theatre Movement see Raphael Samuel (ed.), *Theatres of the Left 1880-1935:*

Workers' Theatre Movements in Britain and America (London: Routledge and Kegan Paul 1985).

30   *Daily Worker* 9 January 1932; NUWM Branch Activities Monthly Reports February and March 1931(MML: Hannington and Brown Papers A1 and A2); Phyllis Short, interview with Peter Brabban 1979.

31   Minutes of the NAC Meeting February 1933 (WCML); *Unemployed Leader* vol 2 no 3 November 1933.

32   Minutes of the NAC Meeting May 1932 (WCML); *Unemployed Leader* no 10 February 1933.

33   Minutes of the NAC Meeting September, December 1932; February, May 1933 (WCML); *Unemployed Leader* vol 2 no 9 April 1934.

34   *Northern Echo* 27 October 1932; *Newcastle Journal* 30 September 1932; *Daily Worker* 4 October 1932.

35   Sue Bruley, *Leninism, Stalinism and the Women's Movement in Britain 1920-1939* (New York: Garland Publishing 1986, p. 247); Peter McDougall (ed.), *Voices from the Hunger Marchers: Personal Recollections by the Scottish Hunger Marchers of the 1920s and 1930s* Vol 1 (Edinburgh: Polygon Press 1990, p. 51); information about the Airey family connection from Dave Atkinson (1915-2007) of Newcastle, who knew them both; Phyllis Short, interview with Peter Brabban 1979.

36   Phyllis Short, interview with Peter Brabban 1979.

37   Sue Bruley, *Leninism, Stalinism and the Women's Movement in Britain*, p. 248; Phyllis Short, interview with Peter Brabban 1979; *Daily Worker* 10 October 1932; Hester Barron, *The 1926 Miners' Lockout: Meanings of Community in the Durham Coalfield* (Oxford: Oxford University Press 2010).

38   Report of Assistant Commissioner Metropolitan Police to Home Office 3 November 1932 (NA: HO 144/18187). On the ILP see Gidon Cohen, *The Failure of a Dream: The Independent Labour Party from Disaffiliation to World War II* (London: I.B. Tauris 2007).

39   Report of Assistant Commissioner Metropolitan Police to Home Office 3 November 1932.

40   *Unemployed Special* no7 December 1932; *Blaydon Courier* 6 May 1933; *Northern Echo* 5 November 1932.

41   *Newcastle Journal* 2 November 1932; Peter Kingsford: *The Hunger Marchers in Britain 1920-1940* (London: Lawrence and Wishart 1982); Richard Croucher, *We Refuse to Starve in Silence: A History of the National Unemployed Workers' Movement 1920-1946* (London: Lawrence and Wishart 1987).

42   See *Unemployed Leader* no11 March 1933; *Blaydon Courier* 21 January 1933; *Chester le Street Chronicle* 16 February 1934. The Commissioners administered the Means Test in County Durham until the establishment of the Unemployment Assistance Boards in 1934/5.

43   *Blaydon Courier* 4 February 1933; *Northern Echo* 27 January 1933; *Heslop's Local Advertiser* 10 February 1933(GLS).

44   *Northern Echo* 30 and 31 January 1933; *Newcastle Journal* 31 January 1933.

45   George Short, interview with Peter Brabban 1979; *Northern Echo* 30 and 31 January 1933.

46   *Newcastle Journal* 10, 11and 25 April 1933; *Northern Echo* 25 April 1933.

47   George Short, interview with Peter Brabban 1979; Phyllis Short, interview with Peter Brabban 1979; *Northern Echo* 4 April 1933.

48   Minutes of the NAC Meeting December 1932 (WCML).

49   *Blyth News* 19 October 1933; *Gateshead Labour Herald* April 1933 (GLS); *Daily Worker* 27 September 1933; *Heslop's Local Advertiser* 13 April 1933(GLS).

Hunger March meeting at Newcastle Bigg Market, 1930 (*Newcastle City Library*)

Children in an NUWM demonstration in Felling, 1930s – Jim Ancrum is in the background (*Ancrum Collection, Gateshead Local Studies*)

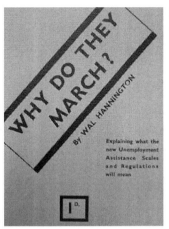

Pamphlet on the 1934 Hunger March
(*Gateshead Local Studies*)

NUWM banner in an Aid for Spain demonstration, Felling circa 1938 (*Ancrum Collection, Gateshead Local Studies*)

Delegates at the NUWM National Conference 1939 (*Ancrum Collection, Gateshead Local Studies*)

Tommy Richardson campaign leaflet, 1945 General Election (*author's collection*)

MAN OF THE PEOPLE.

THE RECORD OF A MAN WHO HAS ALWAYS FOUGHT FASCISM AND DEFENDED THE INTERESTS AND RIGHTS OF THE PEOPLE.

Councillor Lieut. T. A. Richardson was fighting the Fascists long before the outbreak of this war in 1939. He did not wait until Hitler had double-crossed Chamberlain before learning to hate the Nazis. The little story told at the foot of the page is striking proof of it.

He is an ex-miner thrown out of a job in the depression years known so well to the workers of Sunderland and Durham County. In 1936 he led the Houghton contingent of the Hunger Marchers, who tramped from the North East Coast to London to protest against the Means Test and the general miserable conditions of the unemployed. His valuable work for the people of Houghton won recognition when they elected him to the Houghton-le-Spring Urban District Council in the same year as the Hunger March. As local organiser of the National Unemployed Workers' Movement he was untiring in his efforts with cases before Courts of Referees and with the million and one jobs people were constantly asking him to do.

His work in the Houghton-le-Spring Council has been a model. Unfailing in his attendance before the war and taking up the problems of the people. During the war, too, wherever a period of leave gave him the opportunity, he has fulfilled his duties to the electors.

Chapter 6

FIGHTING THE UNEMPLOYMENT ACT

The Unemployment Assistance Act and the 1934 Hunger March

The previous chapter illustrated some of the consequences of the rejectionist approach of the Communist movement to all sectors of the Labour Party, the trade union leadership and the ILP. At the height of 'class against class' the *Daily Worker*, the public face of the Communist Party, included reports of Chester le Street, with its Labour MP and Council drawn often from DMA officials, as a 'stronghold of social fascism' and could describe even local left trades unionists like George Harvey of Follonsby lodge as 'on the side of the boss'. As we have seen though this had shifted by 1933; by then of course Hitler had achieved power and the international Communist line had moved in response to this further success for fascism in Europe. Indeed, the fierce division between the Communist and social democratic parties in Germany, which had been fostered by the Comintern line, had been an important factor in Hitler's assumption of power. Therefore Communists began to move towards trying to build a united front of all working-class and progressive organisations against fascism, war, and in Britain the National Government. The further assault on the unemployed and their families represented by a new Unemployment Act was also an opportunity to promote this.[1]

The Unemployment Assistance Act was put forward in November 1933 for implementation by 1935. This proposed to maintain the cuts to unemployment benefits imposed as an emergency measure in 1931. Part II proposed that the benefits system would be administered by local Unemployment Assistance Boards independent of local PACs, whom the government thought were responsible for raising costs by paying the maximum on a benefits scale. For the first time since the introduction of the original Poor Law a century earlier the administration of long-term unemployment support was to be taken away from locally elected bodies. The role of PACs would be confined to support for some children, disabled, and frail elderly people, and supplementary grants for special needs, all still from local rates. This was because the government recognised that local authorities were open to lobbying and this, it thought, was the reason behind the continuous rise in transitional benefit costs as Councils applied the higher scales. The UABs would determine new transitional payments scales too, and it was expected that these would be lower. Further, to keep their benefits long-term unemployed men could be required to go to one of the Ministry of Labour's Instructional Camps (immediately dubbed 'slave camps' by the NUWM) to carry out manual work at pocket-money rates.[2]

The response of the NUWM leadership to the draft Bill was to organise another nation-wide Hunger March to London, the first section setting off from Scotland on 22 January 1934. All the different contingents were planned to reach London for a major rally in Hyde Park on 25 February, so that they would be in London as the Bill was being debated. This was to be followed by deputations to Parliament and further demonstrations. The march aims included scrapping the Unemployment Bill, the Means Test, the Anomalies Act and the 'slave camps'; restoring the 10% cut and increasing benefits, a 40-hour week and public works at union rates to combat unemployment. As was the case with other marches though there was an additional political agenda besides the immediate demands of the march.

By 1934 another objective was unity in action with the Independent Labour Party, in marked contrast to the 1932 march when as we have seen the ILP, along with the TUC and the Labour Party leadership had been denounced as an arm of the capitalist state. The NUWM sought and achieved support from three MP s – Maxton and McGovern for the ILP and Aneurin Bevan for Labour – for the march and the national Unity Congress which was to be held in London during its conclusion. The Labour Party itself and the TUC declined the offer of joint action against the Unemployment Bill and continued to rebuff working with 'non-affiliated organisations'.

There are NUWM internal circulars available about this march that show in detail how these initiatives were organised, or perhaps how they were intended to be organised. 'Every recruit must be fully aware that the march means hardships' … and must be 'fully conscious of the importance of this great activity and who can be thoroughly relied on to conduct themselves accordingly, such as accepting the orders of the march leaders'. The best way to ensure this was not just to select for physical fitness but also to insist that recruits were elected by a trade union, Co-op Guild or other meeting; thus 'every man or woman should feel that he or she represents a definite body of workers, so that they are marching not as individuals but as delegates of the masses'. It was pointed out that on previous marches 'much trouble had been caused by people starting without proper equipment' and this must be avoided, such as by each contingent carrying a field kitchen with them. Each contingent should be divided into companies under a company leader, who was to see that the marchers kept to a steady, swinging step: 'this has a more striking effect on the public, and demonstrates efficiency and control, and further it is possible to cover much more ground with a minimum of fatigue'.[3]

This was accompanied by as much emphasis on building the united front as on supporting the march. The local reception committees who organised, where possible, food and accommodation were referred to as 'united front committees' for example, and expected to demonstrate participation by a range or organisations with this common political purpose.

The North East United Front March Committee issued a 'call for unity of action' to 'all trade union branches and working-class organisations' in Northumberland and Durham in early December 1933. This set out how the proposed 'drastic change to the whole system of unemployment insurance will bring untold suffering and hardship to millions' on top of the 'intense drive against the workers' by the appointed Commissioners in Durham. It drew attention to how local Medical Officer of Health reports were pinpointing the health effects of bad housing and diets due to poverty and unemployment. The traditional line of the NUWM and its predecessor continued – 'the unity of the employed and unemployed which will hold up and drive back the starvation offensive of the National Government'. Recipients of the appeal were urged to elect delegates to a conference later that month, whose purpose would be to mobilise support for the North East contingent on the Hunger March, elect a deputation to the Durham PAC and delegates to the national Unity Congress.[4]

What was the North East United Front March Committee? The appeal signatories were Mrs Chater, Jim Ancrum and Tommy Richardson from the NUWM (and also of course the CP), Jim Stephenson and 'Comrade Charles' of the ILP; others were listed by their union, but would have been known as CP activists: miners Billy Todd, George Cole and Matt Burdiss for example or Jim Holdcroft of the GMWU. Others were Will Pearson, the Marsden checkweighman, who was a former member from the 1920s dual membership days, and Mrs. Forster from the Co-op Women's Guild who seems to have been a sympathiser at least since the 1932 march. Their unions were listed but there was no suggestion that they were delegated to represent them on this Committee. The appeal would have been recognised by its target audience as an NUWM-CP initiative and seems to have drawn the usual negative response from the mainstream labour movement. The

NUWM reported that the Tyneside contingent would be marching 'with mass support from the Durham miners' although in fact only Follonsby, Heworth, New Hartley and Mainforth lodges had committed donations.[5]

There were certainly examples of unity with the ILP being achieved in the North East besides the United Front March Committee. In Gateshead, for example, where of course the ILP had been involved in unemployed struggles since 1920, 'One of the largest demonstrations ever seen in Felling Square' gathered to send off the local section of the Tyneside contingent. In what must have been a visually striking event they set off through Gateshead in a torchlight procession led by the ILP band, and a Gateshead ILP activist who had been a councillor before disaffiliation marched with them down as far as Yorkshire.[6]

There were around 120 marchers from Tyneside, south Northumberland and Teesside. Another contingent from Cumbria joined up with the Scottish marchers in Carlisle and came south by a different route. The leadership of the Labour Party and the TUC maintained their policy of not supporting marches by 'non-affiliated bodies' and this meant discouraging trades councils and Labour Party branches from organising accommodation, food and collections for the marchers along the route. Nevertheless, again as with other Hunger Marches, there were many examples of local branches ignoring this guidance. Where they did not ignore it there were examples too of church groups, Co-op Societies and the ILP coming forward to help. Again, overnight and rest stops were an opportunity for public meetings about the march and about politics.

One marcher was John Longstaff from Stockton, then fifteen years old, unemployed and living with his grandmother. He was not eligible for a transitional payment and so they were both struggling to survive on her 10s a week pension. He didn't understand what the march was about; he thought it was a search for jobs, and tagged along until he was allowed to join it. He was apolitical at that time – 'I did not know then what Socialism, Communism, Fascism, Capitalism or any other ism meant' – but became more politically minded along the way. Later he was to serve with the International Brigade in Spain. He recalls:

> All the marches and I didn't know this at the time, all the hunger marches had been proscribed by the General Council of the TUC. The Labour leadership had told the Constituency Labour Party organisations to give no help or support to the unemployed … but … we went on for the main reason which was to try and get a job or to make the country realise what was happening in many other parts of Britain, in Glasgow, Newcastle and

Middlesbrough, Liverpool and all the other places. Very few men were politically, what I would call now politically conscious.

As with the previous marches though there were opportunities to learn more:

The political aspect came in wherever we stopped, whether it was in a village or a town or anywhere. One of the leaders would always get up and try and get as many people from the town or the village to come and listen to the arguments that the unemployed were using to get work and it was then that those men, experienced men, would give the political reasons as to why we were marching. They were explaining what capitalism meant, what socialism meant ...

He remembered very positive responses along the route too:

On arriving at any town or village all the marchers' heads would be held up high with everyone marching in step...My main memory of the march was when we arrived at some small town to find the local people, with tears in their eyes, cheering at the sight of us for our plight was also their plight...Even in Grantham, despite the fact that Mrs Thatcher came from there, the people in that town met us and took some of the men in to sleep in their homes. Others were taken into chapels and churches and given accommodation by the churches whatever it may be, whether it was Catholic, Protestant, Methodist or what. Our reception with the people was excellent.[7]

As with the previous two Hunger Marches there was a women's contingent in 1934. As NUWM headquarters instructed, '... Do not wait until the men set out and then do something about the women'. A special effort to reach Co-op Women's Guilds was recommended, although as was noted in the previous chapter the practicalities meant that it was likely that only those from politicised family circumstances would take part. In the second week of February 75 women marchers left from Derby, where they had been accommodated by the Co-op Women's Guild. This was a noticeably larger contingent than in the past. Their route took them through Derbyshire, Warwickshire and Northamptonshire. One of their leaders – all of whom 'had a splendid record in their localities' – was Mrs. Chater from Gateshead, 'who has led many a local struggle'. She was one of the speakers at meetings along the route and indeed the main audience seems to have been Co-op

Women's Guilds. She described how organising the march had helped to reinvigorate the Gateshead NUWM, and also something of her own circumstances. Her husband Alf, a long-standing activist as we have seen, had been unemployed for the last four years. She had become active, again as we have seen, around the 1932 march and her involvement had been a source of great amusement to her friends at first. They had been gradually won round apparently until they had come to realise along with her that it was 'only through struggle that working-class people gain anything'.[8]

The men of the North East group were supported by the University Socialist Society during their stop in Cambridge. This support, as the Blyth correspondent on the march put it, 'must have been disconcerting to the ruling class', coming as it did from 'one of the twin strongholds of British imperialist teaching'. Fifty years later one student who remembered the North East marchers was Margot Heinemann; the encounter was important in her own political development:

> ... early in 1934, I certainly remember there was a demonstration to go out and greet the contingent of Hunger Marchers from the North East coast, who were passing through Cambridge. We marched out to meet them and marched back with them. Their reception was organised, they slept in the Corn Exchange as I remember, medical students were organised to treat their blisters and deal with their feet, and then there was a meeting in the town in the evening which was addressed by the leader of the contingent, Wilf Jobling from the North East coast. I remember that as a landmark because for the first time it occurred to me that the working class could have a leading role, the central role, in politics, and that working-class leaders could have a central role. He was an unemployed miner, a very fine speaker...[9]

Nevertheless it must also have been a sociologically interesting encounter. John Longstaff recalled an incident involving right-wing students that has not been mentioned in the 'official' accounts of the march:

> This time we did meet some trouble but it was some students in the University...about 30 of them ... they'd thrown things at us, pieces of wood, eggs, tomatoes and such like. Well, some of the lads just got their sticks and they chased them and, if they got them, they would have got more than a bloody egg on their face.

Once they were in the suburbs of London each contingent was co-ordinated to join together into a single final procession into Hyde Park on February 25th, where they were greeted by a 100,000 strong crowd organised by the London labour movement. This came about because the Federation of Trades Councils in the capital had side-stepped the wishes of the Labour leaders and the TUC and organised a mass welcome. John Longstaff recalled the biggest crowd he had ever seen, but as a teenager who had never left Stockton before, he found the locals bewildering:

> More and still more people had joined the marchers. These marchers were, I was told, from the East End of London. I could not understand what they were shouting or even talking about, it was like a foreign language; no doubt they also had great difficulty in understanding our north east accents.

The response was, he remembered, class determined, as he discovered during one of the post-march demonstrations:

> Away we went, passing through the City of London, where some better dressed men started shouting at us - "Bloody Reds, you all want shooting." Others were shouting, "Go to Russia where you came from." And they were frightened of us in those days, a few unarmed ill clad, badly clothed and half starving men; they were frightened of us – for what?

In London he recalled his contingent carrying – with 'great precision', it was carried by ex-servicemen – 'a cardboard coffin and the slogan on that was He Died of Starvation'. As we will see the use of a coffin on demonstrations is associated with the protests of 1939, but this account points to the idea being developed earlier.

The climax of the 1932 march had been violent disorder and the arrest of what was virtually the NUWM leadership. Such scenes are not associated with the 1934 march, although John Longstaff has another account of the entry into Hyde Park:

> I noticed that there was fighting taking place and what it was the police who were hitting the hunger marchers. The reason being was that they were attempting to split our march up into many different groups. This in itself would have meant that it the march have not been one continuous organization and on top of that men would have been waiting, 6 or 8 hours on the pavements ... it was the mounted police who came along

with thick truncheons … the unemployed men coming from all over the country, all over the British Isles, they were fighting back with the placards that they had, the banners they were marching alongside with and they were making sure, if they could possibly do so, to try and unseat the policeman from his horse … I think there was one that I saw, yes there was only the one and he did get a roughing up by the men, he was now no longer six foot higher than the men.

Some of the men were badly hurt and it was the bystanders, the London people who took them away, got them into hospitals and things of that nature … in Hyde Park itself, a lot of the women who had turned out, tearing up their underclothes to bandage the men's faces and heads up with.

William Tatham, a marcher from Whitburn in County Durham, who had been a platform speaker at an earlier meeting, was one of those who returned home with a bandaged head from this encounter. The police later congratulated themselves over how the massive crowd had been handled without any trouble and even Wal Hannington's account of the march mentions that there were 'only one or two incidents' when the marchers entered Hyde Park. In contrast John Longstaff's recollection shows how major an 'incident' can seem to those in the middle of it.[10]

After Hyde Park there were other rallies, including one of an estimated 6,000 people in Trafalgar Square at which Sam Langley and Mrs. Chater were once more among the many speakers. Langley appears to have adopted the new approach to the ILP without any visible effort. The Unity Congress took place and attracted 1,000 delegates. The North East contingent met the Northern Group of MPs at the House of Commons, government representatives having refused to meet them, and the *Newcastle Journal* reported that the meeting had strengthened the MP s' determination to lobby for the restoration of the 10% cuts. The paper regretted, of course, 'this unfortunate exploitation of the workless by the Communists'.[11]

Historians have identified some gains from the 1934 march. On Budget Day April 1934, two months after the Hunger March had arrived in London, the government announced that the cuts of 1931 in the standard rates of unemployment benefit were to be restored, and a modest increase in the allowances for children granted. This 'u-turn' was hailed as a victory by the NUWM. There were however some recriminations within the organisation. On one hand the NAC reported that it had been '… the biggest thing ever done by our movement … it made the working-class United Front a reality … and roused the country on the demands of the unemployed as never before'. Nevertheless the North East contingent –or rather the majority male contingent -featured quite prominently in the discussion of 'weaknesses', and it was agreed that Harry McShane would lead an inquiry into the responsibility for recruiting 'bad types' into the Tyneside section:

> ... insufficient care was taken in the Tyneside contingent to see that suitable types were recruited and properly equipped. This resulted in a number of Marchers having to be expelled by the leadership whilst on the road. In all contingents (except South Wales) insufficient was done to get marchers elected or endorsed by trade unions or mass meetings. There was insufficient political discussion by company leaders.[12]

Unfortunately there was no information given about what was meant by 'bad types' or what they had done. Problems might purely have been the result of the lack of political awareness that John Longstaff recalled among many of his fellow marchers. The comparative weakness of the CP in the region and its detached position from the mainstream trade union movement is evident from the people making up the March Committee. They could not ensure that their quota consisted entirely of unemployed men with the political or trade union background the movement would approve of, and instead made up the numbers with whoever was reasonably fit and ready to come forward. The reference to 'not properly equipped', something bound to have caused problems on the road, suggests that Tyneside NUWM could not raise enough support in the region to equip them properly. There was a suggestion of this in 1929 too; it has been mentioned that spectators in the Bigg Market donated overcoats to some men who needed them, and so therefore there had been equipment problems even then. The aspirations of the National Hunger March leaders could not be realised on Tyneside at this stage. Despite, as we will see, the evidence of local activity and even some success, the NUWM in the region was seen to be struggling by the national leadership.

There were local efforts to sustain the momentum of the united front. In April 1934 representatives of the 'Chopwell United Front Committee' – including Wilf Jobling and Maggie Airey – led a small march 'which included in its ranks a number of women' to the local PAC meeting. Having 'sung their way into Blaydon' their deputation and petition were received by the PAC. There, Maggie Airey explained that it was common for women, including her, to have rent problems, and that:

The trouble with them is that they sit within the four walls and keep their troubles to themselves, whereas if they would get out onto the streets and advertise the fact they might get a little more support, especially from those who are supposed to represent them.

In making this point she was articulating one of the purposes of the NUWM which was to encourage unemployed people to look beyond their personal circumstances and see them as a consequence of how society was organised. Collective action to achieve change was then the next step. This should also include women who, although not claimants themselves, were still struggling with poverty as a result of unemployment and the Means Test. Her colleague Mrs. Holliday set out her own household budget and explained the problems she would have feeding her children properly after the proposed cuts in benefits. The PAC expressed its support for them but as always drew attention to its limited powers.

At the elections to Blaydon UDC in May 1934 the United Front could claim a sort of success, but not one that was appreciated by the ruling Labour group on the Council. Alongside the Communist candidates such as NUWM activist Wilf Jobling there were two 'United Front' ILP candidates including Jim Stephenson. When they lost these two seats to the ILP candidates the ruling group promptly excluded the ILP members from Committees, sparking a brawl in the Council chamber; ironically this disturbance prevented an NUWM deputation led by Jobling and Airey from being heard.[13]

Trades Council Unemployed Associations

The last chapter made mention of attempts by the TUC to organise the unemployed through local trades councils, clearly as an alternative to the NUWM, its politics and its Hunger Marches; this seems to have been pushed more after the 1932 Annual Conference. It did acknowledge a problem in that some trades councils were reluctant to establish associations that would put trades unionists and non-members on the same footing. We have seen how the Wallsend equivalent in 1931 'would only give assistance to trade unionists'. Again, the same issue as in the 1920s: trade unions existed primarily for their members and for some organisations it was a serious culture shift to do otherwise. This is clear from the reports of the Annual Conferences of Trades Councils in the 1930s. It was reported to the 1932 conference that there had been resistance to the TUC organising unemployed associations, some trades councils felt that the unions should organise their unemployed members and that a separate unemployed association gave the impression that they were not able to do so. The delegate from South Shields Trades Council, Alfred Gompetz, told the 1936 conference that 'the industrial north had not taken kindly' to unemployed associations, but he did not explain why. By 1935 apparently 130 out of 420 trades councils in England and Wales had an affiliated unemployed association, which means that they were operating on a much more limited scale than the NUWM.[14]

Hannington's accounts dismiss these associations as primarily social clubs and the historian of the NUWM agrees with him. Their judgement is not necessarily accurate. Certainly the associations did provide this social function but the one established in 1933 by Newcastle and District Trades Council reported two years later that 'Many cases have been contested at the local Court of Referees, and the vast majority have resulted in obtaining benefit for the applicants.' The following year it could be reported that there had been a 'big increase in membership' of the unemployed association, whose members appreciated the opportunity to express their views at trades council meetings. By 1936 the Newcastle Unemployed Association had four branches and 'Our representatives have assisted their members who had difficulty with the PAC, Courts of Referees, and the Labour Exchange … We can claim that many families with unemployed or sick members have received benefits they would not have got but for the efforts of our organisation'.

The Association claimed that it was not receiving the support that was needed from the local unions but clearly though this trades council organisation of the unemployed was functioning and effective. Likewise the Gateshead association, formed in 1934, reported the following year that it had 2-300 members, and along with a football team, club room and library on the Bensham Road it had a local expert on 'Exchange cases' who ran a weekly advice bureau. As in the 1920s again, trades unions and in particular the DMA represented their members with benefits claims. Ellen Wilkinson wrote of Jarrow that the local Trades Council and Labour Party had undertaken the work done elsewhere by the NUWM, and built an effective organisation to do so. At least two of its activists had been involved in the former NUWCM in the 1920s.[15]

The Sunderland Labour Party and Trades Council too were active, although its annual reports do not mention an unemployed association. In 1931 the council was clearly engaged on issues around task work set by the PAC, on wages for public work schemes, and the inconvenient meeting times of the Court of Referees sessions. In 1936 it dealt with 'the method for interviewing applicants (for benefits) at the Area Office which was settled to our complete satisfaction' … Various matters have been taken up with

Labour Exchanges and the Local Employment Committee'. The evidence from the Trades Council does point to a more low key activity rather than the open-air public meetings near the labour exchanges that the NUWM carried out. This is probably why Sunderland NUWM veteran Nick Rowell, in the early 1930s an unemployed driller, recalled that, 'The Labour Party in Sunderland took up some cases but seemed scared to take a lot on'. Similarly George Short recalled that 'The trades unions here in Stockton didn't play a part but it is true to say that in Stockton, I can only speak for Stockton, the political agent of the Labour Party did take up cases.'[16]

By 1935 there is some evidence that the TUC was making an effort to organise the unemployed, in response to the Unemployment Assistance Act and to provide an alternative to the NUWM. It published a pamphlet, 'Unemployment Hardships – Don't Struggle by Yourself' intended to support recruiting for the trades council associations. It claimed that the penny a week subscription 'may put pounds in your pocket by successful claims and additional benefits and relief'. Besides this the associations could 'organise demonstrations for the removal of the Means Test', appeal on claimants' behalf, check UAB determinations, - they knew 'all the intricacies of the UAB determinations' – and send a friend with claimants to tribunals, advise on UAB clauses and make representation to the PAC for special allowances. There was an attempt to build a National Federation of Unemployed Associations ('to obtain one organisation for the unemployed') and this did oppose 'the so-called United Front and Hunger March' in 1934. It seems that hardly any records of the Federation have survived at the TUC, but what little there is suggests that there were major disagreements with the TUC over how the organisation should be run. For example the TUC insisted that a trade union official or a clergyman be the association treasurer and not an unemployed worker, whereas the Federation believed, like the NUWM, that organisations of the unemployed should be run by the unemployed themselves. Here again therefore is an important difference between the NUWM, which was an organisation of as well as for the unemployed, and the trades council unemployed associations. This alongside the others which have been noted: the NUWM felt no constraints about trade union membership for claimants, and had a very public presence wherever possible.[17]

In the eyes of the Communist national leadership however the ideal recruit to the NUWM would be a trade unionist, already inculcated into the value of organisation and already with some political awareness. Such a recruit would also be good material for CP membership. Therefore it expected the NUWM to have a role with the Trades Council Unemployed

Associations despite the several years of political history that lay between them. This was certainly the case by 1934 and 1935 when the Party and the Comintern had moved on from its sectarian position. Further criticism was to be levelled by the Party leadership at the NUWM leadership over relations with the Trades Council Unemployed Associations. These local bodies appeared, to repeat, to have access to exactly the sort of recruit the Party wanted – trade unionists – and through the trades councils the unity with employed workers the militant unemployed movement had always sought. Therefore during 1934 and 1935 branches were encouraged to 'develop a constructive attitude' to the Unemployed Associations and approach them about potential joint campaigns, and thus 'win them over' to the NUWM position. As we will see this pressure was to increase later in the decade.[18]

Poverty and the Public Health in the North East

By the early 1930s the health effects of the poverty generated by unemployment benefit scales was recognised by even the mainstream medical profession. The agitation over the 1934 Act coincided with controversies between local doctors, public health specialists and the government about the impact of low incomes and health. This became part of the context in which reactions to the government measures took place.

In November 1933, the same month in which the Unemployment Act was put forward, the British Medical Association published a Report by its Committee on Nutrition. This demonstrated, essentially, that the benefits paid to unemployed people were too low to ensure an adequate diet for their families. Its author was Dr. McGonigle, the Medical Officer of Health for Stockton whose own local research on the subject (*Poverty and the Public Health*) was eventually brought together as one of the first Left Book Club publications in 1936. The BMA report was seized on by the labour movement as a campaign tool and it formed a continuous battleground with the Ministry of Health, who rejected its findings. The North East featured in March 1934 when Prime Minister Ramsey MacDonald initiated a survey into malnutrition amongst the unemployed on Tyneside, and specifically Newcastle, Gateshead and Jarrow. This was done quickly and reported in May that the nutritional status of the unemployed was low, but this had always been the case, that the incidence of rickets and tuberculosis was high, but it always had been high, and had not been affected by unemployment; in fact 'there was no evidence of a deterioration in the health of the unemployed or their families'. The survey was condemned as superficial by the campaigning doctors who had formed the Committee against Malnutrition in 1934. They compared it unfavourably with local research, based on a thorough study of cases and not quick examinations, and which was telling a different story.[19]

A well-known example at the time was the work carried out by Dr. J.C. Spence in Newcastle. This research compared the height, weight and health of 125 working-class children (of whom 103 were from unemployed families) with a similar number of children of professional people. Examinations for comparison included blood tests and X-rays, and height and weight were compared to the average recorded in Newcastle child health clinics. Spence found that over a third of the working-class children were below the average for height and weight, were unhealthy and appeared malnourished. The conclusion was that, 'Even if we allow for the all too frequent self-sacrifice of the mother of the family...it is still certain that in many of our poorer homes child and adult alike have an inadequate diet'. A pamphlet version of his work was published by the Newcastle Co-operative Society.[20]

Inside Parliament and Whitehall there was also the well-informed lobbying by the independent feminist MP Eleanor Rathbone. She argued that the government's desire to cut costs and by-pass local authorities would prevent the reasonable maintenance of unemployed people and that the health of their children in particular would suffer. At a meeting in the House of Commons in February 1934, coincidentally when the Hunger Marchers were arriving in London, she set up the cross-party Children's Minimum Campaign Committee. Its objective was to establish the principle that relief scales should ensure that children would not be deprived of food and necessities because of their parents' low income. Rathbone attributed the changes introduced by the government after the 1934 Hunger March to this lobbying.

Thus a diverse collection of lobby groups, made up of doctors, scientists and political activists kept up pressure on the government over its neglect of nutrition. Their evidence was used by the NUWM in its *Manifesto of the National March and Congress* in 1934, and North East branches made use of their Medical Officer of Health Annual Reports for campaigning too. A growing consensus was building which went further than the traditional labour movement and the left, and its potential to embarrass the government over its record on nutrition added to the pressure to give some ground over benefits scales.[21]

'Slave Camps'

The Ministry of Labour Instructional Camps were a campaigning issue for the NUWM until the outbreak of war in 1939. In September and October 1934 the North East NUWM campaigned for their local PACs to financially support any man whose benefits were stopped because he refused to go to a 'slave camp'. Largely initiated through the 1934 Act they were not in fact intended to train or instruct the unemployed, but to 'rehabilitate' long term claimants into the habits of work. This was generally in the form of manual labour in road-mending and forestry in rural settings. Those sent to an Instructional Camp did not necessarily go to a local one. There were Camps at the Kielder and Hamsterly Forests in Northumberland and in County Durham, and others in North Yorkshire, but Bobbie Qualie from Sunderland was sent to Fermyn Woods near Kettering in Northamptonshire. He recalls his time there as not being exactly constructive:

> When I went to the instructional camp they'd stopped my dole for six weeks. I went down to a place near Kettering. There we had to live in army huts. Over the top of us was a an ex-army colonel: every morning we had to parade as if we were in the armed forces, roll-call, your bed had to be rolled up, and what we got was six shillings a week pocket money. What you had to do, you had to go into the forest and cut the grass between the small oak trees. They were the property of the big landlord nearby. I was down there for six solid weeks. If you succeeded in doing what you were supposed to do you got a job. But none of us that went there at least at that time did get a job. We had to go into a quarry and dig out the stone to repair the road that they were putting through the forest. When I did come back I got my dole back, the 11s and 3d. I think these camps were just set up to cut down on the dole costs.[22]

Complaints about food and conditions in the camps were recorded by the NUWM and set out in one of Hannington's books. Bad conditions were Bobbie Qualie's experience too:

> The conditions there were so bad, so bad that there was a protest, we wouldn't sleep in the huts, wouldn't sleep in them at all, because they were bug-ridden, there were lice. They burnt all the beds and the blankets and put disinfectant all around the place. You were given a shirt and a coat, and boots; you could bring your boots back with you at the end. The food was bad, so bad people wouldn't eat it because the earwigs used to drop off the ceiling into the food when they were cooking. Earwigs! They were in the soup; you were always picking them out of your food.

The brother of ILP and NUWM activist Len Edmondson was involved in a strike in a Camp in County Durham against the food and the conditions.

They were successful but the members of the strike committee were dispersed to other Camps around the country. Despite these episodes the impression is often of an apolitical atmosphere in these Instructional Camps. According to Bobbie Qualie the NUWM did not necessarily find them fertile ground:

> Those of us who were in the NUWM were putting the line over, the NUWM line over, and like myself, and I think that's why we didn't get jobs afterwards, our names were blacklisted. We didn't get many recruits for the NUWM in the camp, in fact not any at all. They were only there for six weeks and in an out of the way place. If you'd really revolted say and got kicked out of the camp you wouldn't get any money for six weeks when you came home.

This is borne out too by evidence from Scotland that there was no widespread NUWM presence in these Camps, and that inmates could actually find the regular food, exercise and communal life a positive experience after their prolonged periods of unemployment and deprivation. This was the image put forward by the local press, particularly after the Conservative MP for Newcastle Central visited young North East men in a Camp at Carshalton. This, he said, was in response to allegations being made about the Camps by the Communists, allegations which constituted 'the greatest political lie of this generation'. The men he and a reporter spoke to said they were enjoying the experience and rejected the criticisms that had been circulating about the regimes.

The personal evidence from Bobbie Qualie and Len Edmondson's brother does of course come from two individuals who were highly politically aware. It cannot be assumed that this could be said for most of the young unemployed in the Camps, who may well have interpreted their experience differently. At the same time it is worth noting the incident at the Hamsterly Camp in 1939, when most of the inmates walked out and went home in protest about a lack of food and 'class distinction'. What cannot be disputed though is that Bobbie Qualie and most of the thousands of others found that a term in the Camps was no guarantee of skill training or work at the end of it, and nor was their participation really voluntary.[23]

The Act Comes into Force

In January 1935 Part 2 of the Unemployment Act was implemented and the realities of the new benefits scales devised by the UABs became clear. Len Edmondson was an engineering worker from Gateshead who was twenty years old at this time, and unemployed for almost a year. He was an ILP member active in the NUWM. He remembered some of the effects of the new scales:

I clearly recall at that time the case of two brothers who were unemployed and living together in a house – probably the house in which their late parents had lived. They were each in receipt of 15/3d per week unemployment benefit but, under the new regulations, they were classed as "man and wife" and given 23/3d between them.[24]

Most claimants in the region were much worse off under the new UAB rates and action soon followed. As we have seen the NUWM in the North East had a well-established system of open air speakers and public meetings in the 'speakers' corners' of each town where it had a presence: the Bigg Market in Newcastle, Windmill Hills in Gateshead, the West Park in Sunderland, the Market Places in South Shields and Blyth, Harbour View in North Shields. In 1934 and 1935 Frank Graham was active in the NUWM in Sunderland and he recalled some of the political culture of the time:

... we had a lot of people who were extremely good speakers. And particularly at the open air rallies they could put across a case clearly and in a popular way that moved people ... Of course in those days you had to be a good speaker because you could always have faced heckling and if you couldn't put a case over in an open air meeting the audience would disappear anyway ... but it was no problem to any orator in those days – and there were literally, I can think of at least six – a dozen – people on Tyneside who were absolutely first class orators, who were superior to practically any Labour Party or Conservative member of parliament today. And they knew what they were talking about, they were – because you see an unemployed agitator was a full time politician in a way, because that was the main thing he did – he had no work to do.[25]

Len Edmondson explained how local demonstrations of the unemployed were organised:

The organisers of the demonstrations had no funds so they could not publicise the intended marches by posters or leaflets, and the press and the radio did not give any publicity to intended marches or demonstrations in those days. The whole of the organising had to be done by chalking the streets, calling upon everyone to assemble at a particular place and line up for a march against the dole cuts or to demand employment.

Sometimes to announce the demonstrations a few men would go into the streets, ring a bell, and when the people came out they announced that a march was to be held and called upon everyone to join in.

In January 1935 the NUWM in Felling and Gateshead organised a mass rally against the Act. Len Edmondson recalled the demonstration and its leader, the Communist Jim Ancrum, and also what they achieved:

> … they had a chap called Jim Ancrum from the Felling who had a powerful voice. He was speaking on this new Act which had been introduced. There had been a lot said in the press that many were going to get an increase. Jimmy Ancrum, who had a terrific voice and a great crowd around him, he said "Well we'll see where these increases are." He says "I've got an increase here from the Felling. He was in receipt of thirty-one shillings a week. He has got a decrease down to six and a tanner a week. A twenty-five and sixpence a week reduction!" He said. "And, he said, "I've got a lot more here in my pocket with reductions ranging from five shillings up to a pound!" And he announced that they were going to have a mass march from the Felling and they wanted all the Gateshead people to join in at the end of Sunderland Road where Felling meets Gateshead. March to the Unemployment Assistance Board which used to be just a bit further over on Windmill Hills. I think he marched about six thousand from the Felling alone and all the Gateshead people joined in and all the unemployed that saw it. People were joining in on the pavements and all over. Well it was estimated that there were twelve to fifteen thousand people assembled outside the Unemployment Assistance Board offices and the Unemployed Workers Movement at the Felling, through Jimmy Ancrum, had made arrangements first of all for the manager to receive a delegation. A short meeting was held therefore outside the offices and Jimmy Ancrum had mentioned that he had made arrangements with the management for to receive a delegation, four or five going in and had arranged for a speaker to keep the meeting going while they were in. That was the Gateshead NUWM Secretary, John Henderson. They went in and he said he knew the manager because the manager used to be at the Felling in some position.[26]

Clearly the NUWM had learnt from Durham in 1933 where the crowd had been left to its own devices whilst a deputation of its leaders left; it now had an organised way of keeping their interest during the wait. Len Edmondson heard the outcome:

He reported that they had been treated with courtesy when they went in and they put the case to the management for the withdrawal of the 1934 Act, the complete withdrawal. They couldn't ask the manager to send a telegram demanding the withdrawal he would have got the sack. What they asked him to do was to send a factual telegram, a statement that there was about twelve to fifteen thousand unemployed assembled outside his office demanding the withdrawal of this 1934, so called Unemployment Assistance Act. And he gave an undertaking that he would do it immediately. That was the way that the Unemployed Workers Movement operated in those days. Always marching to a particular place and always asking the manager or someone like that to send a factual statement. You couldn't get them to send one demanding the withdrawal. But they would send a factual statement down to the Prime Minister.

This was not the only action in Gateshead. Len Edmondson continues the story:

… and then on the Friday night of that same week, Oliver Stanley the minister who had introduced this bill was speaking in the City Hall allegedly to explain the meaning of this bill as though the unemployed didn't know it. The unemployed assembled in the Bigg Market for a meeting and it was announced to elect a delegation to meet to get into the City Hall and meet the minister … When we got up to the City Hall the delegation couldn't get in. It was admission by ticket only. So there was an appeal made to the unemployed there who had tickets. Well, I don't know how they got tickets but they got the tickets for the delegation and the delegation went in. One policeman came and he said that we couldn't remain on the road outside like this. So we decided to march round and round the City Hall and keep moving. An Inspector came over and he was much more civil, accommodating and pleasant with it and he said "look if you just remain there on the other side of the road so that the traffic can get by it will be all right for us, the easier it will be for you the easier it will be for us". And so we were able to remain there.

They received a report later from their deputation:

I think there were about twelve on the delegation, lined themselves up in front of the platform, raised their clenched fists and declared "In the name of the unemployed of Tyneside we demand the withdrawal of this bill!" There was a move to get them away from the front but not a move to get them thrown out of the Hall. A large number of the unemployed had managed to get in and there would have been eruptions if the police or the stewards had attempted to get them out of the hall. When they came out we marched through the town to the Bigg Market to receive a report of all the activity that had taken place.[27]

Estimates of the numbers involved in Gateshead were prone to exaggeration at the time. The NUWM leader Wal Hannington's summaries of the local agitations state that'... in Tyneside, 30,000 marched on the streets'. The *Daily Worker*, apparently in consultation with Gateshead activists, reported that 20-30,000 had participated, and presumably this was the source of Hannington's figure. Jim Ancrum, the leader of the NUWM march, wrote in his local paper that fifteen thousand had taken part; this figure was not challenged by local people in the paper and Len Edmondson's recollection of the number is along the same lines. However his memoir reminds us too that we should also take account of the numbers who supported demonstrations more passively from the pavement or who did not march but joined the outdoor meetings. This would increase the numbers of participants quite considerably. Although the scale of the protest on the streets cannot be ascertained exactly there is no doubt that the Gateshead demonstrations were the biggest the town had seen for many years.[28]

Gateshead had the biggest but certainly not the only demonstration in the region against the new scales. In Sunderland, in the last week in January, the NUWM organised a rally in the West Park attended by 1,000 people. A week later Billy Booth of the NUWM chaired a meeting addressed by speakers from different shipyard unions, Ryhope and Wearmouth Durham Miners' Association Lodges, Sunderland ILP and the CP. The meeting called on the T.U.C. to organise a one day general strike against the Bill, and agreed to mandate their members who were on public bodies to 'refuse to implement the parts of the Act relating to work camps'.[29]

At the end of January 1935 the NUWM organised a demonstration of 3,000 people at the Tynemouth Borough Council meeting in North Shields, complete with placards of 'Down with this baby-starving government' and 'Workers of the World Unite!' In 1932 the NUWM anti-Means Test march in the town had resulted in violent clashes with the police and subsequently the arrest and imprisonment of the North Shields NUWM leadership. Now the antagonists were lined up again, and the newspaper report communicates a tension between them that is almost tangible. The demonstration went on for most of the afternoon and the evening, police reinforcements were called in and a confrontation was narrowly averted when they attempted to prevent the crowd from marching up and down outside the town hall during the Council meeting. The Council itself had obviously given up its previous policy of not receiving deputations if a demonstration was also involved, because it received one on this occasion which consisted of Walter Harrison, William Carr and Mrs. Mulholland, 'representing the women'. They wanted the Council to forward their protest about the UAB scales to the government, Tynemouth PAC to make up any cuts made by the UAB, and to investigate some local cases.

The comments made by Tynemouth Borough councillors during this meeting illustrate how feelings about the Act were running high among local authorities as well as claimants. The Council, which was not controlled by Labour, agreed to 'protest against the hardships that were arising in the borough under the administration of the UAB scales, and suggest that the regulation be quashed'; this resolution to be forwarded to the Prime Minister, the Minister for Labour, and the local Members of Parliament. One councillor expressed alarm at the cuts being made, and another was convinced that the town was going to suffer. Councillor Stanley Holmes, an old antagonist of the NUWM, rejected the idea of 'lax administration' on the Council's part over the benefit scales they had previously been responsible for implementing. They also agreed to investigate complaints against local Relieving Officers.[30]

Jarrow Labour Party organised a demonstration in the town against the Act in February, and the 500 people it attracted doubled to 1,000 for a public meeting in a cinema. Here the local Conservative MP tried to defend government policy but the audience reaction was such that the police had to escort him from the building. In Blyth, at the end of January, the Council received a deputation following an NUWM rally, condemned the UAB scales and agreed to join a deputation to the Ministry of Labour.

In Blaydon the Council condemned the UAB scales and received an NUWM deputation led by Mrs. Clarke and Charlie Woods. The Council was urged by them to 'do something more than lodge a protest', by 'actively taking part in the agitation that is being generated'. It agreed to hold a town protest meeting 'for all organisations regardless of politics' and call for a regional local authority conference to agree how to 'obstruct and fight against the Act in every way possible'. Woods later spoke at this town meeting against the Bill organised by Blaydon and Winlaton Labour Party, alongside Councillors Jim Stephenson and Steve Lawther.[31]

As with the earlier Means Test protests all this was, it must be stressed, part of a national movement. In fact the agitations in the North East were on a much smaller scale than in other areas of high unemployment. Riots occurred in Sheffield and Merthyr. In South Wales as a whole an unprecedented mobilisation involving political parties, churches, chapels and shopkeepers as well as the unemployed themselves came together. Demonstrators there were numbered in the hundreds of thousands, the product of an altogether different trades union and political culture, one which called too for a one-day general strike. Nevertheless the extent of the protest in the North East, where militancy was not a byword, shows the depth of the anger.[32]

A Partial Victory

On 5 February 1935 the Minister of Labour, as Wal Hannington put it, 'had to bow before this mighty storm': he announced in the House of Commons that applicants for transitional payments would now get either their original scale or the UAB one, whichever was higher, and arrears would be paid to those who had seen their benefit reduced. The movement kept up the pressure to ensure that all this was actually implemented and arrears paid without any delay. In Blyth for example around 200 demonstrators assembled in the Market Place and marched to form a rally outside the PAC offices, 'where their numbers were doubled by onlookers'. A deputation from the NUWM successfully met officials who agreed to process arrears quickly.

The months of agitation had definitely achieved a result. Wal Hannington and the activists of the NUWM hailed this as a vindication for their campaigning; Len Edmondson in old age spoke for NUWM veterans when he described the government retreat of February 1935 as 'a victory for the organised working class'. Also, consider the opinion of a medical historian writing about the British income and nutrition campaigns of the 1930s:

> All the arguments of the campaigning groups and the concerned politicians, doctors and scientists, appeared to have fallen on deaf ears. However, after the UAB came into operation in January 1935, their scales were quickly defeated, not by science-based lobbying, but by protest meetings, marches and riots, after many claimants found that their unemployment assistance was substantially less than the Transitional Benefit they had received previously.

The MPs, UAB managers and local councillors would have been in no doubt about the effects of the cuts and the depth of public anger about them. As was done in Felling, Gateshead, Blyth and Tynemouth they would have communicated this to the government. Significant too was the loss at this time of two safe Conservative seats in by-elections; with a General Election due later in 1935 this loss would have helped to focus the government's mind. Nevertheless the victory was partial. The Means Test remained, as did the 'slave camps' and the local Unemployment Assistance Boards. Government-funded employment schemes continued to be minimal. Moreover the suspension of the new scales was not permanent; new draft rates were to be published in 1936, and as we will see this necessitated a new phase in the unemployed struggle.[33]

NUWM Branch Activity

NUWM membership in the early 1930s was reported to be 40,000 in the summer of 1932, but 20,000 by the following February and back up to 35,000 at the beginning of 1936. As we have seen a modern analysis has put the national membership at a peak of 50,000 at the height of the Means Test protests; by any reckoning it was a mass organisation by the standards of the political left of the time. Nonetheless it was a poverty-stricken movement and Headquarters published a regular litany of financial problems. As we have seen it could not sustain a regular newspaper, and even attempts to raise money through the 'unity football pools' scheme failed; 'it seems that many of our comrades prefer to support the capitalist pools schemes …' These head office circulars do help to provide a picture of action on the ground in the region, for example when the branches which owed money for literature were listed. In the North East these were: Sunderland, Ferryhill, Felling, Shildon, West Hartlepool, Blyth, Newbiggin, Hetton, South Shields, Birtley, Houghton and Stockton. Therefore as well as the main centres where NUWM activity had appeared there were active branches, or at least ones active enough to owe money for literature, in the smaller mining villages too.[34]

The branches' activities were never solely about national issues. Again, Charlie Woods' description of activity around 'every aspect' of what faced poverty-stricken families is borne out at this time. In North Shields a slum clearance programme was moving tenants to the new Ridges Estate by 1934; the NUWM campaigned, but without success, against the Council's policy of stigmatising their new tenants by requiring them and their household effects to undergo a fumigation process before moving in. On the Ridges Estate itself there is an account of the NUWM acting as an intermediary between local residents, the Council and a 'problem' unemployed family, preventing an eviction; action to stop evictions for non-payment of rent also took place. Chester le Street NUWM secretary G. Clark referred to a branch membership of 300 in his letters lobbying the Council about overcrowding cases in housing and the lack of transparency in how the Council selected unemployed men for temporary work schemes. Members of the Morpeth branch borrowed bicycles to travel 30 miles into Northumberland to brief 40 unemployed workers about to be interviewed by the UAB in August 1935. Newbiggin branch, also in Northumberland, claimed success in a community effort to prevent threatened evictions from council housing. In Blyth Ned Breadin, Terry Mooney and Bob Elliott claimed victory in negotiating outdoor relief and not the workhouse for a teenager without parents, and for successfully getting 'scores of cases, where relief has been reduced, brought back to scale.'[35]

According to Breadin the Blyth success was due to 'taking the issues to the workers for support' just as George Short as we have seen did at Stockton Cross; negotiating a case with UAB officers was supported by 'the mass of Blyth workers, men and women, who turned out to demonstrate.' This was in line with the guidance from NUWM headquarters in 1935. According to this it was 'beyond all doubt that that mass agitation leading up to demonstrations and deputations to the authorities responsible for bad treatment or benefit or relief reductions is the most effective means of getting such cases rectified.'[36]

In the eyes of the Communist Party leadership however there was a lack of *political* activity by the North East NUWM in mid-1935, and this was a serious weakness. For example the District NUWM had planned another County Hunger March which could have built on the success of the UAB agitations in early 1935 but this was called off. An NUWM deputation (under the banner of the 'Durham United Front Movement') was received constructively enough by the Durham PAC – the Councillors on that occasion at least were clear that they wanted to avoid a repetition of the 1933 disturbances – but it was not accompanied by a demonstration. The CP Central Committee reported that it had 'had to take strong measures to try and remedy this position' but there is no mention of what, or indeed why the County demonstration had not materialised.

At the end of 1934 Alec Henry had admitted that his comrades in the region 'tended to be isolated from the more advanced sections of the movement' but he believed that the joint work they were doing with individual Labour Party members would benefit the united front as their influence would push local Labour leaders towards 'working-class politics'. Party recruitment was slow; non-existent in Newcastle but with about 40 across Blyth, North Shields and Sunderland, all towns, of course, where the NUWM was active. This critique of the political role of the Party and the

NUWM in the region was to continue as the unemployed struggle entered another phase from 1936.[37] There were, however, the demands of the routine work to deal with as well.

Notes

1   *Daily Worker* 8 April and 25 March 1930; Noreen Branson, *History of the Communist Party of Great Britain 1927-1941* (London: Lawrence and Wishart 1985).

2   Noreen Branson and Margot Heinemann, *Britain in the Nineteen Thirties* (London: Granada Publishing 1973); Bentley Gilbert, *British Social Policy 1914-39* (London: Batsford Press1970).

3   National Congress and March Council Bulletin no.5 and no.6 January 1934 (NA: MEPO 2/3071 Part 5).

4   North East United Front March Committee Appeal 11 December 1933 (DCRO: D/X 411/271).

5   National Congress and March Council Bulletin no.2 February 1934 (NA: MEPO 2/3071Part5).

6   *Heslop's Local Advertiser* 16 February 1934 (GLS); *Daily Worker* 2 February 1934; Len Edmondson, interview with Ray Challinor 1986.

7   John Longstaff, interview with Duncan Longstaff.

8   National Congress and March Council Bulletin no.1 January 1934 (NA: MEPO 2/3071 Part5); *Daily Worker* 13 and 17 February, 3 March 1934.

9   *Blyth News* 26 February 1934; Margot Heinemann, interview 1986 (IWMSA ref 9239).

10   John Longstaff, interview with Duncan Longstaff; information from Bill Tattam's relative Sheila Gray.

11   Metropolitan Police Special Branch Report to Home Office 4 March 1934 (NA: MEPO 2/3071 Part1); *Newcastle Journal* 1 March 1934.

12   Minutes of the NAC Meeting April 1934 (WCML).

13   *Blaydon Courier* 21 April, 19 May 1934.

14   Report of the Annual Conference of Trades Councils 1932, pp. 20-22; 1936, p. 21; 1935, p. 31 (TUC: HD 6661).

15   Richard Croucher: *We Refuse to Starve in Silence: A History of the National Unemployed Workers' Movement 1920-1946* (London: Lawrence and Wishart 1987, p. 157); Newcastle and District Trades Council: Annual Report of the Executive Council 1935, p. 7, 1936, p. 5 (TUC: JN 1129 NEW); *Gateshead Labour Herald* May 1934 and February 1935; Ellen Wilkinson, *The Town That Was Murdered* (London: Victor Gollanz Left Book Club 1939, p. 193); Matt Perry, *The Jarrow Crusade: Protest and Legend* (Sunderland: Sunderland University Press 2005, p. 37).

16   Sunderland and District Trades Council: Annual Report and Balance Sheet 1936 (TUC: JN 1129 SUN); George Short and Nick Rowell, interviews with Peter Brabban 1979.

17   *Unemployment Hardships -Don't Struggle By Yourself,* National Federation of Unemployed Associations Monthly Report July 1934 (TUC: Pamphlets HD 5767.)

18   Minutes of the NAC Meeting February 1935 (WCML); *Unemployed Leader* September 1935; NUWM Headquarters Circular D16, 30 December 1935 (MML: NUWM Bulletins and Circulars); Minutes of the Central Committee of the Communist Party of Great Britain 26 April 1935 (LHASC).

19   G.C.M. M'Gonigle, *Poverty and the Public Health* (London: Victor Gollanz Left Book Club 1936); on the Left Book Club see John Lewis, *The Left Book Club: An Historical Record* (London: Victor Gollanz 1970); David F. Smith: 'The Context and Outcome of Nutrition Campaigning in 1934' *International Journal of Epidemiology* Vol 32 No 4 (August 2003pp. 500-502); *Malnutrition Among the Unemployed, Tyneside, Survey March 1935* (NA: MOH 79/332, pp. 19-20); *Committee Against Malnutrition Bulletin* 9 (July 1935, WIHM).

20   J.C. Spence: *Investigation into the Health and Nutrition of Certain Children of Newcastle upon Tyne Between the Ages of One and Five Years* (Newcastle upon Tyne: Newcastle on Tyne Co-operative Society 1934). See also the Newcastle Dispensary *Annual Reports* for 1931-34 (TWAS: HO.ND/3/1-33.

21   Susan Pedersen: *Eleanor Rathbone and the Politics of Conscience* (New Haven: Yale University Press 2004, pp. 234-7); *Newcastle Journal* 16 February 1934; *Manifesto of the National March and Congress* (1934, WCML).

22   Bobbie Qualie, interview with Peter Brabban 1979.

23   Bobbie Qualie, interview with Peter Brabban 1979; Dave College, *Labour Camps: The British Experience* (Sheffield: Sheffield Popular Publishing 1989); Wal Hannington, *The Problem of the Distressed Areas* (London: Victor Gollanz Left Book Club 1937, pp. 92-140); Len Edmondson, 'Labour and the labour camps' in Keith Armstrong and Huw Beynon (eds): *Hello, Are You Working? Memories of the Thirties in the North East of England* (Whitley Bay: Strong Words Publications 1977); Lorraine Walsh and William Kenefick: 'Bread, Water and Hard Labour? New Perspectives on 1930s Labour Camps' *Scottish Labour History* Vol 34 1999, pp. 14-34; *North Mail* 13 September 1934, 21 and 23 March 1939.

24   Len Edmondson, 'Labour and the labour camps', p. 68

25   Frank Graham, interview with Jim McGurn 1986 (BMSA ref 2007.29).

26   Len Edmondson, interview with Karen Grunzweil 1999 (BMSA ref 1999.9).

27   Len Edmondson, interview with Karen Grunzweil 1999 (BMSA ref 1999.9); *Newcastle Journal* 9 February 1935.

28   Wal Hannington, *Unemployed Struggles 1919-1936* (London: Lawrence and Wishart 1979, p. 312.); also his *Ten Lean Years: An Examination of the Record of the National Government in the Field of Unemployment* (Wakefield: EP Publishing 1978, p. 136.); *Daily Worker* 5 and 7 February 1935; *Heslop's Local Advertiser* 15 February 1935(GLS).

29   *Sunderland Echo* 26 January and 2 February 1935.

30   *Shields News* 31 January 1935.

31   *Shields Gazette* 23 February 1935; Minutes of Blyth Town Council General Purposes Committee 29 January 1935 (NCRO: NRO 00880/60); *Blaydon*

Courier 23 February 1935.

32   See Stephanie Ward, 'The Means Test and the Unemployed in South Wales and the North East of England 1931-1939', *Labour History Review* Vol 73 No.1 (April 2008, pp. 113-133).

33   Hannington, *Unemployed Struggles, p.* 313; *Blyth News* 14 February 1935; Len Edmondson, interview with Ray Challinor 1986; David F. Smith: 'The Context and Outcome of Nutrition Campaigning in 1934'pp. 50.1

34   Minutes of the Central Committee of the Communist Party of Great Britain 4 June 1932, 18 February 1933 and 4 January 1936 (LHASC); Sam Davies, 'The Membership of the National Unemployed Workers' Movement 1923-1938,' *Labour History Review* Vol 57 No.1 (Spring 1992, pp. 29-37); NUWM Headquarters Circular circa 1934 (LHASC: CP/IND/HANN/01/07).

35   North Tyneside Community Development Project Final report Vol.1: *North Shields: Working Class Politics and Housing 1900-1977* (Newcastle on Tyne: Benwell Community Project 1978, pp. 27, 38); G. Clark, letters May – September 1935 ('Correspondence with Chester le Street Unemployed Association 1925-1938' – DCRO: UD/CS 203/23-30); NUWM HQ Newsletter no 9 August 1935 (LHASC: CP/IND/HANN/01/04); *Unemployed Leader* May and June 1935.

36   *Unemployed Leader* June 1935; NUWM Headquarters Circular circa 1935 – '*Notes on How to Form an NUWM Branch*' (LHASC: CP/IND/HANN/1/11).

37   *Blaydon Courier* 4 May 1935; Minutes of the Central Committee of the Communist Party of Great Britain 26 April 1935; 14-16 December 1934 (LHASC).

Chapter Seven

CAMPAIGNS, POLITICS AND MARCHES

Advocacy and Campaigns

Throughout the decade advice and representation continued to be the key activity of an NUWM branch. The changes in benefit systems and regulations from Boards of Guardians to the Means Test, the Unemployment Assistance Boards and the new or proposed rules, all created a need. There were always the potential too for a special needs claim and applications where the Boards or Committees had some discretion in the interpretation of benefits rules. All in all, according to George Short, it 'produced among the unemployed a whole list of amateur lawyers, who were really clever at it too, we had them all over'. NUWM Headquarters advised branches to have a claims committee that would have ready access to all the relevant legislation, but which would avoid leaving all the work to one or two individuals; the 'most capable comrades' should aim to educate others to avoid this happening. They should go into all the facts of a case very thoroughly and be prepared to 'do the talking' if the claimants were too timid to be coached in doing it themselves. As we have seen particularly gross cases of injustice could be accompanied by deputations and demonstrations.[1]

In Sunderland there was a large and active branch and the claims committee has been recalled: 'Billy Booth and Jock Dewar used to take cases. So did Billy Masheder, he was a miner who'd been blacklisted ever since a dispute in 1927. Billy Booth was probably the best. He was a plater but he was a marked man, blacklisted'. The branch held regular meetings outside the General Post Office in the town centre, where people would attend if they needed help. Eventually their activity expanded so that:

The advisers were on the job every day of the week except Sunday at the rooms in Norfolk Street. The rooms were also the CP offices, joint rooms between the two organisations to save on the rent. They were near to the main labour exchange. The rooms were open every day for unemployed to come with cases and to pass the time.

Both Nick Rowell and Frank Graham have said that about a third of the cases they took up became successful claims, and there is evidence that this was the case with NUWM branches in general. It has been established too that appeals where the claimant had representation were much more likely to be upheld at this time. Graham even recalled one occasion when the manager of the main labour exchange in Sunderland came over to the NUWM advisers in Norfolk Street for their opinion on whether he'd interpreted a rule correctly. They did not seem to have experienced any discrimination in terms of their own claims because of their activity with the unemployed; in fact Bobbie Qualie remembered the manager of the Sunderland labour exchange shaking his hand when Bobbie returned from a Hunger March, saying that he admired what he'd done. In South Shields on the other hand NUWM branch Chairman Anthony Lowther campaigned against decisions that he believed had been made against him because of his support for claimants; a UAB inspector on a visit to his home had described him as 'a man of extremist views'. After protest meetings Lowther won his appeal to the UAB and also confirmed the right of the local NUWM to negotiate with it.[2]

There were other issues and campaigns, some with at least partial success. After the 1934 Hunger March there had been an increase in the unemployment benefit scales for a family with children, and so the NUWM lobbied for a corresponding increase in the PAC scales for children whose families were long-term unemployed. This would help to prevent a reduction in the support for children when the eligibility for unemployment benefit came to an end. Between October and December 1934 Sunderland NUWM sent five deputations to the Council and the PAC about this, accompanied on at least one of these occasions by 'scores of unemployed' in a demonstration. Billy Masheder, Joe Wilson, Mrs Wilson, Ed Houghton and Bob Mackie made up the deputations, who cited local Medical Officer of Health reports in support of their case for higher scales to combat the health consequences of malnutrition. They were supported by Jimmy Lenagh, who had been elected as an independent socialist councillor again in 1931. When Labour took control of Sunderland Council in November 1934 they agreed to increase the PAC scales in line with the NUWM demands that December, despite Tory protests about the cost to the rates. They raised them again for children a year later and thereby ameliorated a little of the poverty for 3,000 children.[3]

In South Shields Lowther and his NUWM colleagues used the success in Sunderland to press their own case to the Council a few days later – 'what could be done in Sunderland could be done in South Shields'. Lowther,

John Mitchell, Mrs Smith and Mrs Allen argued for a major effort of slum clearance as a public works scheme at trade union rates, free school meals and milk for necessitous children, extra winter relief and higher relief scales. They explained the effects of rising rents and living costs and the additional fuel required by winter on the budget of an unemployed family, and again quoted the Medical Officer of Health's reports about malnutrition that resulted when spending on food had to be reduced. The Labour councillors supported them and carried a resolution that an NUWM deputation be received by the PAC. They were a minority on the Council though and the PAC meeting again referred matters to its sub-committees that December; a month later the agitation over the UAB scales implemented in January 1935 would have eclipsed the issue in terms of attention. In Newcastle and Gateshead however the PACs either refused to raise scales on cost grounds or referred issues around their various sub-committees to bury the issue whilst appearing to be still engaged with it.[4]

There was evidence of good relations between the Sunderland NUWM and the Labour Party a year later, during the general election campaign of November 1935. The two Labour parliamentary candidates spoke at a rally organised by the NUWM on the Sunderland Town Moor, where a Communist Party presence was very much in evidence. Billy Masheder spoke for the NUWM and one of the Labour candidates, Leah Manning, invoked the movement that had halted the Unemployment Act when she called for 'a united front of all the working- class movements of the country … that would sweep the National Government out of power'. This is a significant example of a joint platform in the region and Manning's words could have come straight from the NUWM.[5]

Each of these efforts included women in the deputations and made a major point about the links between low relief scales, malnutrition and poor health, and quoted local medical evidence to support their case. This could take advantage, too, of the growing publicity being given to medical views about deprivation, diet and health that was noticeable at the time of the 1934 Hunger March. The NUWM made this one of its national campaigning issues in 1934 and 1935 and it was expected that the women's sections would play a leading role. The use of the legislation on the 'Feeding of Necessitous Schoolchildren' in the 1920s was discussed earlier, but, unsurprisingly in view of the continuing poverty of long-term unemployment, it remained an issue through the 1930s also. The NUWM policy was that which had been adopted by Durham County Council during the mining lockouts: free school meals should be provided according to parental income and not dependent on a medical examination, and provided on the rates or through government funding. As Mrs Allen had told South Shields Council at the time of a royal wedding in 1934, 'If there is money for this sort of thing there is money for the children, whose health should be of paramount importance'. Early in 1936 a Board of Education circular did indeed confirm that low income was itself a sufficient criterion for free meals. Although the NUWM hailed this as a victory for campaigning the fact remains that in the North East the take-up of the meals remained very low; one factor was that PACs could, and did, reduce the family's weekly relief by the cost of the meal.[6]

Another prominent issue was over what was called 'extra winter relief'; winter brought increased needs for coal, fuel and warm clothing for unemployed people and their families and the NUWM established that the UABs had 'considerable discretion' over making payments for them. PACs making payments also had the ability to raise their scales to meet additional needs. 'Discretion' had always meant 'room for negotiation' to the unemployed movement. Winter relief was included in the demands from 1934 onwards and CP or NUWM candidates in local elections – in Tynemouth, South Shields and Blyth, for example – included it in their manifestoes. By 1935 the Blyth NUWM activists Ned Breadin and Bob Elliott were Communist Councillors on Blyth Council and Breadin also had a seat for the same ward on Northumberland County Council. They urged Blyth Council to support the NUWM's request that they lobby the UAB about additional winter benefits and also Northumberland County Council's PAC; they had a limited level of success in that both Councils agreed to protest about UAB scales. Northumberland County Council had agreed to raise its scales for families with children, something the NUWM claimed as a victory for its work. 'Extra winter relief' was to continue as a campaign issue until the outbreak of the war.[7]

The police surveillance and information-gathering that had accompanied the movement in the 1920s continued. It was not just the Hunger Marches that were kept under close observation but local activity as well, something those involved seem to have been well aware of. George Short for example recalled that:

> The police, they were part of the other side. They tried to bribe the unemployed to give them information about us. Believe me we had an excellent way of dealing with this. It was to report back at the Cross meetings, give all the lurid details, in such a way as to make the police look a laughing stock, ridicule was the best weapon not only against them but against the men they'd been trying to use. The infiltration was by

giving the unemployed fella a new pair of boots or trousers or something like that. In fact if an unemployed fella started wearing a new pair of boots and he was in the NUWM you were very careful to ask him where he got them from.

Although Communist Party membership in the region, like the rest of the country, noticeably revived through its activity in the unemployed movement it only recruited, or only recruited and retained, a comparatively small number of those who passed through the NUWM. This was certainly the Sunderland experience as Nick Rowell explained:

A number came in to the Communist Party through the NUWM, they were politicised there. Others just did a lot in the NUWM. Others were in it but they got their own issues resolved and then never came back, they'd got what they wanted, that's a fact. I still see them around the town.[8]

This returns to the issue raised in earlier chapters, the relations between the Communist Party and the NUWM.

Communist Relations: United Front and Popular Front

By the time of the sixth and last National Hunger March to London in 1936 the international Communist movement had gone through several policy changes and they all had consequences for the NUWM. These were not just in terms of its policy but also in terms of the operating relationships between the leaderships of both. The 'class against class' policy has been described, and it was during this that the Red International of Labour unions, a branch of the Comintern in Moscow, issued a policy resolution that British Communists in the NUWM would have been expected to follow. The veteran's reference to 'joint rooms between the two organisations to save on the rent' in Sunderland (and it was the same with the Party rooms on Westgate Road in Newcastle) is on the surface a practical observation but it also reflects how inter-twined the two organisations were. Similarly local NUWM branch officers and the 'amateur lawyers' were almost invariably Party members too.

In 1930 the Comintern claimed that there had been political failure due to the '... incorrect policy of the NUWM leadership in confining its activities almost wholly to those workers unemployed for a long period.' Workers recently made unemployed were thought to be far more responsive to the message of revolutionary politics than those who had been out of work for an extended period, which in sociological terms was plausible enough.

Those who still felt anger rather than resignation at their circumstances would be a more fertile recruiting ground for the revolutionary left. An alleged concentration on representing the workers' cases at appeal at the expense of political work was criticised, and a new strategy for building an unemployed movement was put forward. According to this the model should be local 'unemployed councils' in which membership would be open to the employed and unemployed, and membership fees voluntary. The focus here would be on political organisation rather than on a 'trade union for the unemployed' with all the great effort required of activists to maintain the workload of advice, representation and appeals.[9]

In Moscow Hannington vigorously defended the role of the NUWM, the nature of its organisation and the value of casework in attracting unemployed workers to the organisation. Although NUWM national conferences stressed the importance of building unemployed councils as opposed to NUWM branches, in practice there seems to have been no local efforts to build them. Local NUWM activists were either not interested or saw no possibility of their success. In the North East the reports of activity being supplied to NUWM Headquarters and the *Daily Worker* at this time refer to NUWM branches being formed, not unemployed councils. Hannington was already marked as a critic of the 'class against class' policy and now he was upbraided for not implementing the policy of unemployed councils. In what were clearly stand-up rows in the CP Central Committee, during which attempts were made to manoeuvre Hannington into having to resign, the unemployed movement leader behaved with agility. In the autumn of 1933 it was explained at the Central Committee regarding the NUWM that 'the fact that we are not able to assist them financially in any way strengthens the feeling of independence from the Party. Many times any attempt to try and force our line would have meant a serious breach of relations with the NUWM'. Hannington, it was reported, 'has extraordinary mass support throughout the country amongst the unemployed' but he 'passionately sees the NUWM as a special field of activity against the line of the Party'. Therein, as far as the Central Committee loyalists were concerned, lay the problem: Hannington and other NUWM leaders like Harry McShane in Scotland could not be relied on to carry out instructions they did not agree with, but their standing among the unemployed was too high for them to be moved aside without damaging the movement.[10]

Their only solution was to try to improve Party 'fraction work' in the NUWM, whereby those loyal to the Central Committee approach would operate as a co-ordinated group to make sure that their line was carried out. Even so success was far from guaranteed. Sam Langley had been a North East representative on the NAC during 1932, one of those described in Hannington's memoirs as 'an excellent team of fearless and devoted comrades' and he also worked at NUWM Headquarters in the early 1930s. There was an attempt by loyalists to use Langley to 'strengthen the leadership's position' there in the autumn of 1933, but it was reported to the CP Central Committee that 'Comrade Langley has not been a help as far as the Party is concerned, in fact a hindrance, so he had to be moved again' and he returned to Tyneside. Therefore there is some evidence that the tensions between the CP leadership and Hannington's group were known to North East activists although how far all this was communicated cannot be known. Changes in national Communist policy did cause problems with Communist supporters in the North East and elsewhere, as we have seen, and a future chapter will examine how they caused problems for a least one NUWM branch in the region too.[11]

By January 1936 Communist Party General Secretary Harry Pollitt was clear that the NUWM too had to change direction. It was 'in a rut' and 'resting on past history'; its 35,000 members were mainly long-term unemployed, and had no working contact with the trades unions; the big part it had played in the fight against the UAB had not been consolidated in terms of Party membership. On the North East coast, apparently, there was little Party work done amongst the unemployed. At the same time there were thousands of unemployed trade unionists in the trades council unemployed associations. The united front as applied to the unemployed should now be to 'create one united unemployed association under the direct control and leadership of the TUC' so that there was one single fight against the Means Test, for public works at trade union rates and to bring about the defeat of the National Government. The memoir of Hannington's colleague McShane, written many years later when he had left the CP, confirms that Pollitt insisted that this aimed-for single body should be subordinate to the TUC.

The response of Hannington and McShane was once more, as their critics in the Party leadership put it, 'to go through the motions of agreement' whilst claiming 'the need to face up to the difficulties'. According to the NUWM leadership there was a significant presence of 'non-Party elements' in most NUWM branches and so they 'couldn't just mechanically announce a change and approach the TUC'. Having been criticised for not building unemployed councils during the revolutionary and sectarian phase the NUWM leaders were now taken to task for not working to submerge the NUWM into a radical TUC body. This was the context for the next phase of the unemployed struggle as the government returned to the rest of its Unemployment Act.[12]

The Cuts Appear Again

The protests against the cuts represented by the Unemployment Assistance Act in 1935 had not prevented their implementation, of course, they had simply delayed it. New scales and Means Test regulations were published in July 1936 with a view to implementation the following November. They proposed severe cuts in the allowances paid to sections of the unemployed, particularly single people, and triggered another wave of protests.

There was nothing new, as we have seen, in the official labour movement of the North East denouncing the UAB regulations but by the summer of 1936 its voice was noticeably more militant than in previous years. In Sunderland's West Park that August 3-4,000 people attended a rally organised by the DMA and Sunderland and Houghton Labour Parties. The CP and the NUWM also took part, an innovation that did not go unnoticed by Sunderland Conservatives. The rally demanded the abolition of the Regulations and the Means Test, and called for government intervention to ensure work or full maintenance for the unemployed. Although the rally made an open commitment to support 'any action taken by the National Council of Labour to implement the demands' George Harvey from the platform stated that 'direct action was needed, not resolutions'; he wanted a general strike to smash the Means Test and the government.

During the same month 2,000 people attended the rally organised by the DMA and Seaham Labour Party at the Eppleton Colliery Welfare Ground where Councillor Moore, who was also the DMA Financial Secretary, stated that 'mere demonstrations were insufficient to cause the withdrawal of the regulations' and so therefore 'their trade unions and political movement would have to threaten some industrial action'. Sam Watson, DMA agent, told a 'large crowd' at New Washington Welfare Hall that strike action against the Means Test would be required. By this time Will Lawther was on the DMA Executive and was Vice-President of the Miners' Federation of Great Britain. He drew attention to the success of earlier demonstrations against the UAB Regulations as signs of public support for serious action; the miners, he claimed, 'wanted something very drastic'. These were not just the voices of scattered militants. The DMA Executive requested the National Council of Labour, which was the joint policy forum for Labour's National Executive and the TUC, to call a one day general strike against the UAB regulations. Will Lawther and Sam Watson were a new generation of leaders in the DMA; in contrast to their predecessors like Peter Lee they were, at this time, on the left of the movement and not adverse to working with Communists. They were also reflecting the anger of the mining communities at the effects of the Means Test system.[13]

The Miners' Federation of Great Britain - whose members, of course, lived in the areas most affected by long-term unemployment and the Means Test - pursued the industrial action proposal at the TUC Annual Conference that September. Delegate Sam Watson provided examples of how this was an issue for people in work as well as the unemployed, which was one of the consistent themes of the unemployed movement. A worker earning £2 a week could have to contribute 12s a week towards the sustenance of an unemployed parent. In County Durham, he said, a wage increase the DMA had successfully negotiated had almost been wiped out from family incomes. This was the effect of the Means Test requirement to reduce the unemployed father's assistance allowance by a corresponding amount. Therefore he concluded that:

> It is because we feel bitter at the imposition of the Means Test that we think the General Council should get down to considering not only the question of demonstrations and speeches but the question of industrial action.

However this position failed at the Congress. TUC Chairman Walter Citrine's judgement remained consistent throughout the 1930s:

> If we cannot, by reason and by argument, convince the people of this country that the regulations are inequitable and that they mean misery and poverty for hundreds of thousands of our people, we can never expect their backing if we try to force Parliament by extra-constitutional means.[14]

This was a similar situation to the Labour Party Conference of 1932 in that the suggestion of radical action ran counter to the culture of the organisation urged to take it. The TUC General Council was not going to seek a confrontation with the government regardless of the 'misery and poverty for hundreds of thousands of our people'. The problem with constitutional, parliamentary methods was the Conservative majority at Westminster. Labour's electoral disaster of 1931 had left it with too great a task to secure a majority at the general election of 1935. The Conservatives were returned again, although they kept the term 'National Government' so that they could continue to claim a wider consensus. Labour regained the seats it had lost in County Durham but overall its gains were 'geographically and occupationally limited ... to constituencies dominated by the industrial working classes' and this was insufficient to achieve a parliamentary majority.

The labour movement could not rely on parliamentary action to relieve the burden of degradation from the unemployed and to confine activity to working for a Labour government, eschewing 'extra-constitutional means', meant in effect that action against the poverty of many areas was to be postponed indefinitely.[15]

1936 did see some extra-constitutional pressure in the shape of the sixth, and in fact final, national Hunger March to London; also a superficially similar initiative, the Jarrow Crusade, which was subsequently to become the received image of unemployed protest in the 1930s.

The 1936 Hunger March

In line with the new approach of the international Communist movement this march would 'be different from all its predecessors...' Using the effective joint Labour and CP local agitations against the 1934 Act in South Wales as a template it would also be an opportunity to 'aim for the official support of the Trade Unions and the Labour Party', and in that it was to be more successful than would have been predicted three years earlier. The terrain in that respect was shifting at the grass roots and this was seen in the North East as well. Alongside this political agenda the march demands were for the abolition of the Means Test and the Anomalies Act, for work schemes at trade union rates and the scrapping of the cuts to benefits scales.[16]

The miners' unions raising the issue of strike action was one example of how pressure from below about the Means Test and the UAB regulations was becoming stronger. Both the Labour leadership and the TUC had been criticised for lethargy during the protests of 1935. As a Welsh mining delegate put it, 'the TUC made no appeal for action against the Act until the struggles initiated in the localities were virtually over ... Conference should insist that the General Council act in a speedier fashion and mobilise the struggle more effectively in the future'. Similarly the Labour National Executive had played no leadership role in those protests, so that those in the North East and elsewhere that had featured Labour had been local initiatives. There is evidence too that by this time the longstanding opposition of the TUC General Council to Hunger Marches was not necessarily shared by its constituent bodies. In 1937 the General Council issued a questionnaire to affiliated trades councils who had been on the routes of Hunger Marches to ascertain if they had supported them and whether the effort had been justified. The returns had been mostly positive on both counts (albeit from a low response rate) although this was distorted by the TUC in its final report. Some local trades councils had actively supported the marches and valued the stimulus they had given to local activity when they passed through.[17]

One consequence was that of all the NUWM Hunger Marches it was this one in 1936 that attracted the most support from the mainstream labour movement. This was the picture in the North East too, with Tyneside District reporting that it was 'co-operating with the Labour Party in the numerous meetings and demonstrations in the district', which had indeed been the case. Newcastle and District Trades Council supported the Hunger March, although it declined to organise a contingent from its own unemployed association to join it. In October the Trades Council arranged a conference on the new UAB regulations and following this they 'associated themselves' with the North East March Council, and made a donation to the funds. This seems to have been the first time in the decade that a North East Hunger March contingent had been supported by a local trades council.[18]

Support from local authorities, including Labour ones, was to prove a different matter. In Blyth Bob Elliott was by now a Communist town councillor and a Council sub-committee agreed that Councillor Elliott should be its official representative on the march. He was one of the local organisers. However the full Council, despite his protests, quickly quashed this proposal. It seems likely that despite their initial sympathy over the issues at stake the Council was moving back into line with official Labour and TUC policy on not supporting marches by 'non-affiliated organisations.'[19]

Conservative Gateshead Council received a deputation from the 'Unemployed Association' which requested financial help for 10 men to join the Hunger March and support for their dependents whilst they were away. In reply to the Mayor they denied that their organisation was 'an offshoot of the Communist Party' and that the march was 'a Communist stunt'; they denied this and stated that it was 'organised by the unemployed themselves'. It could be that this was a group from the trades council unemployed association and not the Gateshead branch of the NUWM; if so it suggests, as with Newcastle Trades Council, a new co-operation between the NUWM and the local official movement. In any event the Council, despite opposition from Labour members, refused financial help. In South Shields the Council was lobbied by the 'Campaign Committee of the National March to London against the Means Test': it wanted the Council to protest about the Regulations and a grant for equipment for the marchers. 'Political objections were raised' however by the Conservative councillors, who refused a grant and would only protest the Regulations if they placed a burden on the Council. Tynemouth Labour Party decided to 'take no action' in response to a request from North Shields NUWM to support their contingent.[20]

Other, Labour, Councils were more supportive. West Hartlepool donated money, food and blankets as well as overnight accommodation. In Blaydon the Council chairman was Harry Bolton; his expulsion by the CP from dual membership in 1929 was described earlier but despite this he remained sympathetic to the Communist position until the end of the 1930s. He addressed the Blaydon contingent at their eve-of-march rally, to which the local Labour MP William Whiteley had also sent a message of support. Bolton told the marchers that the UAB regulations and the Means Test were examples of 'class war legislation' and that 'They had the beginning of the international class war in Spain and this government was showing its hand both at home and abroad in the interests of the idle class'. This reference to the struggle of Republican Spain will be pursued in the next chapter. Besides Wilf Jobling the Blaydon contingent included at least two other Communists, William Watson and Joe Woods, as well as James Batey, Ernest Henderson and Patrick Gorman. There were three women from the area: Rose Hutchinson, Olive Airey, niece of Charlie Woods, younger sister of Communist and Co-op Women's Guild campaigner Maggie Airey, and Emmie Lawther, a left-labour activist for over a decade. These three had been funded for boots and clothing by the Co-operative Movement.[21]

In all of these cases, and in others such as Durham, the march organisers were trying to get a commitment that the Public Assistance Committees would grant outdoor relief to the marchers' families while they were away. As in every previous march the Ministry of Labour would not permit claimants to 'sign on' along the route and so the knowledge that their families had some support would reassure those marchers who had dependents. It could also make the difference between taking part or not. In the examples above only Blaydon (with its 'Labour PAC' as Wilf Jobling put it) made this commitment, the others took refuge in the rules and only undertook to treat each case on its merits. Blyth and Morpeth branches did obtain an assurance that no action would be taken against marchers whose families became claimants of the PAC; this was important because they were technically open to legal allegations regarding 'desertion'.

Once more there was financial support from some miners' lodges such as Follonsby, six were represented on the March Committee and several called for the DMA to support the march officially. Tyneside District Secretary George Aitken reported to the Central Committee that the DMA Executive had decided against this but by just one vote, although no details were given. For the first time the Northumberland Miners' Association made a donation to the March Council.[22]

As in Felling in 1934 there was support too from the wider community. Marchers Frank Graham and Nick Rowell recalled that a number of small businesses in Sunderland responded to the NUWM appeal for boots and clothing, one local tradesman actually ensuring that each marcher had a new pair of boots. In Felling the 20 men who took part were equipped by local donations: Jim Ancrum listed the street and estate collections together with the donations from tradespeople and 'working- class organisations'. Again the Co-operative movement was to the fore, with the Teesside District Women's Co-operative Guild pledging to 'give every possible support to the Hunger March'.[23]

There was at least one local demonstration against the Regulations just before the Hunger March began. In North Shields Walter Harrison led 300 unemployed behind a 'Unity against Hunger' banner, from a larger mass meeting at Harbour View to the UAB office in Queen Alexandra Road. This was a protest against the 'National Government's new attempt to lower our standard of life and further enslave the working class of this country'. The press noted 'a large number of women among the marchers including one or two with a child in their arms'; wider community support too is suggested by the four Tynemouth Borough Councillors who had signed the marchers' appeal. One of those was Stanley Holmes, an opponent of the NUWM earlier in the decade. A deputation entered the UAB office to request that the manager forward their protest to the Ministry of Labour, as had been done in Gateshead the previous year, but all he undertook to give was a personal assurance that he would investigate any cases of hardship. North Shields NUWM members were pleased with the response to the anti-Means Test petition they were organising. This was aimed in good part at the professional classes, a tactic that has been a source of sarcasm for one historian, but in fact was a justifiable recognition of how far doctors and teachers, for example, were speaking out against poverty and unemployment and thus becoming potential allies of the unemployed movement.[24]

Around 150 men made up the North East contingent that left from the Bigg Market in the second week of October. The Felling marchers, with banners carrying slogans such as 'Felling unemployed demand the withdrawal of starvation scales', had left once more with a torchlight procession, band and mass send-off. The Sunderland contingent included the youngest member of the Hunger March, Paddy Durkin who was 15, whilst Blyth contributed the oldest member, Boer war veteran Alec Vettern who was 64. The women's section on this occasion assembled at Coventry, the North East marchers travelling there by organised buses. Two women from Sunderland were involved along with those from Gateshead, Chopwell and Blaydon. The North East male contingent was led by NUWM activists and Communist Councillors Tommy Richardson from Houghton le Spring and Bob Elliott from Blyth, with Councillor Jim Ancrum from Felling for part of the way. The March Committee also included George Short and David Catterick from Stockton, Joe Woods and Philip Reed, and a 'youth named Graham of Sunderland' who, the police, thought, 'seemed to be one worth watching.'[25]

Footwear and feet understandably crop up in marchers' recollections. The donation of boots that Frank Graham refers to was actually a mixed blessing:

> ... and in some cases we had quite a measure of support from local businessmen. For example one businessman in Sunderland gave all the hunger marchers a pair of boots, which was quite expensive in those days. It was a mistake of course because unfortunately the boots weren't worn in, and they had a lot of trouble with marching down in boots that were practically new, as it were.

Fellow marcher Nick Rowell recalled his boots too:

> The NUWM asked for donations of boots and clothing for marchers who didn't have them, and in Sunderland a number of small tradespeople also contributed. I got a new pair of boots. I was hoping to keep them to wear when I got back, but my own boot soles were so thin that I got my feet hurt and so I had to use the new boots. I wore them out, too. The march was a great experience. But when I got home I had fourteen blisters on one foot to cure![26]

The police reported that the conduct of the North East group was good, with the leadership of Elliott and Richardson being effective, even though most of the marchers were young and 'clearly of the corner boy type'. Once more a disparaging reference disguised the reality that it was single young people who were often bearing the brunt of the Means Test. In any case the North East contingent did not experience the disciplinary problems sometimes encountered in earlier marches. This could have been because more of them, for example as was claimed in Felling, had actually this time been selected by trade unions as the March Committees intended. Nevertheless Sunderland marcher Nick Rowell recalled one untoward episode:

> There were about 25 on that march from Sunderland. Some of them had no idea about politics that was the trouble. They were there because they

were physically fit enough to do the march. One of them, he was seen in a pub, he'd been singing in a pub or two along the way to get beer money. So the Committee decided to send him back, they didn't give him the money for a ticket they bought it for him and put him on the train. But generally the lads conducted themselves very well.[27]

The welcome meeting for the march in Hyde Park was supported by the London Labour Party and Trades Council and addressed by Clement Attlee, leader of the Parliamentary Labour Party, who also presented the marchers' petition to the House of Commons and led in the subsequent debate about the Means Test. At the end of the round of demonstrations and meetings there was a 'farewell' rally of some 4,000 people in Trafalgar Square, with more than 20 short speeches from the plinths, the speakers being national figures or local march leaders. Emmie Lawther was one speaker, on the same plinth as Communist Party leader Harry Pollitt, Aneurin Bevan MP and Councillor Bob Elliott from Blyth. This place in the running order suggests that Emmie Lawther was one of the women's section leaders. Tommy Richardson, recently elected as a Communist to Houghton le Spring Council, spoke from another. The co-operation of the Labour Party and trade unions was unprecedented and reflected the pressures from below described earlier.[28]

The BBC had agreed to broadcast some women marchers putting their case but later cancelled the idea; another example, according to the *Daily Worker*, of the BBC 'standing by its old custom of censoring anything likely to give publicity to working class wrongs'. The Committee against Malnutrition, the network of campaigning doctors mentioned in the previous chapter, responded by organising a public meeting on 'Unemployment and the Housewife', at which three of the women marchers were invited speakers. One of them was Mrs Holliday from Chopwell, presumably married to Steven Holliday, a Chopwell miner and Communist since the 1920s. She explained that her husband had been out of work for twelve years (probably blacklisted, although this was not mentioned), the budget her family had to live on and the effects it had on their health. This served as an expressive accompaniment to a speech by Dr Shirley Summerskill on poverty and child mortality in Britain.[29]

The NUWM claimed that the march was an unqualified success. Politically there were many positive elements, with far greater support and participation by trades union and senior Labour figures than ever before. Historians have identified some practical achievements too. For the first time the Minister of Labour actually met a NUWM deputation; he agreed to suspend the introduction of the new scales for two months pending a review; any alterations in the existing allowances would be phased in over eighteen months.[30]

The Jarrow Crusade

While the Hunger March was at the planning stage Hannington was contacted by Ellen Wilkinson, who had won the Jarrow constituency for Labour in 1935. She wanted to discuss the plans of the Town Council to organise a march to London by unemployed men to petition the government. Their aim was to lobby for shipyard and other contracts to alleviate the devastating unemployment and deprivation in the town. The new Jarrow MP had long been a sympathiser of the NUWM and it was logical for her to turn to the organisation for advice; their expertise in these matters was by now of course considerable. Hannington recommended that the Jarrow marchers join the North East contingent of the national Hunger March that the NUWM was planning for around the same time. At the end of their series of discussions Wilkinson reported that she had in fact recommended this to the Town Council but they had rejected the idea in favour of a separate march of their own. In Hannington's view this reflected the negative attitude of the official Labour Party towards the NUWM and a wish by the Council to maintain the Jarrow shipyards as the sole focus of its efforts. It also reflected a determination among the Jarrow organisers to avoid 'politics' in order to achieve more support and make a better case to the government.

Nevertheless Hannington's account shows that he went over all that was involved in planning a march to London with Ellen Wilkinson, and it is worth speculating how the Jarrow Crusade might have fared without his early input. Locally too Wilf Jobling made an offer to help the Jarrow men but this seems to have been ignored. Both Hannington and the CP thought the Jarrow March would be a useful way to draw attention to the poverty in the town and so they supported it throughout.[31]

The TUC and the Labour Party though refused to support the Jarrow March, despite Ellen Wilkinson's furious efforts at the Labour Party conference. The leaderships of the official movement maintained their opposition to marches to London, even one as politically innocuous as this one. Apart from the taint of the NUWM that was attached to them they believed such marches to be ineffective and a distraction from constitutional approaches to political change. Like the Hunger Marchers, the Jarrow men were refused permission to sign on at labour exchanges along the route, and so application had to be made to the PAC to support their families while they were away. In the Jarrow case however all the families concerned were already 'a charge' on the PAC and so they would be granted relief; Durham PAC were advised that this might not be the case with the Hunger Marchers and so each application would be assessed on its merits. Unlike some of the Hunger Marchers then the Jarrow men started with the assurance that their families would be supported.[32]

The progress of the Crusade was similar to that of the Hunger Marchers. Some local Labour Parties and Trades Councils were willing to ignore their leaderships' position and supported the marchers by providing food and accommodation. Where they would not some Conservative Associations stepped in: this action both reflected the blessing the Jarrow Association had given to the march and the opportunity to appear more concerned than their Labour opponents. Otherwise of course the local workhouse had to be used, but there seems to have been no effort to enforce the workhouse regulations regarding 'casuals' on them. The Jarrow men might not have known that this more relaxed attitude had in fact been struggled for and established by the NUWM Hunger Marchers of previous years.

March Marshall and Labour Councillor David Riley rebuffed any attempts to help from Communists along the route, even when it was in the form of financial donations. Ostensibly this was to maintain the non-political character of the event but he did accept donations from the Conservatives. This political decision suggests that the image he was striving for was more to do with respectability than being seen to be above party politics. Like the Hunger Marchers, the Jarrow men held public meetings along their route but they were significantly smaller in number than those held by the 1936 Hunger March; they were also solely concerned with the plight of their town. The marchers did not know that local Communists canvassed the unemployed to attend some of these public meetings, another example of the practical support they were willing to provide. The end of their march in London lacked the welcoming rally that had been a feature of the NUWM initiatives because they had not thought to organise one in advance, or to link up with the labour movement in the capital. Instead Communists at one of their own rallies in Hyde Park moved as a block to provide a welcoming audience for their speakers.[33]

Therefore it is worth observing that although the Jarrow Crusade rejected any association with Communists and the NUWM it owed quite a lot to both: Hannington's early planning input, the flexible response of workhouse managers, support along the way and at the end; it is also worth reflecting on how likely it would have been for Jarrow Council to conceive of a march to London if they had not had the precedent of the NUWM Hunger Marches before them.

The marchers believed that they were going to be able to present their petition to the House of Commons and discuss what Jarrow needed with government ministers. Instead there was no meeting with ministers, the petition was presented in the absence of the marchers themselves and it generated only a short and inconsequential series of questions in the Commons. This angered the men but respectability prevailed and a move for a sit-down protest at Westminster evaporated. Unlike any of the NUWM Hunger Marches the Jarrow Crusade cannot claim any results. Notwithstanding the efforts of Ellen Wilkinson at the Labour Party Conference it caused no ripples in the mainstream movement either, unlike the 1936 Hunger March which had provoked considerable manoeuvring among the leaderships about how far support should be expressed. Jarrow marcher Bob Maugham reflected in the 1980s:

Everybody thought something would happen. Nothing happened, after a couple of months things were just the same ... just carried on as usual. Never felt a change, it had done nothing... and it took them years before they remembered it, it was forgot about until just this last ten year. They took no notice of wor down there, not one iota.[34]

According to a police report Hannington was frustrated by the favourable press publicity that the Jarrow March had attracted, although he must have been calmed and encouraged by the later success of the NUWM march shortly after it. Frustration about the Jarrow March was to stay with the NUWM Hunger March veterans in the North East, but for a different reason. Frank Graham, probably the longest surviving one, explained this in an interview fifty years later:

... A great deal of confusion in the air exists about the hunger marches and the Jarrow marchers, and in most people's minds they are mixed up. Of course, the Jarrow marchers have received such enormous publicity that the hunger marches are almost forgotten, but they were of course, at the time and still are, much more important ... The difference between them and the Jarrow March was that the Jarrow march was really a begging march – it went to London to beg for work. The hunger marchers were much more militant, and they went to London with specific demands, and usually these demands were not only for work but for improvement in the system whereby people received dole and so on, because in those days there were such a number of people out of work that the conditions on the dole were of paramount importance to them.[35]

Frank Graham was also known to say that the Jarrow marchers 'went down there with a begging bowl and a lot of good it did them.'[36] It is indeed commonplace to find, not only that they are mixed up, but that Jarrow has served to eradicate the memory of the NUWM marchers. The Conservative MP David Davis is the grandson of North Shields NUWM activist Walter Harrison, and stated that his grandfather had taken part in the Jarrow March, unaware that it had in fact been the 1936 Hunger March. John Pemberton was one of the medical students who treated the feet of Hunger Marchers in London and witnessed a mounted police baton charge against them, erroneously recalling, decades later, that this had been the Jarrow March. Unfortunately too Emmie Lawther's daughter believed that it was the Jarrow March that her mother had taken part in, writing to *The Guardian* in 2003 to 'correct' their report that the Jarrow Crusade had had a policy of not including women. One reason for 'such enormous publicity' – and its effect on the memories even of those close to the actual events - is simply the consequence of government attempts to marginalise the Hunger Marches at the time.

For example Home Office discussions about responses to the 1934 Hunger March made the point that during the 1932 march all the newsreel film companies apart from one had given 'voluntary assurances' that they would not screen footage of it, on the grounds that this would be 'contrary to the public interest'. This was the case too in 1934 and 1936, and in the last example at least the Home Office reported that 'The BBC is understood to have refused on its own initiative to allow a representative of the NUWM to broadcast on the subject of the new regulations'. We have seen how it would not broadcast interviews with any of the women marchers even on a human interest basis. As a result the voice of the Hunger Marcher was not recorded at the time and later generations of documentary film makers had easy access only to footage of the Jarrow March. Thus it became by default the standard image of unemployed protest marches in the 1930s. Another reason was that at the time, and ever since, the Jarrow Crusade fitted convenient political agenda which the Hunger Marches did not.[37]

The Return

The return of the North East contingent of Hunger Marchers and the Jarrow Crusaders also provides a political contrast. The people of Jarrow gave their marchers a fulsome reception when they arrived back but there were recriminations within the Labour group on the Council. Within a short space of time the four left-wing councillors who had been central to the March had been expelled from the Labour Party for, among other allegations, attacking the role of Ellen Wilkinson in the failure to have the petition presented to the House of Commons. Frustrated at the outcome of the Crusade they had also proposed a second and more political march from Jarrow against the Means Test. This was symptomatic of the general political divisions and factionalism within Jarrow Labour Party that Ellen Wilkinson had to balance. The rebel councillors subsequently stood, with some success, as 'New Labour Party' candidates, and later associated themselves with the ILP. This attempt to build a left alternative in the town, fuelled in no small part by the perceived failure of the Jarrow Crusade, came to nothing and the rebels eventually returned to successful careers in the Labour fold.[38]

The North East Hunger Marchers on the other hand shared a feeling of success. Blaydon Council held a civic reception for their contingent on their return and this was another opportunity for the leaders to put their political message across. Describing the Means Test as 'one of the worst forms of class war legislation ever to reach the statute book' Harry Bolton claimed that a 'united front of the people' could sweep away the Means Test, the regulations and the government itself, and 'secure a new social order'. This theme was continued by William Watson and Wilf Jobling, the later stating that it was now time for 'the workers to build up a united front and abolish the present capitalist system so that there would be no need for hunger marches'. Olive Airey, apparently the youngest in the women's contingent said that it had been a tremendous experience that had left her ready to carry on the work of the last three weeks. Emmie Lawther described the impact the women had had in explaining the realities of life under long-term unemployment to those in more prosperous areas. She attacked the privation and vicious injustice of the Means Test and stated that women were the people who suffered the most under it. Therefore, she said,

> We believe that women should take their place with the men in the fight against this vicious Means Test, we believe we can help our men in this struggle, just as the Russian women have stood side by side with their men, and the Spanish women are fighting alongside their men for democracy.[39]

Calling for women to get involved, to take their rightful place in the struggle had been a mission for Emmie Lawther since the miners' struggles of the 1920s, and it was one also for women active in the North East NUWM. Their role as the household manager was undermined by the poverty of unemployment and what had been called earlier the 'inquisitorial methods' of the benefits system; the comparatively few in the region who worked after marriage faced the injustice of the Anomalies Act. The references to the crisis of Republican Spain that we have seen in the context of this march are the theme of the next chapter. A good many active members of the North East NUWM were to take part in the Spanish Civil War during the next three years.

Notes

1   George Short, interview with Peter Brabban 1979; NUWM Headquarters Circular circa 1935 – *'Notes on How to Form an NUWM Branch'* (LHASC: CP/IND/HANN/1/11).

2   Nick Rowell, interview with Peter Brabban 1979. Billy Booth later became President of Sunderland Trades Council (*Sunderland Echo* 5 March 1956); Richard Croucher: *We Refuse to Starve in Silence: A History of the National Unemployed Workers' Movement 1920-1946* (London: Lawrence and Wishart 1987); Frank Graham, interview with Don Watson 1996; Bobbie Qualie, interview with Peter Brabban 1979; *Shields Gazette* 9 March and *Daily Worker* 30 March 1938.

3   *North Mail* 11 October, 6 November, 4 December 1934.

4   *Shields Gazette* 6 and 28 December 1934; *North Mail* 4 and 10 December 1934.

5   *Sunderland Echo* 12 November 1935. The Labour candidates lost in Sunderland. At this election the CP only stood two parliamentary candidates (one of whom, Willie Gallacher, won in Fife) and in the interests of a united front campaigned for Labour.

6   NUWM Circular D30 on Women's Sections 4 January 1935 (MML: NUWM Bulletins and Circulars); *Shields Gazette* 6 December 1934; Minutes of the NAC Meeting February 1936 (MML: Hannington D Miscellaneous); *Malnutrition among the unemployed: arrangements for local investigations 1934-35* (NA: MH 79/334); Charles Webster, 'Health, Welfare and Unemployment during the Depression', *Past and Present* No 105 (November 1985, p. 204-2300).

7   NUWM Headquarters Circular D91 29 November 1935 (MML: NUWM Bulletins and Circulars); Shields News 30 October 1934, Shields Gazette 1 November 1934;Minutes of Blyth Council 20 and 26 November 1935, 9 January and 13 February 1936 (NCRO: NRO 00880/61); Minutes of Northumberland County Council 7 February 1935, 6 February 1936 (NCRO: CC/CM/CC 45 and 47); Report of Towns where Concessions have been granted in Agitation for Extra Winter Relief', *Report of the 9ᵗʰ National Conference of the NUWM 1935* (LHASC: CP/IND/HANN/01/06).

8   George Short, interview with Peter Brabban 1979; Nick Rowell, interview with Peter Brabban 1979; Andrew Thorpe, 'The Membership of the Communist Party of Great Britain 1920-1945' *Historical Journal* Vol 3 No 43 (2000, p. 777-800).

9   *Daily Worker* 11 March 1930. A detailed account of relations between the CPGB and the NUWM is provided in Alan Campbell and John Mcllroy, 'The National Unemployed Workers' Movement and the Communist Party of

Great Britain Revisited' *Labour History Review* Vol.73 No.1 (April 2008, p. 39-61).

10   Richard Croucher: *We Refuse to Starve in Silence*; see for example *Daily Worker* 9 January 1932; Minutes of the Central Committee of the Communist Party of Great Britain 4 June 1932, 20 February and 9 September 1933 (LHASC).

11   Minutes of the Central Committee of the Communist Party of Great Britain 9 September 1933 (LHASC); Wal Hannington, *Never On Our Knees* (London: Lawrence and Wishart 1967, p. 248).

12   Minutes of the Central Committee of the Communist Party of Great Britain 4 and 5 January 1936 (LHASC); Harry McShane and Joan Smith, *No Mean Fighter* (London: Pluto Press 1978, p. 220).

13   *Sunderland Echo* 17, 19 and 24 August 1936; Huw Beynon and Terry Austrin, *Masters and Servants: Class and Patronage in the Making of a Labour Organisation – the Durham Miners and the English Political Tradition* (London: Rivers Oram Press 1994, p. 361).

14   *Report of the 68th Annual Trades Union Congress* (London: Trades Union Congress 1936, p. 289-90; p. 295).

15   David Howell, 'The British General Election of 1935', *Socialist History* No. 28 (2006, p. 60-76).

16   Minutes of the Central Committee of the Communist Party of Great Britain 5 June 1936 (LHASC); Minutes of the NAC Meeting August 1936 (MML: Hannington D Miscellaneous).

17   *Report of the 67th Annual Trades Union Congress* (London: Trades Union Congress 1935, p. 257); *Report of the 69th Annual Trades Union Congress* (London: Trades Union Congress 1937, p. 255-6); *Report of the Annual Conference of Trades Councils 1937*, p. 20 (TUC: HD 6661); For a full account see Mathias Reiss, 'Circulars, Surveys and Support: Trades Councils and the Marches of 1936' *Labour History Review* Vol.73 No.1 (April 2008, p. 89-112); relevant too is Matt Perry, 'The Jarrow Crusade, the National Hunger March and the Labour Party in 1936: A Re-appraisal' *Socialist History* No. 20 (2001, p. 40-54).

18   NUWM HQ Newsletter 24, 5 August 1936 (MML: NUWM Bulletins and Circulars); Newcastle and District Trades Council: *Annual Report of the Executive Council 1936/37*, p. 4 (TUC: JN 1129 NEW).

19   Minutes of Blyth Council 22 September and 8 October 1936 (NCRO: NRO 00880/61)

20   *Newcastle Journal* 24 and 25 September 1936; *Shields News* 2 October 1936.

21   *Daily Worker* 3 and 16 October 1936; *Blaydon Courier* 17 October 1936.

22   *Blaydon Courier* 17 October 1936; *Daily Worker* 14 and 18 September 1936; Minutes of the Central Committee of the Communist Party of Great Britain 5 June 1936 (LHASC); NUWM Hunger March Bulletin 30 September 1936 (MML: NUWM Bulletins and Circulars); *Blyth News* 17 September 1936.

23   Frank Graham, interview with Jim McGurn 1986 (BMSA ref 2007.29); Nick Rowell, interview with Peter Brabban 1979; *Heslop's Local Advertiser* 11 December 1936; *Daily Worker* 29 September 1936.

24   *Shields News* 12 October 1936; see Harry Harmer, 'The Failure of the Communists: The National Unemployed Workers' Movement 1921-39' in Andrew Thorpe (ed), *The Failure of Political Extremism in Inter-War Britain*

(Exeter: University of Exeter Press 1989, p. 29-49).

25   *Sunderland Echo* 5 October 1936; *Heslop's Local Advertiser* 16 October 1936; *Daily Worker* 14, 16 and 19 October 1936; Metropolitan Police Special Branch Report to Home Office 22 October 1936 (NA: HO 144/20 696).

26   Frank Graham, interview with Jim McGurn 1986; Nick Rowell, interview with Peter Brabban 1979

27   Metropolitan Police Special Branch Report to Home Office 22 October 1936 (NA: HO 144/20 696); Peter Kingsford: *The Hunger Marchers in Britain 1920-1940* (London: Lawrence and Wishart 1982); Nick Rowell, interview with Peter Brabban 1979.

28   Report of the Metropolitan Police Commissioner to Home Office, 16 November 1936 (NA: HO 144/20697). See also Matt Perry, 'The Jarrow Crusade, the National Hunger March and the Labour Party' (p. 46-47).

29   *Daily Worker* 10 November 1936; *Unemployment and the Housewife: Report of a Public Meeting at Essex Hall 10 November 1936* (MML: Hannington and Brown Papers Aiv-Av).

30   Richard Croucher, *We Refuse to Starve in Silence* (p. 181)

31   Wal Hannington, *Never On Our Knees* (p. 314-5); Matt Perry, *The Jarrow Crusade: Protest and Legend* (Sunderland: University of Sunderland Press 2005, p. 61); Minutes of the NAC Meeting August 1936 (MML: Hannington and Brown Papers Aiv-Av).

32   *Sunderland Echo* 25 September 1936. This contrast between the Jarrow and Hunger Marches was noted at the time during PAC discussions, and several councillors were unhappy about the position of the Hunger Marchers: *Newcastle Journal* 25 September 1936.

33   Matt Perry, *The Jarrow Crusade* (p. 85); Richard Croucher, *We Refuse to Starve in Silence* (p. 180-181); Wal Hannington, *Never On Our Knees* (p. 315-6).

34   Robert Maugham; interview 1983 (BMSA ref 2007.94).

35   Report of the Metropolitan Police Commissioner to Home Office 6 November 1936 (NA: MEPO 2/3097); Frank Graham, interview with Jim McGurn 1986.

36   Frank Graham, interview with Don Watson 1996; for an example of favourable reporting at the time see the *Sunderland Echo* 5 October 1936; Matt Perry, *The Jarrow Crusade*; John Pemberton, 'Origins and early history of the Society for Social Medicine in the UK and Ireland' *Public Health Policy and Practice* Vol 56 No 5 (May 2002, p. 342-6); see also his 'Some reflections in 2003 on the 1930s', *International Journal of Epidemiology* Vol 32 No 4 (August 2003, p. 496-8); Mary Cowlyn, letter in *The Guardian* 20 September 2003.

37   Notes of Conference at the Home Secretary's Office 6 February 1934 (NA: MEPO 2 307 pt.1); Home Office Report on the Hunger March 1936, 19 January 1937 (NA: HO 144/20697). The ideological meanings attributed to the Jarrow March in recent years are analysed in Matt Perry, *The Jarrow Crusade*.

38   Details are provided in Matt Perry, 'The Jarrow Crusade's Return: The "New Labour Party" of Jarrow and Ellen Wilkinson MP'. *Northern History* Vol 39 No 2 (September 2002, p. 265-279).

39   *Blaydon Courier* 21 November 1936.

Chapter Eight

THE UNEMPLOYED, FASCISM AND THE SPANISH CIVIL WAR

The Spanish Civil War

Almost at the start of its service in Spain the British Battalion of the International Brigade suffered devastating losses at the Battle of Jarama. Later it erected a memorial to fallen comrades in the hills above the village of Morata de Tajuna. On it was listed the 17 names of those who had been killed during what were actually two mismanaged attacks by the Battalion. The memorial was later destroyed by fascist troops but there is a large contemporary photograph of it in the village museum, and on this copy the names of those killed can be made out. They include four militants from the National Unemployed Workers Movement in the North East of England: Wilf Jobling, Tom Carter, Jack Palzeard and Tommy Dolan. The dates on the memorial indicate that they were all killed in the same week in February 1937.[1]

A year earlier in 1936 a coalition of progressive parties in Spain won the general election and embarked on a programme of social and economic reform. This programme, modest as it was, threatened the vested interests of the right-wing to the extent that most of the armed forces rose in revolt. Under the leadership of General Mola and then General Franco the Spanish armed forces rebelled against the democratic republic and initiated three years of civil war. The army revolt was in alliance with the Spanish fascists and openly supported by Hitler and Mussolini, who contributed troops and aircrew. In contrast Britain and France imposed a policy of 'Non-Intervention' by which the Spanish government was not to buy or be supplied with arms; on paper this was designed to limit the conflict but in practice it was blatantly ignored by Fascist Italy and Germany. As a counter the Communist International called for volunteers to fight with an International Brigade of the Republican Army against Franco's rebels. It fell to the individual Communist Parties to organise volunteers and because recruitment was soon declared illegal by the British government it had to be clandestine.[2]

Spain had been an issue for the British labour movement two years before. In 1934 a general strike called there against a right-wing assumption of power had been put down with savage repression, again supervised by General Franco. Amidst international labour movement protest the NUWM National Administrative Committee passed an emergency resolution 'in support of the Spanish workers' and proposed to organise a food ship 'as an act of working -class solidarity.'[3] The food ship does not seem to have materialised but this does illustrate an early awareness of the political situation in Spain. The election of the Popular Front government there in 1936, the start of its reform programme and the military revolt against it are events that would have been followed by many NUWM activists.

It had been evident during preparations for the Hunger March in the autumn of 1936 that an association between British unemployed struggles and the situation in Spain was being made. As we have seen Labour left-wingers Emmie Lawther and Harry Bolton at Blaydon had drawn parallels between the emerging conflict in Spain and the fight against the Means Test. Twenty men from Felling took part in the Hunger March, and the money to equip them was raised from trades union branches, shops, the Co-ops, street and estate collections. The organisers obviously believed that it was appropriate to donate 13s from the total raised 'to the Spanish Aid Ambulance' in order to 'assist the Spanish people to resist Franco the fascist leader'. As the Marchers approached Hyde Park one of their slogans was, 'the Means Test shall not pass', which made a clear link between their own struggle and the one in Spain. 'They shall not pass' was a translation of the Spanish slogan 'no pasaran!' which had been coined by the Republican orator Dolores Ibarurri, better known as La Pasionaria. It had also been the slogan of those who had thwarted the march of the British Union of Fascists at Cable Street in London the previous month.[4]

In October 1936, before the Hunger March had reached London, the NUWM National Committee called 'for the utmost activity on the part of the British working class in support of the Spanish workers fighting to defend a democratic republic,' and urged 'all branches to associate themselves with other working-class organisations in solidarity activity with the Spanish workers'. They were to 'link the fight against the Unemployment Assistance Board regulations with the campaign to build working-class unity against the Baldwin government and against Fascism'. The link between the UAB regulations and the threat to the Spanish Republic may not seem immediately obvious but it was entirely in keeping with the Communist International's analysis of fascism. The inter-twined nature of the CP and the

NUWM meant that the analysis was shared by both. A crucial intervention by Comintern General Secretary Georgi Dimitrov in 1935 had set out a strategic response to the growth of fascism. This political phenomenon was the last stand of capitalism in decline: when the democratic structures of a bourgeois society were no longer serving its interests capitalism would erode them and introduce fascist measures that would serve them better. Successful opposition to this process would require 'popular fronts' of all who were opposed to fascism regardless of their political allegiance, all who were prepared to defend democracy against the preparatory stages of fascism. In the case of Britain the 'National Government' was creating conditions that would make a transition to fascism easier through maintaining capital at the expense of working-class standards of living, and oppressing the unemployed by the Ministry of Labour 'slave camps' and punitive conditions of life.[5]

Therefore it was predictable that NUWM branches would be among the first to organise solidarity work with Spain, and certainly in the North East branches were doing this and linking it to their own immediate struggles. This was evident soon after the military revolt and before the National Committee resolution. In South Shields for example the NUWM held open-air meetings attended by 'several hundred people' where they called on the TUC to give 'practical support to the heroic workers and peasants of Spain' that July. In August their public meetings were both condemning the unemployment scales and regulations and calling for an end to Non-Intervention in Spain. In Blaydon the Hunger March leader Wilf Jobling had been organising public meetings on the issue that September. In Blyth the NUWM was the first working-class organisation to mobilise for the Republic, in contrast, they claimed, to the local Labour Party.[6] It was on their return from the Hunger March that NUWM activists like Frank Graham in Sunderland, Wilf Jobling in Blaydon and Bob Elliott in Blyth began the process of volunteering and discussing recruitment for Spain.[7] This chapter examines how many actually took that step and what lay behind their motivation.

Volunteers

It is notoriously difficult to use accurate numbers when it comes to the British volunteers in the International Brigade. The records were often less than adequate, they were dispersed, and they have not all survived. At the time the estimate was over 2,400 British volunteers, which is around 400 more than the numbers given in the first official history published later in 1982. A later figure of 2,500 is the accepted working number at present but it could well be revised upwards in future. Most of them took part at various times between December 1936 and October 1938; 526 of them were confirmed killed and a large number of the survivors were wounded.[8]

The latest and most extensive history of the British Battalion has explored the difficulties of estimating just how many of the volunteers actually were unemployed. The Battalion records, themselves incomplete, usually state the trade or trade union of each individual but not whether they were working at their job at the time of enlistment. Some will have preferred to record their trade rather than the fact of their unemployment and in the North East at least there are obvious cases where this happened with known NUWM activists. For example Frank Graham from Sunderland is listed as a 'student' although he was unemployed having left his course two years earlier; Bobby Qualie from Sunderland is down as a shipyard plater, William Dean of Gateshead as a bricklayer and Harry Reynolds from Newcastle as a dock labourer, although all had been long-term unemployed before joining the Battalion. Nevertheless the account does quote with approval an estimate of between one eighth and a quarter being out of work: in other words between approximately 313 to 625 volunteers out of an estimated total of 2,500. This could be an under-estimate, though, for the recording reasons previously described.[9]

The Eleventh (and, although they were not to know it, the final) National Conference of the NUWM was held in September 1939, when the Spanish war was over and the world war about to begin. Here delegates were told that '500 members of our Movement served with the International Brigade in Spain'. This seems a conveniently round number but the NUWM was the organisation best placed at the time to produce a figure. The number of 500 is within the range estimated by the latest history of the Battalion; so around 20% of the volunteers in the British Battalion were members of the NUWM. Interestingly, the phrase 'members of our Movement' does not make it clear whether the 500 were just current members or whether they also included former members, those once in the NUWM but who had found work, for example by moving south, before going to Spain. If former members are not included then the total number of volunteers with experience of NUWM membership could be much higher than 500.[10]

Between the end of December 1936 and mid-January 1937, 45 volunteers from Tyneside, County Durham and south Northumberland had formally enrolled into the British Battalion. At least 40 more would join the Brigade over the next eighteen months but these 45 constituted the first wave of local volunteers who responded to the formation of the International Brigade. They are particularly interesting because they represent the initial response to the appeal to defend the Republic. There is evidence from police reports, newspapers, oral testimony, and NUWM documents that 22 of the 45 had been active in the NUWM before going to Spain. This is a provisional figure and the actual one, if finding it ever proves possible, could probably be higher. This is because the names appearing in the sources mentioned tend to be the activists or those with leadership roles in the movement – speakers at meetings, members of deputations, Hunger March committees – or the names of those appearing in court following demonstrations. There may be others who were active but never had their names recorded. Even on this basis though it can be said that the NUWM was the biggest single organisation in the North East from which the first volunteers were drawn. This seems to have been the case too in South Wales and Scotland where the NUWM was particularly strong, although with much larger Communist Parties and a more militant trade union culture the overall numbers of volunteers from these areas were significantly higher.[11]

This first wave of North East volunteers, like that from other parts of the country, included NUWM activists of a high calibre. Bob Elliott from Blyth was an elected councillor at a time when the Communist Party had only around 50 in the country; his death at the Battle of Brunete warranted inclusion in a telegram to Communist leader Harry Pollitt in London. Sam Langley had had national as well as district roles with the organisation. Wilf Jobling as we have seen had been an NUWM leader in Blaydon for several years, and had attended the National Administrative Committee. There has been speculation among historians of the Spanish Civil War as to whether national Communist Parties were each given a numerical quota of volunteers that they were expected to fill. Although this has never been confirmed it would explain why so many men of this experience and ability were allowed to volunteer in the first place. An alternative possibility is that the enterprise was initially just hasty and haphazard. The British Party, and particularly its North East District, was consistently the smallest and hence the most over-stretched of the European Communist organisations. It would not be able to sustain the same levels of political activity if a number of able cadres and activists were in Spain. At the same time this recruitment does demonstrate how seriously the rise of fascism was being taken.[12]

Unemployment

The fact that a noticeable number of British volunteers for the International Brigade were unemployed before going to Spain has not gone unremarked. It has led to assumptions that just escaping unemployment was the real reason for their recruitment. This was voiced at the time by the mother of

Sunderland NUWM activist Tommy Dolan after he was killed, for instance, and it is probably the explanation that would come readily to the minds of families who did not share or understand the politics of the deceased. Certainly the first official account of the British Battalion published in 1939 felt it necessary to take issue with this view, and it stated that the unemployment of some who joined had in fact generated greater sympathy with 'the down-trodden of Spain'. Another example is the autobiography of Charlotte Haldane, who had been involved in Communist international work at the time and had processed many of the British volunteers on their way through Paris. She says that 'They were mostly unemployed lads, miners, often, from the valleys of South Wales, or the mining villages of Scotland. Years of depression and the dole had forced them into enlistment.'[13] This explanation for their involvement needs to be seen in the light of her book's intended role as a Cold War intervention, in which all Communist efforts are to be disparaged wherever possible, but the 'desperate to escape the dole' explanation for volunteering seems to persist. Some later historians have taken a similar line, arguing for example that, 'Recruitment to the Brigades is understandable when we remember the psychological and material effects of the depression and the sense of despair it left in the working classes'. Similarly a popular military historian's account of the Spanish Civil War states of the International Brigade volunteers that 'some of them were glad to escape the apathy of unemployment.'[14]

Other historians have probed the issue of unemployment and volunteering for Spain more thoroughly. A detailed study of the Welsh brigaders showed that a large proportion of the unemployed volunteers, largely miners, had been victimised for trade union activities. Further, it estimates that 29% of the volunteers from the Welsh coalfields were NUWM members and of these nearly half had been Hunger Marchers. Another account has concluded that, in the British Battalion generally, those who were unemployed at the time of volunteering were likely to be members of the NUWM; this has been confirmed by the major study of the North East and the Spanish Civil War. The latest and most extensive history of the British Battalion identifies an NUWM background for several Battalion commanders, and also makes clear that for a number of volunteers going to Spain was a logical progression from their participation in NUWM activity such as the national Hunger Marches. For these men the NUWM had provided the very antithesis of the 'apathy of unemployment.'[15]

Therefore the contribution of the NUWM to the International Brigade has been acknowledged but it is worth considering in more detail. This is because it adds to our understanding not only of the International Brigade but of the NUWM itself as a significant radical working-class movement of the inter-war years. The roots of this awareness of the situation in Spain lay in two key and under-explored areas of local NUWM activity evident before 1936: political education and anti-fascism.

Political Education

The NUWM is celebrated for its organisation of national Hunger Marches and local agitations against the Means Test, and for its work in representing unemployed claimants. But it also had another local role that would eventually prove relevant to recruitment for Spain. This was in providing, through its branch life, political education and discussion. An NUWM organiser in the Scottish mill town of Hawick explained that 'The main training of this organisation consists of... public speaking, social evenings, and general discussion of any question relating to working-class conditions'. This was part of an appeal for funds and so the organiser was possibly a little economical with the details but as we have seen this was a principal aim of the militant unemployed movement since the formation of the NUWCM. It sought to convince the unemployed that they were not to blame for their situation, that the capitalist system was dysfunctional and that only a socialist system of society could ensure the end of mass unemployment.[16]

Frank Graham has recalled how political education and discussion could be popular, and not unusual, for the Sunderland NUWM:

... Because in those days there were a lot of working-class people who were very, extremely, well educated. Particularly amongst miners, there were a lot of people who studied, even when they were unemployed, they'd spend a large amount of their time reading and studying. And miners who were working were extremely interested in books on economics, social history and so on. You'd come across quite a number of people , some of them quite young, who were well educated, could express their ideas clearly and so on, who were not university educated , in fact were not grammar school educated even ...

I remember organising a series of lectures every Sunday at the Big Lamp on Buchan Street, at the Co-op hall there, and every Sunday we had a capacity audience of 120 people, who came along to listen to a serious lecture lasting about half an hour, and then a question and answer meeting afterwards. And the standard of participation was extremely high. That would be, say, 1935. And I mean there were really large numbers of meetings held.[17]

Stockton NUWM secretary George Short has described how his branch organised some political education in the town, even in the most basic of circumstances:

> Actually you know where the church is at the bottom end of Stockton, the bottom end of Yarm Lane, it was the site of one the first classes on labour history in Stockton. In summer this was, sitting beside the gravestones, because we had no premises. But a couple of dozen unemployed used to come there. We had classes, some of them weren't at a very high level, but the unemployed used to come and ask questions. We had a lad, his idea of Marxist theory, the only thing was he never got past discussing the theory of value, he hadn't time for anything else but there were some very interesting discussions.[18]

What Graham and Short are describing here is in fact part of a tradition of working-class education in Britain. Classes on subjects of interest to politically minded workers had long been organised by the Plebs League and the Central Labour College movement, but they also occurred more informally as Short recalls. He demonstrates that even with no resources other than the interests and knowledge of the membership discussion classes could still feature in branch life.

Economics, particularly the critique of capitalism and the potential for an alternative, would clearly be a popular subject for the long-term unemployed who had been discarded by capitalism. The Communist Party on Tyneside had included economics as a major part of the syllabus in the 'Workers' Study Circles' it had organised, and even when it was as small and isolated as it had been in 1931 it was still providing learning for 75 workers in 4 study circles. 14 Communists from the North East also attended the International Lenin School in Moscow during the 1930s and of these 10 were activists in the NUWM. The quality of the process ILS students went through and their effectiveness in the movement on their return has been queried, as indeed it was by some in the Party at the time, but at least Wilf Jobling as we have seen was regarded as 'a very good speaker,' as was John Henderson too. Both of these NUWM activists, and Brigade volunteers, ran economics classes in Blaydon and Newcastle.[19]

Economics was by no means the only subject. Sunderland Hunger Marcher Bobbie Qualie, who volunteered for Spain with Frank Graham in 1936, remembers NUWM political education about fascism and its threat to peace:

We organised groups or what we used to call schools to keep up the political education. We got books. When it came to the period of 1935 we were campaigning against Mussolini and what he was doing in Abyssinia. We did a lot of work about what fascism was about, we exposed a lot about what was going on in Germany. [20]

NUWM HQ encouraged branches to subscribe, if they could, to the Left Book Club which was established in 1936 and became the first publisher for Hannington's books. This would help them to make 'a library of working-class literature available to members' that could be used for 'programmes of education and campaigns'. As we shall see NUWM activists in Sunderland were definitely familiar with the Left Book Club texts that could support their rent strike campaign in 1939.[21]

Therefore at least a number of those who had spent time in the NUWM would have been exposed to a level of political analysis and discussion that, when the call came to defend the Spanish Republic, enabled them to identify with another struggle against economic and political oppression. Their understanding of and opposition to fascism was active as well as theoretical though, as local fascist supporters discovered.

Anti-Fascism in the North East

Sir Oswald Mosley had, originally, the image of something of a left-winger in Britain. In 1929 – the year when he had been an invited speaker at the Durham Miners' Gala - he had broken with Ramsay MacDonald's Labour Cabinet when it refused to consider his plans to combat unemployment through state intervention. His 'New Party' did initially attract some interest on the left but it quickly became clear that it was to be a vehicle for his own his egotism and ambition. Before long he was admiring, and seeking funding, from Mussolini's Italy and in 1932 he founded the British Union of Fascists. The BUF was a quasi-military organisation uniformed in black shirts which subsequently supported and drew inspiration from Hitler's Nazis. His attempts to build his organisation in places like the North East were vigorously resisted by the left and although the BUF had a presence it was prevented from exerting influence.[22]

British Communists had identified the fascist potential of the 'New Party' at an early stage. Mosley's European mentors had used the unemployed on their roads to power and so the NUWM was particularly alert to the danger the BUF represented. Indeed at least two prominent local leaders in the original NUWCM – Sam Langley and Alf Chater – were, as we have seen, involved in organising the Labour League of Ex-Servicemen in the North

East in 1927. Among the objectives of the LLX was to act as a 'workers' defence force' against police attacks during demonstrations and pickets, but also against threats from supporters of the Italian *Fascisti*. Thus Langley and Chater of the NUWCM were among the first anti-fascists in the region.[23]

Frank Graham, before his return to Sunderland and involvement in the NUWM, had been politically active as a student in London. There he had been part of the demonstration that had attempted to disrupt Mosley's mass rally at the Olympia in 1934 and was obviously keen to continue this work in Sunderland. Fifty years later he recalled that the size of the anti-fascist movement managed to prevent Mosley from making any headway in the region as a whole:

> Invariably he tried to have open air rallies. And of course they arrived, about thirty or forty of them from outside the area. Every time they had a meeting a certain number of people were drafted in say from Manchester or somewhere like that, maybe a few local people and they attempted to hold open air meetings. And I think they were never at all successful. They were always broken up by the crowds who shouted at them and jeered at them, and although they received, always received, very strong police support, none of the rallies – I can't remember a single fascist rally in the area that proved successful … except of course when they had private meetings in halls on their own.[24]

There is certainly evidence to bear this out, including examples of the NUWM itself being in the forefront of anti-fascist activity in the North East. As early as 1931, for example, before the BUF was formed, the Sunderland branch reported that it had been 'instrumental in breaking up the local branch of Mosley's bright young things.'[25] It was in 1934 and 1935 though that the fascists made their real attempts to secure a foothold for regular public activity in the area. In this they failed.

In July1934 at Harbour View, the 'speaker's corner' of North Shields, 'a fair sized crowd' at an NUWM meeting 'heckled away' a British Union of Fascists speaker when the BUF attempted to hold a meeting there. A week later there was a more serious clash between the two rival meetings. A crowd 'of around a thousand...including many women' heckled the fascist speaker, James Nichol. This man was a former Communist (although the North Shields branch unconvincingly denied this) and NUWM activist who had been gaoled with Spike Robson and Walter Harrison after the disturbances in the town in 1932. On this occasion he fell from his platform when the NUWM leader and former boxing champion Robson 'appeared to collide' with him. Robson was arrested and subsequently gaoled after he refused, as he had done in 1932, to be bound over by the magistrate's court and refrain from any future activities like this. His colleague from Blyth, the long-standing NUWM activist Bob Elliot, was fined for the same incident, although Walter Harrison was not arrested. If Nichol had been attempting to re-invent a political role in the BUF the chances are he was to be disappointed. In that year Mosley purged his organisation of ex-Communists so as not to deter 'a better class' of recruit.[26]

Two years later Robson achieved international attention when he led the crew of the merchant ship the *S.S. Linaria* in a strike; he believed the ship was carrying potential munitions to Nationalist Spain. After a long legal battle the crew won their case against the criminal charges brought by the shipping company, a battle supported by campaigners for Republican Spain in Liverpool and North Shields. Robson was opposed by the very same National Union of Seamen officials he had clashed with as an NUWM activist in 1931.[27]

Several key confrontations took place in Newcastle. In mid-May 1934 John Beckett (formerly of the ILP and once a Labour MP for Gateshead) led a group of fascists in a march to Cowan's Monument in the city centre. This provoked running fights with anti-fascists in the city centre area where at one point mounted police had to cope with 'a thousand anti-fascists'. The BUF had to retreat back to its office whilst their opponents packed the Palace Theatre in the Haymarket to hear ILP Member of Parliament Jimmy Maxton. The next day Beckett attempted to hold a rally at Gateshead Town Hall, where he found his members outnumbered by anti-fascist hecklers. Calling it off, the BUF needed a massive police escort to escape over the Tyne Bridge in the face of 'several thousand protesters'. William Young, an anti-fascist later killed in Spain, was arrested on this occasion. The next month Mosley announced that he would hold a rally on the Town Moor, but had to 'postpone' after police advised him that they could not guarantee his safety: local announcements had made it clear that the North East trade union, Co-operative and left political movements intended to counter-demonstrate on a huge scale. A police presence of an unprecedented level allowed Mosley to hold a rally there at the end of July but even so the interruptions and heckling were effective. His two attempts to hold a rally in the City Hall also dissolved into disarray when anti-fascists disrupted the proceedings. The BUF, led by Mosley's henchman and future Nazi propagandist William Joyce, tried again in Newcastle in 1935. His rally at the Town Moor had to be abandoned because of the size and strength of the heckling crowd, one of whom, NUWM activist Tommy Richardson, was arrested for disorderly behaviour.[28]

May 1934 also saw disturbances in Sunderland; BUF meetings on Gill Bridge Avenue were heckled and disrupted and on at least one occasion the local fascist leader was knocked from his box by the crowd. Later unemployed Thomas Jobling, who later joined the International Brigade, was charged with assault over this but given the benefit of the doubt by magistrates. In November 1935 eight people, five of them fascists, were injured during fighting at a BUF rally at the Palace Theatre in South Shields. Hecklers drowned Mosley out for much of the meeting and more than fifty opponents including 'Communist leaders' were ejected after violent scenes with the stewards. Outside the police prevented an anti-fascist demonstration from forming up by keeping the 'large crowds' moving, but action was still taken. Two coaches had brought fascist stewards from the Midlands to the meeting and as they left demonstrators pelted one with half-bricks, breaking all the windows and injuring several of the occupants. In July of that year a fascist meeting in Sunderland was closed by the police because of a threatening crowd; a week later in West Sunniside in the centre a fascist leader was assaulted when his open-air meeting was brought to a halt by anti-fascists. On that occasion a protestor was fined for assault, with Mick Morgan, an unemployed miner who later served in Spain appearing as a defence witness.[29]

They were particularly concerned to prevent the fascists from organising among the unemployed, as they had done successfully in Italy and Germany. Local NUWM activists like Frank Graham claimed that their work with claimants made it difficult for the Blackshirts: when they tried to spread propaganda about the 'reds' in Sunderland, for instance, unemployed people remembered that it was 'the reds' who had helped them out and so they were disinclined to pay much attention to the fascists. Obviously it is difficult to test this claim, but the local press does provide some support for it. In April 1934 the fascists attempted to hold a meeting at Windmill Hills, the 'speakers' corner' for Gateshead, only to be 'chased by an angry group of unemployed' from the nearby labour exchange. In the same year Jack Cogan, an Independent Labour Party activist who had been regularly involved in the unemployed movement since 1921, is reputed to have led a group of unemployed workers to break up the BUF office in Gateshead. Also in Gateshead NUWM member Alf Chater reprised his 1927 role with a 'workers' militia'. This was not the Labour League of Ex-Servicemen this time but the 'Greyshirts', a 'defence' squad for the Newcastle and Gateshead Anti-Fascist League, about half of whose members were unemployed. They were thought to be responsible for the damage to the BUF office although they denied any involvement.[30]

Clearly NUWM activists were heavily involved in the successful initiative to prevent the BUF from gaining influence on Tyneside, although they did not have a monopoly of anti-fascist work by any means, as the large numbers turning out against the fascists show. In the words of a local observer at the time, 'there was always one event that brought the Communists and most of their critics together. This was the arrival of Sir Oswald Mosley's Blackshirts'. It seems likely though that this active role of physical confrontation with fascism was part of the mental atmosphere that underlay volunteering for Spain. In this context John Henderson, at one time secretary of the NUWM branch in Gateshead, provides an interesting example of how activists could put pressure on themselves when it came to volunteering. He recalled:

> A number of my comrades from the Party and the NUWM around the Tyne had volunteered and it was on my conscience that me, who'd been shouting his bloody mouth off about fascism and Spain and how we had to do something, well, I felt I had to go.[31]

However the influence of other factors besides political awareness and opposition to fascism needs to be considered.

Motives and Motivation

It is not necessary to accept the position of some of the writers quoted earlier to acknowledge that other factors besides politics could have been at work here. It is not difficult to imagine that volunteers could easily have seen Spain as an escape to a political adventure and away from boredom, frustration and a meaningless existence. Pointers to this can be seen in the lives of some of the North East volunteers. For example Harry Reynolds from Newcastle, who was killed at the Battle of Jarama, was an NUWM member who had taken part in the 1930 Hunger March. He had served in the British army and his brother has recalled that at one point during his unemployment he tried unsuccessfully to join the army again, under a false name.[32] For some political activity, even if frequent, stimulating and absorbing, might only have been a substitute for the purpose and status conferred by a job. Another issue was how the benefits system was administered through the Means Test. As we have seen younger single men, the category most likely to volunteer perhaps, were only entitled to reduced or even no benefits from the PAC after their six months unemployment insurance had elapsed if they were living with parents. This, in effect, made them a financial burden on people who themselves were more than likely to be unemployed or low paid, and guilt about this could add to the feelings of life without purpose generated by unemployment.[33]

Nevertheless if it was simply the case that unemployment was a crucial factor then the International Brigade would surely have been many times larger than it actually was. The political dimension comes with the NUWM and what it could bring to the unemployed working class. In this respect it is likely that some volunteers acted through mixed motives, but neither cancels the other out. Those with a clear political awareness would have felt the strongest reasons to attack the system that had produced their unemployment and been more likely to take the opportunity to fight a symptom of it.

Contribution to the Brigade

Some volunteers who had been through the NUWM made a particular contribution to the Brigade. For example after the battle of Jarama in February 1937, Sam Langley was given the role of political commissar in the hospital where he himself was a wounded patient.[34] His fellow patients, some of whom were seriously injured, had just emerged from a particularly brutal engagement that had exposed the lack of weapons, equipment, training and organisation on the Republican side. Only around 100 of the original 600 British and Irish volunteers were still effective, and many men well known as militants in their localities had been killed. In this situation Langley would have had the task of keeping up morale and a positive approach among the wounded survivors. A veteran Hunger March leader like Langley – an organiser of Tyneside contingents on the marches of 1922, 1932 and 1934 - would have been a good choice. Those marches had given him plenty of experience of maintaining morale and good order in difficult circumstances among men with varying levels of commitment. This role was noted in the recollections of the 1934 Hunger March by Lincolnshire volunteer Walter Gregory, who fought right through the civil war. The examples he used were something of a eulogy:

> The Tyneside contingent was under the leadership of a Communist councillor, Bobbie Elliott. ... He worked many minor miracles on that march to London, ensuring that men who were far from being in peak physical condition after months of unemployment and a poor diet, kept on walking through the winter weather. I was to meet Bobbie again in Spain where he served with the Republican forces as a political commissar
> ...
> Bobbie's immediate subordinate on the march was Wilf Jobling. Wilf

was an extremely attractive personality. He was athletically built, with a powerful voice which was ideal for addressing open-air meetings, and a wonderfully persuasive magnetism. Tirelessly Wilf would walk up and down the length of the marching column of shabbily dressed and weary men, urging them on with words of encouragement and offering advice on how to treat weary and blistered feet. Like Bobbie, Wilf was to fight in Spain and it was a great loss to the cause of working-class radicalism in Britain that both of them were killed in 1937 within a few months of each other …[35]

Although some of these marchers had dropped out for health reasons or been put out for disciplinary reasons the fact is that most of them, by a good margin, completed the trek to London. The Hunger Marches had produced a corps of activists like Langley, who had led men in sometimes trying circumstances and difficult weather conditions; men who would also have had variable degrees of commitment to the cause at hand.

However if it can be argued that the NUWM had a positive effect on the International Brigade and support for Spain, what effect did the campaign to support Spain have on the NUWM?

The Effect of Spain on the NUWM

NUWM branches seem to have absorbed themselves in the Republican solidarity campaigns, just as their national leadership urged, but also just as their early reactions to the military revolt would have suggested they would. The secretary of the West Hartlepool branch reported at the end of 1938, without any apparent complaint, that his twenty-one members had '5,000 Spain leaflets for distribution' as well as their own regular activities. Such efforts were all part of the different support campaigns that were organised in the region, but there is photographic evidence that NUWM branches took part with their own banners in the large demonstrations in the region in support of the Republic. Thus they maintained their own identity as unemployed organisations within the broad campaign. It was openly as Blyth NUWM Secretary that Terry Mooney initiated the door to door collection of food and goods to be donated to a supply ship for Republican Spain. As he said, the NUWM branch recognised that 'this battle for elementary human rights is equally our battle'. Similarly it was as an NUWM group that the Boldon Colliery branch also made door to door collections for a food and medical supply ship.[36] Did this extra dimension to the role of the branches distract from their original role with the unemployed, the role that had after all built the membership?

The national historian of the NUWM has identified a falling-off of militant protest by the organisation from around 1937. One of the causes he puts forward for it is the number of its members who were in Spain, effectively out of circulation for campaigning work in Britain. There were no divisions between the Communist and NUWM leaderships over this; nothing was spared in the struggle for Spain. It has been suggested too that for the North East this effect would have been worse because both the Communist Party and the unemployed movement were small compared to the other regions with high unemployment. The argument here is that after early 1937 there were only a few sporadic and localised examples of Means Test protests in the region, and that this decline must be due to the effect of Spain. It is worth repeating too that the calibre of those in Spain could be very high, both in terms of their level of activism and their abilities. It is surely indisputable that NUWM activity in the North East would have been reduced by the service of some key people in Spain. Nevertheless the evidence, in the context of the movement since the early 1930s, is less clear-cut and there are other factors that need to be acknowledged before attributing a lower level of local campaigning activity principally to the Spanish Civil War. This can be done by examining some of the activity that took place at the time and the attitudes of the Communist leadership towards it.[37]

After the 1936 Hunger march Jim Ancrum, who was now a Communist councillor, did get a unanimous Felling Urban District Council committee agreement to:

> ... convene a conference of all local authorities, religious, social and political organisations and trades unions in County Durham and Northumberland to consider and decide upon the best methods of mobilising massed public opinion against the pernicious legislation of the Government regarding the new Unemployment Regulations and the Means Test.

Despite his vociferous protest the full Council rescinded the resolution the following month. Ancrum had been tasked by the National March Council to organise a protest march against the UAB regulations, and presumably this conference would have been a means to build support for it. In the event the march and deputation to the Area UAB manager took place early in 1937; in theory it was supported by a wide range of working-class organisations but apparently it 'did not attract nearly so many demonstrators as might have been expected ... just a few hundred men and women took part'. The Labour Party banners were far outnumbered by the CP ones, suggesting that once again it had not really connected with the mainstream movement.[38]

In South Shields during the summer of 1937 the NUWM held public meetings in the market place and gathered signatures for a petition to the Council. This was for increased UAB and PAC scales, more government-funded public works and a fair system of allocating jobs under them. The Chief Constable there was known for his reluctance to permit demonstrations by Communists, so there was a demand too for 'free speech for all working-class organisations'. In Jarrow the following year NUWM branch secretary Owen Hunt reported that a meeting of 700 unemployed had 'condemned' the Town Council for calling off a planned march to the UAB District Office in Newcastle. Clearly some branches were still engaged in public campaigning work. The Blyth branch was still active and besides its usual activities continued to organise children's outings for members and others, as it had done since 1935. It continued to lobby for additional winter allowances. NUWM branches dealt with the issues members and local people brought to them and this would, as always, have absorbed a great deal of time. For example in Chester-le-Street the branch at this time was concerned with how the Council allocated temporary work. This was the system whereby work on government-funded temporary employment schemes was provided for the unemployed. There were complaints from the unemployed that this was not being allocated fairly, indeed that there was no public information about what the system was, and the NUWM was regularly trying to engage with the Council to agree what the branch claimed would be a fair and transparent system. It seems that in November 1937 the NUWM sent a deputation to lobby the Durham PAC over higher relief scales but on that occasion it declined to meet it.[39]

One factor which may have deflected local NUWM campaigns was that during the autumn of 1937 the mainstream labour movement itself was campaigning for increased UAB and PAC scales to match the rise in the cost of living. In October Emmie Lawther and Jim Stephenson from Blaydon and Winlaton Labour Party, 'the largest organised body of workers in the district', led a deputation to lobby the UAB manager in Newcastle. The group included Mrs. Clarke, a member of an NUWM deputation in 1935, but although Lawther and Stephenson were NUWM sympathisers there was no indication of a formal involvement by the movement. Later in the month Jarrow Divisional Labour Party and the Boilermakers' Union also sent a deputation to lobby the same UAB manager, who 'passed on their concerns'. Increased benefits scales were the theme of public meetings by left Labour Parties and resolutions from miners' lodges as well as Co-operative groups. The Durham PAC was resistant to higher relief scales on cost grounds, but under pressure it did convene a regional conference of PACs to examine a uniform scale based on the cost of living. This seems to have foundered when the government made it clear that additional funds would not be available.[40] Nevertheless if the local Labour Parties were taking up this lobbying the role of the NUWM could be superfluous.

Another factor that has been identified is the effect the introduction of the Unemployment Assistance Boards had on local protest. Whereas the the Boards of Guardians were elected and the PACs, when they oversaw transitional payments, were part of local councils the UABs were a branch of central government. Therefore there was no effective way for local protesters to influence the benefit levels paid in their areas. The state had in fact structured the scope for collective action.[41] This point should be considered but nonetheless local protests were still being made in the region, as we have seen, and this became important over additional winter relief where local UABs could exercise some discretion.

During the summer of 1937 and up to the end of the year the CP Central Committee dealt once more with the 'failings' of the NUWM and once more the North East coast was used as an example. In August a delegate complained that 'on the North East coast one cannot see the slightest sign of activity so far as the NUWM is concerned' and this he attributed to not working for closer contact with the trade union unemployed associations, which as we have seen is the line the Party leadership wished it to take. In December a critique was levelled by Willie Allan, who by this time had been elected as a Communist to Blyth Council. He had won the seat in the by-election caused when Bob Elliott was killed in Spain. Allan was a Central Committee loyalist of the first order and he repeated what had been the standard anti-Hannington criticism of the NUWM for the last few years. He detected 'an almost complete deadness' regarding agitation among the unemployed nationally, 'with no reports of demonstrations and mass activity'. Predicting a return of national economic recession 'where masses of fresh workers are becoming unemployed … the existing NUWM will constitute one of the biggest barriers and obstacles to us being able to get influence and activity among the unemployed'. This was because despite the debates of 1930 and 1931 the NUWM had not shifted from being an unemployed trades union, a reminder from Allan that its leadership had not delivered the direction the Party required. It could actually be necessary to wind the organisation up if it could not be 'transformed out of recognition' into one 'constantly agitating and struggling among the unemployed'.

Again the North East was an example, according to Allan: despite having some good comrades and a number of branches, they had too many 'lumpen-proletarian' elements or were 'a small club of a handful of people who seem to know everything but who seem to spend all their time in arguing'; as was the case elsewhere, branches were 'dominated by people against the Party.'[42]

This litany seems be evidence of a decline in the local NUWM and support for the case that the likely cause was the departure of dedicated activists to Spain. As we have seen, though, the litany was a familiar one which had appeared well before the Spanish military revolt in 1936. Again as we have seen Pollitt had complained of a dearth of national activity at the start of the year, by which he seems to have meant the activity with the trade union unemployed associations which the political line required. Four years earlier Springhall had attacked the North East District even though there had been promising NUWM activity in North and South Shields and Stockton; not carrying out an unrealistic Party line had been the real problem. The North East District NUWM had been upbraided for failing to organise the planned County Hunger March in 1935, when it could have capitalised on the large agitations against the UAB regulations that year, joint agitations in which it had been heavily involved. The District NUWM also appears to have called off a planned Durham march the previous year. This certainly seems to have been a local organisational failure, for whatever reason, and which indicated that the movement having its activists in place was no guarantee that mass agitation would be carried out.[43]

In Blyth, presumably the NUWM branch that Allan knew most about, there were other factors at work besides the absence of the leading figure Bob Elliott. Problems would have been experienced in the movement there regardless of recruitment for Spain. In November 1937 Blyth CP had announced a decision not to contest a Croft ward by-election, where it already had two councillors, but instead to support the Labour candidate. This will be examined in the next chapter, but at this stage it should be noted that the move away from 'class against class' in Blyth that this represented had split the Communist branch and by extension the NUWM. A number of leading Communists, including their original Councillor Ned Breadin, had been expelled from the Party. Although Allan and Breadin still co-operated with each other in the Council chamber, and Breadin subsequently re-joined the Party, this dissension within the CP branch must have had repercussions for the Blyth unemployed movement. It could explain what Allan meant by the local NUWM being 'dominated by people against the Party', they may have been those who did not accept the consequences of the change in line towards the Labour Party and council elections in the town.[44]

Also, in September 1937 the NUWM National Committee heard that a member in Blyth had absconded with a 'large sum' belonging to the branch and that his behaviour with a cheque had caused the Co-op to involve the police. The branch had ignored an earlier District Committee instruction to expel this individual for a previous theft of funds. Therefore it was agreed that the branch would be 'disbanded and re-formed with those willing to carry out District Committee decisions'. Two months later a letter from the branch appeared in the local press, admitting that there had been 'trouble in the Blyth branch, previous to the District stepping in and disbanding the branch … A number of members were expelled from the movement'. This was a second wave of 'trouble' following the apparent split in the Blyth CP over the stance towards the Labour Party. It is possible of course that had Bob Elliott and the other Brigaders still been present all this would have been ameliorated, but that must remain speculation.[45]

The point here is that although the absence of active volunteers in Spain must surely have diluted the effectiveness of the NUWM in the region it is not the explanation for all its problems, and nor did campaigning for the Republic necessarily halt campaigning work for the unemployed. At least some of the criticism coming out of the Communist Central Committee was, as it had been in the past, the symptom of another agenda rather than an accurate assessment. Nevertheless the commitment to anti-fascism of the unemployed movement came with a price. How the activists like Jobling, Elliott, Dolan and the others who were killed would have developed had they survived, what contribution they might or might not have made, can only be a matter of speculation rather than prediction. At the time though the loss was felt; at the memorial meeting for Wilf Jobling in 1937 it was said that he would be 'sorely missed by the class that most needed him', which was surely undeniable. Charlie Woods had been involved with the unemployed movement since the 1920s and between 1936 and 1937 had acted as Communist Party District Secretary. In that role he had known and facilitated many in the first wave of volunteers. He had also on occasion had the task of informing relatives about the death in action of a son or husband. His reflections fifty years later included this one:

> The toll that was taken of the lads who would have played a leading role in the labour movement was heavy. To this day I have misgivings, not regrets but misgivings, about maybe a mistake was made by the Party, that we sent our best comrades from this area to Spain, they were killed and we couldn't afford that to happen when we needed them as cadres.[46]

The NUWM continued to be active in the North East in different ways until the outbreak of the Second World War and this last part of the decade will be examined later. Some references have already been made to the fact that well-known figures in the NUWM had been elected into local government in the region. This was a revealing episode in the history of the movement in the North East and so it is the subject of the next chapter.

Notes

1   A good reproduction of the photograph is in Frank Graham, *Battle of Jarama 1937: The Story of the British Battalion of the International Brigade in Spain* (Newcastle on Tyne: Frank Graham 1987p. 42). On the British Battalion generally see Richard Baxell, *British Volunteers in the Spanish Civil War: The British Battalion in the International Brigades 1936-1939* (London: Routledge 2004); James K. Hopkins, *Into the Heart of the Fire: The British in the Spanish Civil War* (Stanford California: Stanford University Press 1998).

2   On the civil war see Jim Jump (ed.) *Looking Back at the Spanish Civil War* (London: Lawrence and Wishart 2010); Tom Buchanan, *The Spanish Civil War and the British Labour Movement* (Cambridge: Cambridge University Press 1991). There is a detailed and comprehensive local study of the North East and the Spanish Civil War in Lewis Mates, *The Spanish Civil War and the British Left: Political Activism and the Popular Front* (London: I.B. Tauris 2007).

3   Minutes of the NAC Meeting March 1934 (MML: NUWM Bulletins and Circulars).

4   *Blaydon Courier* 17 October and 21 November 1936; *Heslop's Local Advertiser* 11 December 1936 (GLS); Metropolitan Police Commissioner Report to the Home Office 16 November 1936(NA: HO 144/20697).

5   NUWM HQ Circular E18 13 October 1936 (MML: NUWM Bulletins and Circulars); Georgi Dimitrov, *The Unity of the Working Class Against Fascism: Speech at the Seventh World Congress of the Communist International* (London: Lawrence and Wishart 1935).

6   *Shields Gazette* 28 July and 25 August 1936; *Blaydon Courier* 5 September 1936; *Blyth News* 10 December 1936.

7   *North Mail* 29 December 1936, *Blyth News* 17 December1936.

8   *National Memorial Fund: An Appeal to Co-operators* (MML: International Brigade Archive); Bill Alexander, *British Volunteers for Liberty: Spain 1936-39* (London: Lawrence and Wishart 1982, p. 29); Richard Baxell, *British Volunteers in the Spanish Civil War* (p. 18). Material published by the National Archives in 2011 indicated 4,000 Britons in Spain but closer examination revealed that the list was inaccurate and included visitors and other non-combatants (NA: KV/5/112: *List of persons who fought in Spain 1936-1939*).

9   Information from Jim Carmody, International Brigade Memorial Trust archivist; Richard Baxell, *British Volunteers in the Spanish Civil War* (p. 23).

10   *Report of the 11ᵗʰ National Conference of the NUWM 1939* (MML: Hannington D Miscellaneous.)

11   Information from Jim Carmody, International Brigade Memorial Trust archivist; for comparisons see Lewis Mates, 'Durham and South Wales Miners in the Spanish Civil War' *Twentieth Century British History* Vol 17 No.3 (2006, pp. 373-395).

The 22 men definitely from the NUWM were: Tommy Carter (killed), Steve Codling (killed), George Coyle, William Dean, Tommy Dolan (killed), Bob Elliott (killed), Frank Graham, Richard Hearn, John Henderson, Thomas Jobling, Wilf Jobling (killed), Sam Langley, Bob Mackie (killed), Jack Palzeard (killed), Bill Parlett, Bobbie Qualie, Harry Reynolds (killed), T.W. Richardson, Harry Smith (killed), Bill Tattam (killed), Edgar Wilkinson (killed) and William Young (killed).

12   For the number of councillors see Noreen Branson, *History of the Communist Party of Great Britain Vol. III 1927-1941* (London: Lawrence and Wishart 1985, p. 146); Cable from Will Paynter to Harry Pollitt, 13 July 1937 (MML: International Brigade Archive Box 21/3f); Richard Baxell, *British Volunteers in the Spanish Civil War* (p. 9).

13   Mrs. Dolan quoted in Lewis Mates, *The Spanish Civil War and the British Left* (p. 38); William Rust, *Britons in Spain* (London: Lawrence and Wishart 1939, p. 7); Charlotte Haldane, *Truth Will Out* (London: Weidenfeld and Nicholson 1948, p. 114). Haldane, in fairness, does have other very complimentary things to say about the volunteers.

14   Raymond Carr, *The Civil War in Spain* (London: Weidenfeld and Nicholson 1986, p. 142); Anthony Beevor, *The Battle for Spain: The Spanish Civil War 1936-1939* (London: Weidenfeld and Nicholson 2007, p. 178).

15   Hywel Francis, *Miners Against Fascism: Wales and the Spanish Civil War* (1984, p. 192); Tom Buchanan, *Britain and Spanish Civil War* (Cambridge: Cambridge University Press 1997, p. 126); Richard Baxell, *British Volunteers in the Spanish Civil War* (p. 42) ; Lewis Mates, *The Spanish Civil War and the British Left* (p. 29).

16   See Don Watson, 'Self-Help and Aid for Spain: The Hawick Workers' Mill 1936-1939' *Scottish Labour History* 34 (1999, pp. 119-124).

17   Frank Graham, interview with Jim McGurn 1986 (BMSA ref 2007.29).

18   George Short, interview with Peter Brabbam 1979.

19   Mathew Worley, *Class Against Class: The Communist Party in Britain Between the Wars* (London: I.B. Tauris 2002, p. 219); Margot Heinemann, interview 1986 (IWMSA ref 9239); Len Edmondson, interview with Karen Grunzweil 1999 (BMSA ref 1999.9); John Henderson, interview with Don Watson and John Corcoran 1986.

A detailed analysis of the Lenin School, including a list of the British students, is provided by John McIlroy, Barry McLoughlin, Alan Campbell and John Halstead, 'Forging the Faithful: The British at the International Lenin School' *Labour History Review* Vol. 68 No.1 (April 2003, pp. 99-129). The definite North East NUWM activists who attended were: Jim Ancrum, George Coyle, Richard Hearn, John Henderson, Wilf Jobling, G. Reay, George Short, Bob Smith, Billy Todd and Charlie Woods.

20   Bobbie Qualie, interview with Peter Brabbam 1979.

21   Minutes of the NAC Meeting November 1937 (MML: Hannington D Miscellaneous).

22   On the BUF see Stephen Dorrill, *Blackshirt: Sir Oswald Mosley and British Fascism* (London: Penguin Viking 2006); a detailed study of anti-fascism in the North East in the 1930s is Nigel Todd, *In Excited Times: The People Against the Blackshirts* (Whitley Bay: Bewick Press 1995).

23   County Borough of Gateshead Constabulary Reports 10 and 14 November 1927, 25 May 1928 (NA: HO/144/13864); *Newcastle Evening Chronicle* 10 November 1927.

24   Frank Graham, interview with Jim McGurn 1986; he describes the Olympia episode in his Imperial War Museum interview (IWMSA ref 11877/6).

25   NUWM Branch Activities Monthly Report May 1931(MML: Hannington and Brown Papers Ai and Aii).

26   *Shields News* 4, 5, 7, 11 and 12 July 1934; Stephen Dorrill, *Blackshirt* (p. 323).

27   On the Linaria dispute see Don Watson and John Corcoran, *An Inspiring Example: The North East of England and the Spanish Civil War 1936-1939* (London: McGuffin Press 1996, pp. 15-23); Lewis Mates, *The Spanish Civil War and the British Left* (pp. 132-5)

28   *Newcastle Journal* 14, 15 and 17 May 1934; Nigel Todd, *In Excited Times* (pp. 69-71, 80-82, 87); *North Mail* 4 November 1934 and 2 October 1935.

29   *Sunderland Echo* 15 and 26 May 1934; *Shields Gazette* 4 November 1935; *Sunderland Echo* 26 July 1935.

30   Frank Graham, interview with Don Watson 1996; *Newcastle Journal* 2 May 1934; Nigel Todd, *In Excited Times* (pp. 54-56, p. 68).

31   Quoted in Nigel Todd, *In Excited Times* (p. 82); John Henderson, interview in Don Watson and John Corcoran, *An Inspiring Example* (p. 53).

32   Jim Reynolds, interview with Don Watson and Pauline Frazer 2007.

33   This point is made in Hywel Francis, 'Say Nothing and Leave in the Middle of the Night: the Spanish Civil War Revisited', *History Workshop Journal* No 32 (1991, pp. 69-76).

34   Information from Jim Carmody, International Brigade Memorial Trust archivist.

35   Walter Gregory, *The Shallow Grave: A Memoir of the Spanish Civil War* (London: Victor Gollancz 1986, p. 168). James Hopkins, *Into the Heart of the Fire* (pp. 279, 421) records that Elliott was an official observer at the summary trial of a French commander for espionage; Hopkins cites this as evidence that some figures in the British Battalion were aware of repressive Soviet tactics at the top level of the Brigade. However he also cites the sources for maintaining that this case was genuine espionage rather than a politically motivated charge.

36   Letter from branch secretary Len Afflick to Wal Hannington 24 November 1938 (MML: Hannington Papers A viii-x); Jim Ancrum Photograph Album (GLS); *Blyth News* 10 December 1936; *Shields Gazette* 30 January 1939.

37   Richard Croucher, *We Refuse to Starve in Silence: A History of the National Unemployed Workers' Movement 1920-1946* (London: Lawrence and Wishart 1987, p. 188); Lewis Mates, *The Spanish Civil War and the British Left* (p. 54, p. 216).

38   Minutes of the Felling Urban District Council 5 January 1937 and 22 February 1937 (TWAS: UD.FE/A/1/22); *North Mail* 6 and 26 January 1937.

39   *Shields Gazette* 23 July 1937; 3 and 4 March 1938; Letters in *Blyth News* 27 May and 12 July 1937, 24 October 1938; Letters from NUWM Secretary George Clarke 11 January 1936, 3 March, 7 April and 19 July 1937, 1 March 1938 - Correspondence with Chester le Street Unemployed Association (DCRO: UD/CS 203); letter in *Blaydon Courier* 28 January 1938.

40   *Blaydon Courier* 9 and 23 October, 6 and 13 November 1937; *North Mail* 30 October, 19, 22 and 25 November 1937.

41   This is argued in Paul Bagguley, *Protest or Acquiescence? Political Movements of the Unemployed* (London: Methuen 1991, pp. 85-87).

42   Minutes of the Communist Party of Great Britain 6 August, 3 and 4 December 1937 (LHASC) No discussion about the consequences of Spain for the NUWM or the Party seems to have taken place at the meeting, or at least it was not minuted.

43   *Sunderland Echo* 15 January 1934.

44   Letter from Allan in *Blyth News* 20 December 1937.

45   Minutes of the NUWM NAC Meeting September 1937 (MML: Hannington D Miscellaneous); letter in *Blyth News* 15 November 1937).

46   *Blaydon Courier* 17 April 1937; Charlie Woods, interview with Don Watson and John Corcoran, *An Inspiring Example* (p. 37).

Chapter Nine

SHOP STEWARDS OF THE STREETS –
THE NUWM IN LOCAL GOVERNMENT

It has been mentioned that by 1936 some NUWM activists in the region had been elected as Communists to local councils. This chapter examines the five Communist councillors elected in the Northumberland and Durham coalfields and their activities on their local authorities between 1933 and 1939. Three seats were held in Croft ward in Blyth; Ned Breadin and Bob Elliott were elected to the Borough Council, and when Elliott was killed in Spain his seat was held in a by-election by the erstwhile United Mineworkers of Scotland leader Willie Allan. Breadin also held a seat for the ward on Northumberland County Council. Elsewhere Jim Ancrum was elected to Felling Urban District Council and Tommy Richardson was elected to Houghton le Spring Urban District Council in County Durham. All of these authorities were Labour apart from Northumberland County Council where the Conservatives were in control.

These councillors were all miners except possibly Ned Breadin who was described in election literature as a 'disabled ex-serviceman'. Apart from Allan they were local men who had had extended periods of unemployment. Ancrum as we have seen had joined the CP during the 1926 lockout and in the course of this he had been arrested and gaoled. He came to prominence for his role in organising support during the Dawdon colliery dispute in 1929 and subsequently served briefly on the CP Central Committee. He had been a local leader of the Miners' National Minority Movement in the early 1930s and had been trained at the Lenin School in Moscow. Allan too had a national profile in the CP: his activism went back to the early period of the Party and the National Minority Movement, and he had been a colleague of Ancrum's on the Central Committee. He had led the United Mineworkers of Scotland, a union set up by the CP (and consisting of its members) at the height of the 'class against class' period; its organisational and political failure was one reason why he had sought work in Northumberland. Breadin, apparently a First World War veteran, had been drawn into left politics when the National Unemployed Workers' Committee Movement had been established in Blyth in the early 1920s. Elliott too had joined the CP during the 1926 lockout and Richardson had joined the NUWM and the Party during the Means Test protests of 1931. Each had earned a local reputation as an NUWM campaigner for some time before their elections.[1]

The North East District was consistently the one with the smallest membership of the CPGB. Therefore it is not surprising that by 1938 the District had only nine percent, five out of fifty-four, of the Party's national total of local authority seats.[2] It is that very exceptionality that is interesting, though, and it cannot be a coincidence that all of these individuals had been local NUWM leaders for some time before they were elected. The reputation for effective individual casework across the local community combined with public campaigning, which has been described earlier, could also give NUWM activists a good base for standing in their local council elections.

Communists, the NUWM, and Local Elections

As we have seen, in the North East candidates representing the unemployed had been standing in local elections since the 1920s, beginning with the Boards of Guardians. These candidates had generally (although not exclusively) been of the left and their attitude towards standing against Labour had much to do with the policy of the Communist Party at a given time. Once the NUWM had emerged as the only really national organisation for the unemployed and under Communist leadership an attempt was made at a consistent approach to electoral work.

The 1931 National Conference of the NUWM had criticised 'the tendency on the part of NUWM branches to enter election struggles on a similar basis to the social democrats' and acting as if it was a party organisation putting forward its own independent candidates. It was not the function of the movement to enter elections as a political party. Electoral work should be done in unity with local 'revolutionary organisations'. In some localities circumstances could be such as to justify a candidate drawn from the NUWM branch, where there was no Communist candidate, but again this should be done in unity with the support of the revolutionary movement. In 1933 the NUWM leadership stated again that 'the mass movement of the unemployed is not a political party' and advised against fielding NUWM candidates in elections because it was felt that this would 'narrow the political focus solely to the unemployed'. A year later it still criticised the 'tendency on the part of some of our branches to run independent NUWM candidates'. In line with the changing national policy of the CP it advocated 'workers candidates' agreed through local conferences with the ILP and

Labour where possible. Branches should, though, according to NUWM Headquarters, strive to get the NUWM nominee as the workers' candidate at these conferences; these nominees would presumably be the well-known local activists.[3]

All this suggests some confusion, or autonomous behaviour, by some branches, an example of the 'localism' that could trouble the NUWM leadership. As we have seen, in the Tyneside District the CP had only around 100 members in 1931, and even if this had risen to 200 in 1933 these numbers confirm that the local NUWM activist, Communist, or member of a 'revolutionary organisation' such as the Minority Movement would be likely to be one and the same person. By 1930 some of the active NUWM branches on Tyneside and the Northumberland coalfield were standing candidates in local elections, especially after the introduction of the Means Test which rejuvenated the movement and also kindled a modest growth in the CP. Historians have noted that 'in Blyth and Tynemouth CP members first stood as NUWM candidates, only later changing to an explicitly communist ticket'. If this is a suggestion that some sleight of hand was being attempted then it would have been pointless: given the small pool of 'workers' candidates' the voters would have been aware of the affiliations of the NUWM leaders even without local press campaigns to remind them.[4]

In 1932 NUWM campaigner Walter Harrison stood as a Communist in Tynemouth with J. Fox as NUWM; Billy Booth of Sunderland NUWM stood as a Communist as did Jack Douglas in Morpeth; Breadin and Elliott stood in Blyth as NUWM candidates. In South Shields NUWM activists Andrew Codling and G. Reay were 'Workers' Candidates' and Communist candidates respectively. In any event in the North East NUWM campaigners standing in local elections after 1932 were described in the local press as Communist candidates. Walter Harrison and Spike Robson in North Shields, Wilf Jobling in Blaydon, Jim Ancrum in Felling and Breadin and Elliott in Blyth were all Communist candidates in 1934.[5]

Breadin was elected to Blyth Council in 1933 and to Northumberland County Council in 1934. Elliott was first elected in a by-election in Blyth in 1935. Both had stood for the Council on several occasions before they were successful. When Elliott was killed with the International Brigade in Spain in 1937 Willie Allan was elected to his seat in a by-election a few months later. At this time Allan was the checkweighman at a local colliery and he is one possible exception to the generalisation about an NUWM background for these councillors. But he had been closely associated with the movement and had been active as a speaker in Blyth and the Northumberland coalfield for several years. Ancrum won a Council by-election in Felling in 1935, his third attempt to win a seat in his ward, and stood again at the Council election in 1937 and increased his vote. Richardson was elected in 1936, the year in which he had been a local leader of the Hunger March. That this association between an NUWM profile and election to the Council cannot be a coincidence is suggested in other parts of the country too. In Hawick in 1937 for example the local NUWM organiser was elected as the first, and only ever, Communist councillor in the town. Long standing Staffordshire Communist councillor Fanny Deakin was a formidable local campaigner on unemployment and poverty related issues since before her involvement in the Party. According to Phil Piratin the CP only made a showing in Stepney local elections after its work in tenants' groups and an NUWM branch had become established. In Glamorgan the sole Communist on the County Council, Lewis Jones, toured his constituency in a loudspeaker van to conduct benefits advice sessions. Their success was reported to the Ministry of Health by the auditor, who commented that '… I am informed that a very large number of persons are now applying for out relief, who, were it not for this propaganda, would have refrained from asking for help …'[6]

The CP could draw on election workers outside its own ranks through the NUWM, and in Blyth at least they appeared to have adopted the same street by street tactics that had been used in the pit villages during the 1926 lock out: '… speakers in every street, canvassers in every street, our policy in every home'. Active NUWM branches would have had a public presence all the year round, not just during election campaigns. They fielded candidates whose names and profiles would have been continually in front of their electors through street meetings in the local Speakers' Corners as well as through advice and representation.

Although the electoral position of the North East CP in 1936 was more promising than ever before there was a basic weakness, one that was pointed out at the time. The Felling local newspaper probably summed it up accurately in its report of Ancrum's election in 1935: 'This contest appears to have been fought on an individual and not a political basis … Councillor Ancrum is well known throughout the district and this no doubt accounts for his remarkable victory'. This invites a comparison with Jimmy Lenagh in the Bridges Ward in Sunderland. He had originally been elected to the Board of Guardians as a Communist, then Labour, and later to the Council as an 'independent socialist', and then again, despite a prison term for electoral fraud. Votes were being cast for the respected local campaigner for the unemployed rather than the party he stood for, or even, like Lenagh, if he had no party at all.[7]

Council Work and the NUWM

A political historian has observed that in South Wales during the 1930s the structure in which Council minutes were set out makes it difficult to identify progressive gains that can be attributed to specific Communist pressure. This is true for the North East too, but at least these Council minutes do carefully record the wording of motions, the names of those who moved and seconded them, and the numbers of votes for and against. This does help to identify the actions of Communist councillors and the support they attracted in the Council Chamber.

It is clear that at one level their NUWM role was interchangeable with their Council work. Richardson in Houghton maintained a consistent flow of questions and motions in the Council chamber and much of the material must have come from his NUWM casework. He argued that workers on the government-funded projects for the unemployed should be paid the trades union rate for casual labourers; successfully pressed that the County Council should be lobbied to provide a free hot meal every day for all school children, because of the poor nutritional status of the area. As was done elsewhere, free milk should be supplied during the school holidays. The government should be urged to raise benefit scales in line with the rising cost of living, and 'take steps to control food prices and frustrate the efforts of the millionaire profiteers'. Temporary staff for the Council should be recruited through the labour exchanges to give the unemployed a chance. Councillors on the Public Assistance Committee agreed to his motion that the PAC should meet weekly and not fortnightly so that the hardship caused by the delay in processing claims could be avoided.[8]

Similarly in Blyth the Councillors were a continuous link where possible with the NUWM and its campaigns outside the Council. For example Ned Breadin, at his second Council meeting in December 1933, proposed an NUWM motion (not seconded and declared out of order) on assistance for all necessitous cases among the Blyth unemployed. In 1934 he proposed a sarcastic motion on the Mayor's salary, quoting the Medical Officer of Health's Annual Report on economic distress and ill-health in the borough. More seriously, in 1935 Blyth Council agreed that the Mayor represent the Council on a protest delegation to the Minister of Labour. He also won support for a protest (which bore fruit in this case) against the local UAB practice of reducing the benefits paid to unemployed families where the Council was providing free school meals. The Council investigated, but rejected on cost grounds, the possibility of a 40-hour week for Council employees to create jobs; it agreed to give unemployed workers priority for temporary Council work. These initiatives were all at Breadin's suggestion or formal proposal, and were first raised by NUWM meetings in the town and a deputation to the Council.[9]

The Communist councillors won support for individual NUWM campaigns such as for higher winter benefit scales, for free school milk provision to be extended through the school holidays, and for free school meals for 'necessitous schoolchildren' as defined by the 1921 Education Act. In Blyth, though, the Council was inclined to tone down the wording of the motions from Breadin and his later colleague Bob Elliott. The Labour Groups on these Councils were prepared to support the Communists on these issues but only up to a point. We have seen how in 1936 Ancrum and Elliott gained initial backing from their Council colleagues to support the National Hunger March only to find the full Council overturning those decisions later. It seems likely that despite their initial sympathy over the issues at stake these Councils were moving back into line with official Labour and TUC policy on not supporting marches by 'non-affiliated organisations'. The Labour Groups pulled back from what could have been seen as direct support for the CP or its satellite organisation.[10]

Jim Ancrum had a national role with the NUWM from at least 1938 while he continued his Council work; his name appeared on the NUWM letterhead as a National Organiser until the organisation was formally disbanded. Richardson, Elliott and the regular but unsuccessful Blyth Council Communist candidate Terry Mooney were part of the local leadership of the 1936 Hunger March, with Elliott and Mooney speaking from the platforms at one of the concluding rallies in Trafalgar Square. Elliott played little part in his own re-election campaign in November 1936 because of the March but it was still a success, he and Breadin receiving high shares of the poll.[11]

Ancrum too was a conduit for issues originating with Felling NUWM to reach the Council. Examples are travel expenses for unemployed families re-housed because of slum clearance displacement; ensuring that men in the Ministry of Labour training camps were still eligible for Council temporary jobs whilst there; the financial position of unemployed men whose children had been evacuated as war approached; free school meals funded through the rates. His election campaigns (two out of four of which were successful) always stressed his role in the NUWM in Felling: struggles against evictions, for re-housing and repairs, for free school meals and to ensure the maximum benefits were paid by the Public Assistance Committee and the Unemployment Assistance Board. Besides the NUWM there were issues around, essentially, open government that marked out the Communist contribution in North East local government at this time.[12]

Open Government and the Reaction

Richardson was elected to Houghton le Spring UDC in September 1936 and as a matter of Council routine took over his predecessor's Committees. Little more than a week later he was the object of protest by other Councillors for breaches of procedure, apparently disclosing Council business at public meetings before the Council had considered the reports. He replied that he considered it his duty to keep the electors informed, and regardless of any protests he intended to continue. A resolution passed protesting at his conduct and threatening to 'consider means of restraining his activities'. At the Council meeting the following month, in his absence, he was criticised again for conducting public meetings to discuss committee business before the reports had reached the Council. In December he was accused of 'open defiance' of the Council resolutions protesting at his actions. Richardson claimed that he had never discussed private matters, only procedural ones, and 'resented' the implication that he had. But the UDC found a means to 'restrain his activities': at the Council annual meeting in April 1937 he and a Labour councillor who had supported him were excluded from membership of all Council committees.

Such exclusions were the traditional means for local authority members to neutralise their too awkward or too dissident fellows, or as a political response. Councillors who were not members of Committees would only have a limited knowledge of Council business and therefore reduced opportunities to influence it. Despite his frequent protests ('I am here as an elected representative of the working class and I make my protest on their behalf') Richardson remained excluded from membership of Committees from April 1937 until he resumed his Council work in 1944 following army service. In contrast Breadin and Ancrum were appointed to Committees despite, as will be shown, their own conflicts with Council procedures.[13]

Ancrum too, at least when first elected, was criticised by his Council for being too ready to discuss Council business outside the Town Hall. Early in his tenure he faced criticism for allegedly criticising Council job recruiting at public meetings before the relevant Committee reports had reached the Council. This in turn generated its share of press publicity, but the Felling Labour Group did not exclude him from Committees. Council jobs and tenancies seem to have been seen as being in the gift of councillors and therefore a source of local speculation and discontent.[14]

It seems to have been common practice for activists to 'report back', as they would have termed it, to public meetings about the business they had been involved in as a representative. This could have repercussions, of course. Ancrum for example had been expelled from the Durham Miners'

Association for a time in 1931; he had apparently breached union rules by circulating a 'typewritten document' and 'dealing with Lodge business in Felling Square'. It is probably impossible to determine now whether these reactions were procedurally justifiable or politically motivated. Houghton le Spring Labour Party must have been unhappy about losing a seat to the Communists, and at the height of the 'class against class' period Ancrum was a leader of the Durham Miners' Minority Movement and a vociferous critic of the DMA Executive. Communist councillors in other regions faced isolation too; when Phil Piratin was elected to Stepney Borough Council in 1937 the response of the Labour group was to forbid their councillors to second any of his resolutions.[15]

The 1931 National Conference of the NUWM resolution on electoral work had stated that where elected NUWM candidates must 'regularly report to meetings of the unemployed and other workers an account of their work in these bodies'. But this 'reporting back' was part of the culture of the North East radical unemployed movements these men had come from or even been formed by. As we have seen the unemployed demonstrations and deputations during the 1921 recessions, when the NUWCM was formed, were characterised by the nominated leaders reporting back to mass meetings about the discussions taking place with the councillors and the Boards of Guardians. This continued into the 1930s. This has also been identified as one of the democratic bases of community politics in the 'Little Moscows' of Fife and South Wales. The authority of leaders was drawn essentially from resolutions agreed at public and open-air meetings, and they were seen as having a face-to-face accountability to those who had elected them. Attempts to take politics out of the public arena were to be resisted.[16] Open government appears as an issue in other ways. Ancrum did eventually win a battle to have the Council papers available to the press before the meetings to facilitate local reporting. Richardson too argued, without support from the Labour Group, that his Council should admit the public to its meetings, and hold them in a venue large enough to permit it.[17]

'Corruption' in Local Affairs?

It has been claimed that stories of corruption and nepotism in the Labour Parties of the South Wales coalfield in the 1930s were popularly believed and gained the status of folk legend. Writing of Stepney Council in that decade Phil Piratin states that as a councillor there he occasionally attacked actual corruption; solid Labour majorities, he believed, can start a 'drift to complacency and sometimes corruption'. Events after 1945 in the North East of England and elsewhere serve to demonstrate his point.[18]

Ancrum had been elected in 1935 with a pledge to 'struggle against corruption and graft in local affairs', particularly regarding allegations of Council corruption and favouritism over the allocation of Council tenancies and jobs. Felling NUWM had brought up Council job recruitment, and it was over this issue that he had been criticised for discussing Council business at public meetings. A memoir recalls that local CP officials advised Ancrum to 'tone down his attacks on other Councillors' and 'favouritism in the allocation of work' unless he had firm evidence. He was reacting to local dissatisfaction. Like Ancrum, Richardson took up issues of Council procedures over tenancies and over jobs; in his area too they seem to have been a source of popular resentment. In particular he criticised the practice of the Chairmen of the Council and the Housing Committee, and the Town Clerk, selecting the new tenants when council houses became vacant. This was 'undesirable and unfair to all concerned' and he proposed an open system on a 'points' basis that would prioritise slum clearance families, those suffering from overcrowding and those in substandard accommodation.[19]

Similarly the allocation of temporary Council jobs and the decision making over who was to be kept on longer was apparently 'a source of considerable dissatisfaction' in Houghton le Spring. Richardson had in fact led an NUWM deputation to the Council about the 'unfair allocation' of this work in 1935. There is evidence too that in Blyth and other parts of the North East local NUWM branches (such as Chester le Street, as we have seen) were protesting about 'anomalies' in this system: here again, the councillors were reacting to local concerns.[20]

Political Contexts: 'Class Against Class' and Its End

Earlier chapters have discussed the Communist 'class against class' policy of the early 1930s and the effects this had on the NUWM. In 1929 the future Blyth Councillor Elliott considered that 'the labour and trades union bureaucracy is co-operating with the boss class in reducing working-class conditions in an attempt to stabilise declining capitalism'. Four years later his election literature and that of Breadin stated that 'We are fighting this election on a class basis. Class against class. Communists in the Council Chamber can ruthlessly expose the class nature of the Moderates ... and the role of the Labour Party with its policy of collaboration with the capitalist class'. In Felling Ancrum too had long been a critic of the Labour and DMA leaderships in similar terms. As we have seen abuse of Labour councillors was a regular feature of NUWM rallies in the North East in the early 1930s, particularly where Council meetings refused to receive NUWM deputations.[21]

This was the context in which the first CP councillors in the North East were elected, and it seems to have informed Breadin's early approach in the Blyth Council chamber. Four months after his election standing orders were suspended at a Council meeting to enable a resolution to be passed calling on him to disassociate himself from a Communist election address. This apparently had been a misrepresentation of the work of the Council and had 'the ultimate object of destroying the democratic institutions of this country'. Three months later his motion calling for the Council to do all in its power to obstruct the Unemployment Assistance Board Bill - and to support those refusing to enter the Ministry of Labour 'slave camps' - was ruled out of order; he refused to stop speaking, causing the meeting to be adjourned. The same thing happened when the meeting was reconvened, this time Breadin was ordered to leave the chamber, refused, and was escorted out by the police. All this was accompanied by NUWM public meetings in his support in Blyth Market Place.[22]

By November 1934 the CP approach was to try to persuade potential Labour Party and ILP Council candidates to submit to a 'workers' selection conference' to decide on which of the three parties should stand in a ward, in order to avoid splitting the left vote. The Labour Party almost universally ignored this overture. In Tynemouth the Party appealed to Labour in October 1936 for a united front and for them to support the North Shields contingent, led by the CP Council candidate Walter Harrison, on the 1936 Hunger March. It suggested that a particular Labour activist stand in the ward; the CP would support her, provided that she 'reported quarterly to the electorate' (another example of the 'reporting back' principle) and 'carried out a working-class policy'. Tynemouth Labour Party declined to reply. No agreement with a Labour organisation was ever likely to happen on these terms, as the CP must have known. At the Council elections two months later the CP candidate came second to the Conservatives by seventeen votes.[23]

Willie Allan pursued the same line in Blyth. In November 1937 Blyth CP announced a decision not to contest a Croft ward by-election but to support the Labour candidate. In an open letter less than a month after his own election Allan stated that in view of the likely strength of the Conservative campaign in the by-election, his Party would not 'split the working-class vote' but campaign for Labour. He also requested 'an informal meeting' to discuss 'how best the forces of both organisations could co-operate'. He later claimed in the press that Blyth CP, at his own urging, had been writing to Blyth Labour Party since 1935 'raising proposals for arrangements that would avoid Communists and Labourites standing in opposition to each other in local elections'. But his latest effort was no more successful than his previous ones, as he admitted that 'the Blyth Labour Party has not had the elementary courtesy to even acknowledge our last letter to it ...'[24]

Allan also revealed that this had been a painful process for the local CP. He stated that in trying to build 'the unity of all working-class organisations' he had 'often had to fight against Party members, now expelled, who wanted to oppose Labour on any and every occasion'. He compared this with his own comparative success in the Council chamber when it came to gaining the support of the Labour Group for his initiatives on higher relief scales, Council wages, and conditions for young women at the junior instruction centres. A year later in another letter to the press he stated that 'the Communist Party ended its association with Mr W.H. Breadin more than 18 months ago' and that he now had 'no connection of any kind with it'.[25]

Historians have noted how during his political career Allan 'always followed the script' written by the Communist leadership, but they also explain how his own experience with the CPGB of the early thirties had wrecked his career in Scotland and soured him against whatever smacked of ultra-leftism. Thus his appeals to Blyth Labour Party would have been genuine, but this new line was clearly a step too far for some Blyth Communists. This was a major offering on their part because their years of hard work had been bearing fruit and a third Communist councillor in Croft ward might well have been a realistic prospect. Standing candidates after Labour had ignored the offer of unity through a joint selection conference, as the CP had done in 1935 and 1937 was one thing, but to give Labour a clear run in the ward after the unity offer had been ignored was another. Although Allan and Breadin still co-operated with each other in the Council chamber, and Breadin subsequently re-joined the Party, it was shown in the previous chapter that this dissension within the CP branch also had repercussions in the Blyth NUWM. It seems likely that Allan was 'following the script' about the NUWM at the CP Central Committee when, as we have seen, he disparaged its activity and its politics in Blyth. Any unfortunate effects of the changes in Communist policies themselves were not part of his script.[26]

Political Contexts: National Expectations

The leadership of the CPGB had great expectations of the role its councillors could play in the wider political movement. An example at this time was the Report to the 1938 Party Congress appraising the issue of Communist councillors. Although the new tally of fifty-four was obviously welcome not enough was being done to use this success to build the Party's influence: 'the workers see too much done by councillors as individuals and not enough by them as Party members'. Local authority work was a vehicle to put pressure on and help to remove the National Government. Therefore the monthly bulletin *Party Organiser* set out how this could be translated into action. The keynote of local authority work was to raise every issue affecting 'the mass of the people ... the interests of all workers and the discontented middle class ...' in such a way as to develop a strong movement that 'can sharpen the whole fight against the National Government'.

The strategy for this should be joint activity through 'winning the co-operation of Labour and Progressive councillors for those demands on which we are all agreed'. Communist councillors should campaign to join the Labour Group, but at the same time remember that 'the success of our work depends above all on the extent of the mass movement outside the Council chamber'.

Councillors should take on a leadership role within their local Party branches, and insist that Council matters and how the Party branch could assist be discussed. Branch committees should help councillors with case-work and in preparing cases, and they should take steps to 'appoint qualified comrades to advise on specific problems'. The aim should always be that the councillor was seen as the representative of an organised Party, and hence help to build it and not 'regarded, as it is in most places, as a good individual'. This is an example of what has been described as the recurrent complaint that local leaders such as Councillors were unable to turn their personal success and achievements into organisational success for the Party.[27]

These last points are actually paraphrasing the advice given, as we have seen, by NUWM Headquarters in 1934 about organising local branches. Involving local committees and 'qualified comrades' to help with case work, linking it always to the political context and remembering that success depended on the strength of the mass movement, the ability to exert pressure outside meeting halls. The Party was echoing the work of the NUWM and possibly recognising that therein lay the roots of its local electoral progress. Here too is another aspect of the policy pushed at the NUWM towards local trades council unemployed committees, in this case towards Labour Groups on local authorities.

Some of this would have been recognised and would already have been acted upon by Richardson, Ancrum and the others, but how far would the political instructions have meshed with their realities? Certainly campaigning to join the Labour Group on Houghton le Spring UDC would have been a waste of time. The Houghton Labour Group did not brook dissent: at the time of Richardson's election it had tried to expel a councillor from the Labour Party for proposing a resolution in the Council chamber against its wishes. The only Council ally that Richardson was able to gain in three years had actually left the Group to act as an 'independent trades union socialist' councillor. The ruling group on that Council was an example of a Durham Labour organisation that, in the words of two historians of the DMA, was less to do with socialism than with extending the influence of the local miners' lodge officials. In any case to join such a Labour Group would have meant becoming part of what they had been elected to oppose, not just in policy terms but also as regards their entire way of operating.[28]

How far could they achieve an alliance with progressives in the Labour Groups? Although they undoubtedly secured some gains through the Council chamber the North East Communists often struggled to find seconders for their motions and the unity in action around common issues envisaged by *Party Organiser* rarely looked a realistic prospect. Only one or two Labour councillors ever supported them on a regular basis, and there was nothing like enough 'progressive' strength to overcome official resistance to the 1936 Hunger March for example, as had been achieved in South Wales. The progress of the North East District Party membership figures too does not suggest that the six councillors were instrumental in building up the organisation.

On Northumberland County Council, which was Conservative con-trolled, did the lone Communist member have it any easier? In his first year of meetings he found one Labour ally and they would support each other's motions in Council meetings in favour of local NUWM requests and lobbying, albeit attracting only sporadic support. However the Council did on occasion take up issues with the local Unemployment Assistance Board when urged to by the unemployed movement and others. For example when the government gave way to pressure and suspended key proposals in the 1934 Unemployment Assistance Act, it allowed the restoration of some benefits cuts originally imposed in 1931. Northumberland County Council restored the cuts, and received representation from NUWM branches and local Urban District Councils to further increase relief scales. County councillors on the Public Assistance Committee did take up their arguments with UAB officers, but did not succeed in having the scales increased. It cannot be assumed though that sympathy like this suggested fertile ground for Breadin's work. As we have seen here as elsewhere in the country there was opposition to the original Unemployment Assistance Act even among Conservative and Liberal councillors. They resented the withdrawal of powers from local government that the Act represented, and Whitehall's implication that councils had been profligate with public funds. Some of them in the North East also agreed that the reduced benefits scales originally proposed would create further poverty in their areas. Breadin was however appointed to the Public Assistance Committee, his obvious area of expertise. This may have alleviated situations for individual claimants even if his opportunities to gain support in the chamber for the campaigns outside it were restricted.[29]

By October 1938 *Party Organiser* was sounding notes of realism. Any formal approach by local CP branches would 'in most cases meet the formal rejection required by the Labour Party constitution'. Therefore work with the Labour Party should start on the basis of the Communists' personal contacts with activists where they were fellow members of trades union branches and Co-operative Societies. Talking to fellow election workers for example, 'whilst working side by side for the same cause, can show the artificial character of the barriers erected by the right wing of the Labour leadership against unity'. This was closer to some of the original understandings of the people's front strategy. G.D.H. Cole for example, writing for the Left Book Club in 1937, had argued that the people's front would be a state of mind, a political attitude, and not a piece of electoral machinery, and achieved through joint work in specific campaigns. This was not dissimilar either to Alec Henry's suggestions to the Communist Central Committee in 1934; as was described earlier he had argued that joint working with individual contacts could work while proposing formal joint structures would be ruled out.[30]

As war approached Ancrum was making some limited progress in such joint working between the NUWM and the local 'mainstream' labour movement over issues of common concern. For example in August 1939 he campaigned against moves by the Newcastle Unemployed Assistance Board to compel unemployed youths to decorate an unemployed centre in the city or lose their benefits. He won support from the prospective Labour Prospective Parliamentary Candidate for Central Newcastle (a man who had already shown a limited willingness to share a platform with the CP), a Labour Party District Secretary, the Northumberland Miners Association and the AEU. Ancrum and the others continued to work on NUWM issues until the outbreak of war: Richardson for example lobbying MPs about the large number of additional winter relief claims in his area being rejected with leave to appeal refused, suspecting a campaign to force acceptance of low wages and the Ministry 'slave camps'. Soon, however, such campaigns were overtaken by international events.[31]

Approaching War

The Party's aim to use its local government members as a means of mobilising the opposition to the National Government achieved some success over Air Raid Precautions, another of the priorities for Communist councillors laid down by the 1938 Congress. This was a class issue. Railways, shipyards and factories were at risk of aerial attack and the working-class housing that often surrounded them would therefore be in the front line during bombing raids. Ancrum maintained a routine of critical motions about ARP resources, stating that the Government was providing 'plenty of circulars but no equipment' and arguing that ARP arrangements should be the responsibility of the Council and not the Chief Constable. He argued that with 'emergency' situations being defined by central government and police control of ARP, the result could be wardens being used to break up strikes or demonstrations of the unemployed. Although the Council did not accept his political analysis he was successful in April 1939 when Felling UDC agreed his resolution protesting at the closure of some Felling ARP Warden stations. They too were in working-class areas near factories and railway lines and would be badly needed in the event of raids. In Blyth Willie Allan too was critical of the lack of ARP equipment in the town and the Council took this up with both the County Council and the Government. Houghton le Spring Labour Group actually backed Richardson's protests to Durham County Council and the Home Office about the lack of funding for 'bomb-proof shelters', and his attack on profiteering in shelter materials during the Munich crisis.[32]

Piratin's account states that the CP was the only political party in Stepney campaigning for effective shelters and ARP precautions. It is not so clear that this was also the case in the North East. These three Council Labour groups do not appear to have been as behind the curve as Piratin claims the Stepney Group was, but the Communist councillors seem to have been the more active in terms of resolutions of protest at central government inaction. At the same time the support they were given by their Labour colleagues, not a normal occurrence, suggests that they were pushing at an open door over ARP. There were other issues besides the management and quality of ARP resources. The NUWM had a national campaign to promote civil defence and air raid shelter construction as public works measures to reduce unemployment. Ancrum became a member of the Council Works Committee overseeing local defence construction work, important for an NUWM leader because the movement had also successfully campaigned for this work to be done at trade union rates, and for the jobs to be advertised at labour exchanges so as not to exclude the unemployed.[33]

Attempts were also made to use the Council chambers as vehicles to oppose the Government's introduction of a limited conscription to the armed forces. In April 1939 it was announced that men aged 20 and 21 would be called up for six months military training. Conscription at even this level was unprecedented in peacetime and it was fiercely opposed by all sections of the Labour Party; speakers at May Day rallies throughout the North East denounced it. A prominent feature was suspicion of the motives of the government given that it had never shown active resistance to fascism. South Shields Council Labour Group described conscription as a 'complete shackling of the workers' and Labour speakers close to the CP joined the Party in condemning this 'step towards fascism in this country'. Similarly in June 1939 Allan proposed, and lost, a motion condemning conscription as unnecessary if the correct foreign policy was carried out, and that its introduction 'was not aimed at fascist aggression in Europe, but at the trades union and democratic movement in this country'. However once war was declared three months later Richardson was one of those Communists who quickly volunteered for military service.[34]

Summary

The relative success of the CP in Blyth local elections has been attributed to the 'localised sociological conditions' of the Croft Ward. By this is meant a small and close-knit community in terraced streets with a shared occupational culture of the colliery and the docks. Similarly some Party writers attributed their occasional electoral achievements to the nature of the communities in coal mining areas, which would describe Houghton le Spring although Felling was more occupationally mixed. Piratin in Stepney believed that Party local electoral success depended on its consistency: the same candidates worked the same wards over time, and this was certainly the case in Blyth and Felling. It is likely that all these factors were relevant but the crucial one is surely the common record of the candidates as well-known NUWM campaigners. After all Blyth, Felling, and Houghton le Spring were hardly unique in the North East in socio-economic terms, and nor were they the only towns where the Party fielded local election candidates. Indeed if, as seems likely, the picture of an NUWM background for Communist councillors can be generalised, it points to a political effect of the NUWM that should be recognised by historians.[35]

These Communist councillors were indeed, as a post-war writer put it, 'shop stewards of the streets'. They worked tirelessly on behalf of their constituents in what was essentially an extension of their roles in the NUWM. As with the NUWM they tried to provide a context of political analysis and action for their constituents' difficulties. To a large extent they were the ideal CP role models of the time: grown in their communities and sharing their privations, selflessly active, effective negotiators and open-air speakers, natural leaders whose abilities were honed through Party training and education. The Council minutes tend to suggest that the gains that can be directly attributed to them were comparatively small ones, but, as was pointed out earlier, their effect on people living on the breadline should not be dismissed. They also show a continuous and necessary NUWM-style pressure around public works and employment, housing, nutrition and the roles of key local agencies as well as central government. It is also worth pointing out that their efforts to reform Council procedures over openness to the public, tenancy allocations and employment practice were ahead of their time; a points system for housing allocation for example was not introduced by North East Councils until after the Second World War. Nevertheless these 'shop stewards of the streets' were not operating in a purely local context.[36]

Although the CPGB by 1936 at least had a clear idea of the political function of its councillors as builders of progressive alliances this was not realistic for the North East. Electoral alliances with the local Labour Parties were not going to happen; indeed, often Labour did not even bother to respond to the CP overtures. In the Council chambers it was almost a routine, for several years, for these councillors to fail to secure even a seconder for many of their motions. Where the Communist councillors in the North East did gain support it was generally over issues of a recognisably trades union nature, or over ARP and conscription outside war time where their stance was in line with the national Labour Party. The unity achieved at least temporarily in the Scottish and Welsh 'Little Moscows' could be held up as a national example by the Communist leadership but it could not be generalised. It can only be speculation to suggest that but for the outbreak of war these comparatively improved relations might have matured into anything stronger.

Breadin and Ancrum were first elected on 'class against class' platforms and increased their votes later, whilst Richardson was elected after that sectarian policy had ended but still found rejection by the Labour Group. This suggests that CP policy was much less important in these local elections than the campaigning and casework records of the individuals standing for the Party. This is borne out by events after 1939. During the war Ancrum served as an ARP Warden in Felling and died suddenly in 1946. Labour won his seat back in the subsequent election and continued to hold it easily; the CP appears to have given up contesting it at elections after 1951. 'Lieutenant Tommy Richardson', as he was billed, won 4,500 votes but lost his deposit for a Sunderland seat in the 1945 General Election. He was the only Communist parliamentary candidate in the North East. He resigned from Houghton le Spring UDC on health grounds in 1949, and again Labour recaptured and held his seat. The electoral support these NUWM leaders had attracted could not be translated into support for the Communist Party as such.[37]

Local government elections were suspended for the duration of the World War, so when an elected member resigned or died the convention was that a nominee of the same party would take up the seat without an election being held. Allan resigned from Blyth Council in 1944 for a full-time post with the Northumberland Miners' Association and his seat was taken by the Communist miner Robert Waters. In 1945 both Breadin and Waters were re-elected in Croft ward, although Waters lost in 1947. Breadin was also re-elected to Northumberland County Council in 1946 but by 1948, in the teeth of the Cold War, he had lost both seats and that was the end of Communist representation in Blyth.[38] It was due to the work of the NUWM in the 1930s, and particularly its talented local leaders, that a Communist presence was achieved in these Labour strongholds.

Notes

1   *Newcastle Evening Chronicle* 5 March 1934; *Heslop's Local Advertiser* 20 July 1946 (GLS); Jim Ancrum,'The W.I.R. and the Dawdon Lock-Out' *Labour Monthly* 9 (1929 pp. 555-558); John McIlroy, Barry McLoughlin, Alan Campbell and John Halstead, 'Forging the Faithful: The British at the International Lenin School' *Labour History Review* Vol 68 No1 (April 2003 pp. 99-129); Alan Campbell and John McIlroy, 'Reflections on the Communist Party's Third Period in Scotland: The Case of Willie Allan' *Scottish Labour History* 35 (2000 pp. 33-55); *Blyth News* 3 June 1926.

2   For the number of councillors see Noreen Branson, *History of the Communist Party of Great Britain Vol. III 1927-1941* (London: Lawrence and Wishart 1985, p. 146).

3   *Resolution on the NUWM and Municipal and Parliamentary Elections* (WCML: Report of the 7th National Conference of the NUWM 1931); *Policy of the NUWM in Parliamentary and Municipal Elections* Headquarters Circular 31 1933 (LHASC: CP/IND/HANN/01/06); Headquarters Circular D5 14 August 1934 (MML: NUWM Bulletins and Circulars).

4   Andrew Thorpe, 'The Membership of the Communist Party of Great Britain 1920-1945' *Historical Journal* vol 3 no 43 (2000 pp. 777-800); John Stevenson and Chris Cook, *The Slump: Society and Politics During the Depression* (London: Jonathan Cape 1977, p. 308).

5   *Shields News* 2 November 1932 and 30 October 1934; *Newcastle Journal* 2

November 1932 and 27 March 1934. One exception was William Carr, who stood as an NUWM candidate in North Shields in 1934.

6   *Daily Worker* 1 February 1934; *Heslop's Local Advertiser* (GLS) 18 October 1935 and 18 May 1946; Don Watson, 'Self-Help and Aid for Spain: The Hawick Workers' Mill 1936-1939' *Scottish Labour History* 34 (1999 pp. 119-124); Joyce Holliday, *Silverdale People* (Stafford: Staffordshire Library Service 1996); Phil Piratin, *Our Flag Stays Red* (London: Lawrence and Wishart 1978, p. 35); Charles Webster, 'Health, Welfare and Unemployment During the Depression', *Past and Present* 105 (November 1985 pp. 204 – 230).

7   *Blyth News* 19 October 1933; *Heslop's Local Advertiser* (GLS) 18 October 1935.

8   Chris Williams, *Democratic Rhondda: Politics and Society 1885-1951* (Cardiff: University of Wales Press 1996, p. 186); Minutes of Houghton le Spring Urban District Council 23 February 1937 – 2 November 1937 (TWAS: UD/HS/1/14-15).

9   Minutes of Blyth Council 14 December 1933 – 9 January 1936 (NCRO: NRO 00880/59-61).

10   Minutes of the Felling Urban District Council 5 January 1937 and 22 February 1937 (TWAS: UD.FE/A/1/22); Minutes of Blyth Council 22 September and 8 October 1936 (NCRO: NRO 00880/61).

11   Letter from Eric Edney to Wal Hannington 4 October 1940; Headquarters Committee letter 24 April 1943 (LHASC -CP/IND/HANN/01/02 and 07); *Blyth News* 26 July 1937; Minutes of Blyth Council 9 November 1936 (NCRO: NRO 00880/61).

12   Minutes of the Felling Urban District Council 3 March 1936, 3 May 1938 and 27 September 1939 (TWAS: UD.FE/A/1/22); *Heslop's Local Advertiser* (GLS) 16 February 1934.

13   Minutes of Houghton le Spring Urban District Council 22 September, 3 November and 1 December 1936; 20 April 1937 (TWAS: UD/HS/1/14-15); *Durham Chronicle* 9 April 1937.

14   Minutes of the Felling Urban District Council 4 February 1936 (TWAS: UD.FE/A/1/22); *Heslop's Local Advertiser* (GLS) 14 February 1936.

15   Minutes of the Durham Miners' Association Executive Committee 14 July 1931 (DCRO: D/DMA Acc. 2157 (D) 208); *Daily Worker* 25 March 1934; Piratin, *Our Flag Stays Red*, p. 56.

16   Report of the 7th National Conference of the NUWM 1931 (WCML); Stuart Macintyre, *Little Moscows: Communism and Working Class Militancy in Inter-War Britain* (London: Croom Helm 1980, p. 172).

17   Minutes of the Felling Urban District Council 7 February and 7 March 1939 (TWAS: UD.FE/A/1/22); Minutes of Houghton le Spring Urban District Council 22 February 1938 (TWAS: UD/HS/1/14).

18   Williams, *Democratic Rhondda* (p. 175); Piratin, *Our Flag Stays Red* (pp. 57-8).

19   *Heslop's Local Advertiser* 13 September 1935 (GLS); George Hardy, *Those Stormy Years* (London: Lawrence and Wishart 1956, p. 224); Minutes of Houghton le Spring Urban District Council 5 January 1937, 7 September 1937 (TWAS: UD/HS/1/14).

20   *Durham Chronicle* 2 April 1937; *Sunderland Echo* 10 July 1935; letter in *Blyth*

News 12 December 1938.

21   *Blyth News* 21 September 1929 and 19 October 1933; *Daily Worker* 25 March 1934; *Newcastle Journal* 31 January 1933.

22   Minutes of Blyth Council 8th March, 14th June, 12th and 18th July 1934 (NCRO: NRO 00880/59).

23   Branson, *History of the Communist Party of Great Britain Vol. III* (p. 146); *Shields News* 7 and 12 October, 3 December 1936.

24   *Blyth News* 22 November and 2 December 1937.

25   *Blyth News* 20 December 1937 and 17 November 1938.

26   See Campbell and McIlroy,' The Case of Willie Allan' (pp. 46-47); *Blyth News* 15 November 1937. Breadin was definitely in the CP by 1945 when again he was elected in Croft (*Newcastle Journal* 2 November 1945).

27   *Report of the Central Committee to the Fifteenth Party Congress* (London: Communist Party of Great Britain 1938 pp. 12-13); Editorial: 'The Work of the Communist Councillor' *Party Organiser* 2 (August 1938 pp. 1-3 - NLS); Kevin Morgan, Gidon Cohen, and Andrew Flinn, *Communists and British Society 1920-1991* (London: Rivers Oram Press 2007, p. 111).

28   *Durham Chronicle* 24 July 1936 and 9 April 1937; Huw Beynon and Terry Austrin, *Masters and Servants: Class and Patronage in the Making of a Labour Organisation; The Durham Miners and the English Political Tradition* (London: Rivers Oram Press 1994, p. 263).

29   Minutes of Northumberland County Council 1 February 1934 – 4 May 1939 (NCRO: NROCC/CM/CC 44 - 49). The County Council met quarterly.

30   Hymie Fagan, 'Towards the November Elections' *Party Organiser* 4 (October 1938 pp. 19-20 - NLS); G.D.H Cole, *The People's Front* (London: Victor Gollancz Left Book Club1937, p. 334).

31   *Daily Worker* 18 and 22 August 1939; on the Labour PPC see *Gateshead Labour Herald* (GLS) September 1938; letter from Richardson to Wal Hannington 9 May 1939 (MML: Hannington Papers A vii 4).

32   Minutes of the Felling UDC 2 May 1939 and 2 April 1940 (TWAS: UD.FE/A/1/22); *Newcastle Journal* 3 May 1939; *Newcastle Journal* 12 May 1939; Minutes of Houghton le Spring Urban District Council 9 August, 13 October and 1November 1938 (TWAS: UD/HS/1/15).

33   Piratin *Our Flag Stays Red* (p. 65); Minutes of the Felling UDC 22 November 1939 (TWAS: UD.FE/A/1/22); *Newcastle Journal* 5 January 1939.

34   Charles Loch Mowat, *Britain Between the Wars 1918-1940* (London 1978, p. 640); *Newcastle Journal* 2 May, 8 May 1939; Minutes of Blyth Council 23 May 1939 (NCRO: NRO 00880/64).

35   Stevenson and Cook, *The Slump* (p. 135); *World News and Views* vol 30 no18 (6 May 1950, p. 215); Piratin *Our Flag Stays Red* (p. 55).

36   The phrase is used in *World News and Views* vol 30 no18 (6 May 1950, p. 215).

37   *Heslop's Local Advertiser* 20 July 1946 and 21 May 1952 (GLS); *Sunderland Echo* 26 July 1945; Minutes of Houghton le Spring Urban District Council 20 April 1949- TWAS UD/HS/1/16).

38   *Newcastle Journal* 6 April 1948.

Chapter Ten

AGITATION IN THE APPROACH TO WAR 1938-1939

International Events

The Spanish Civil War accelerated a shift in the focus of the British left towards international affairs and the rise of world fascism. Under its policy of 'Non-Intervention' the British government refused to allow Republican Spain to buy arms for its own defence; simultaneously it ignored the flagrant breaches of the policy by Hitler and Mussolini. The British approach was to become notorious as 'appeasement', whereby Britain and France avoided confronting Fascist territorial ambitions until a world war was inevitable. This became obvious during the Munich crisis in 1938 where British Prime Minister Neville Chamberlain conceded Hitler's plan to annex the Sudetenland. The rest of Czechoslovakia became a German 'protectorate' in 1939. Hitler had an ally in quasi-fascist Japan, which invaded China in 1937 in the first phase of a planned imperial expansion.

The British left largely responded by pressing for the policy of 'collective security'. According to this the two remaining European democracies – Britain and France – should agree a pact with the Soviet Union for mutual assistance against aggression by Germany and Italy. Although this proposal originated with the Soviet Union and so was obviously pushed by the Communist Party, it had a resonance too with those who were not pro-Soviet, including mainstream Labour and others such as the Independent MP and feminist campaigner Eleanor Rathbone. It was believed that such a collective stand would deter further fascist expansion, but the British government never showed any real interest in pursuing it. The opinion of the left was that the Conservatives were more concerned about imaginary threats from the Soviet Union than the genuine threats from fascism.[1]

The perceived urgency of the situation is reflected in the fact that, whereas in 1936 even the mainstream labour movement was organising meetings against the Means Test and the Unemployment Regulations, from 1937 the topic for the public meetings of the left was almost invariably foreign affairs. This is clearly seen in the Durham Miners' Gala and May Day rallies in the region. Spain, appeasement, collective security with the Soviet Union, and as we have seen the oppressive nature of peacetime conscription were the dominant themes across County Durham in 1939; similarly in 1938 and 1939 at both the major Labour and Communist Party public meetings and May Days in Felling, Blaydon and Blyth.[2]

Those former NUWM activists who were still politically involved when they returned from Spain also seem to have concentrated their public efforts on the international situation. Frank Graham spoke as a former International Brigader on the need for diplomatic agreements with Russia at Horden May Day. He also addressed meetings on Spain until the end of the Civil War, on at least one occasion with former Brigader and Gateshead NUWM activist Dick Hearn. Sam Langley, like Graham, was prominent in the Wounded and Dependants' Aid Committee, which raised funds to assist disabled International Brigade veterans and the families of those killed. This was a major campaign in the North East and thus another demand on the activist, but nevertheless it was taken up with commitment and some success.[3]

Therefore it is not surprising to find less public campaign work on unemployment being carried out by the regional NUWM at this time than in previous years. An interesting example of this was Blaydon. In April 1938 Labour left-winger Steve Lawther and Communist Charlie Woods spoke at a public meeting to call for a united front against the 'pro-fascist foreign policy' of the government. The previous month, in the same hall, local Labour MP William Whiteley had held a meeting for those affected by the new Means Test regulations, and having taken the details he took up their cases with the Minister of Labour. This almost amounted to a role reversal: in the same town, the NUWM activist was dealing with foreign affairs and the MP was dealing with benefits legislation and issues. It was recognised at the time that all this was having an effect on political work in other areas. At the beginning of 1939, for example, the British Communist bulletin *Party Organiser* admitted that recently 'international events forced domestic issues into the background. Unemployment is not receiving the attention it deserves either by the Party or by the labour movement in general'. This, then, was the political context in which the unemployed movement in the region worked until war finally broke out. Nevertheless the movement still pursued its traditional concerns.[4]

Winter Relief and Carrying the Coffin

We have seen that the higher coal and fuel costs that winter brought for the unemployed meant that agitating for grants of additional winter relief was a regular issue for the NUWM. During 1937 Hannington discovered that the new UAB regulations, those delayed after the last Hunger March, would mean the end of the discretion that had always been given to the Boards of Guardians and then to the PACs to grant this additional payment. It was eventually clarified that the UABs would have the discretion to grant additional winter payments where local officers agreed that an applicant faced hardship, but only in accordance with a low national scale that was not related to the rising cost of living.[5] The government seemed to be reviewing the allocation of additional winter relief; and benefits levels themselves were not keeping pace with inflation. The effects of the delayed changes to the unemployment regulations originally scheduled for 1936 were also now being felt. In the past all this would have certainly been enough cause to organise a Hunger March. This did not happen though; the memoirs of Harry McShane mention that a decision was taken not to organise one in 1938 but he does not explain why.[6]

There is a possible explanation for this if we recall that there was always a wider context, another agenda, for the 1930s Hunger Marches besides the immediate issues of government unemployment policies. As we have seen 1932 was also about opportunities to condemn the Labour Party, the ILP and the TUC. 1934, in contrast, was also about establishing a united front with the ILP and with the Labour and trade union left. The 1936 March, in line with the popular front, sought to build unity with the mainstream labour and trades union movement, as both the CP and the NUWM leaders believed they had begun to achieve with the mobilisation against the Unemployment Assistance Bill a year earlier. By 1938 the message, reinforced by the Executive Report to the CPGB Conference that year, was to repeat that the NUWM should seek unity in action with the local Unemployed Centres established by the TUC. The Report had called for efforts to 'strengthen the NUWM and the local unemployed associations' to 'effect the closest unity of action between the local unemployed associations and the NUWM' as a medium for developing 'complete unity of all the existing unemployed organisations and their ultimate affiliation to the TUC.'[7]

In this light the decision not to organise a Hunger March in 1938 may be explicable. If unity with the unemployment activity of the official labour movement was the priority then a national Hunger March could not be on the agenda. Such 'extra-parliamentary' campaigning had been shunned by Labour and the TUC for years and so another March would hardly foster the unity with the 'official' unemployed organisations that was now being sought. The NUWM leaders were obliged to submit to or work around the requirements, expressed through the CP leadership, of the Communist International. There is evidence that these requirements did not necessarily match the strength of the movement at a given time. A good example is the imposition of a Hunger March in 1930, a year after the previous one, planned at short notice, and ignoring logistical realities. Therefore had it been deemed politically appropriate to organise a March in 1938 then surely that would have been done regardless of any other factors. It is possible that the exception illustrates the rule: in Scotland the STUC and the Labour Party, for the first time, supported the idea of a Scottish Hunger March to Edinburgh, and one took place in November 1938.

Instead of a National Hunger March the NUWM leadership promoted a series of headline-grabbing initiatives to win public support for additional winter relief. These included a 'lie-down' protest in the House of Commons and in the streets of central London; NUWM members chaining themselves to the railings outside UAB offices and the home of the Minister of Labour; a mass protest in the tea room of the Ritz Hotel in London. Demonstrations in London included the carrying of the mock coffin bearing the slogan 'He Did Not Get Winter Relief'. Although London was the main centre of this activity Hannington envisaged that winter relief protests were to be local initiatives based on ideas from the NUWM Districts.[8] Press reports of such activity in the North East are scanty but one example was Middlesbrough, where Wal Hannington described the climax of one of the demonstrations to the UAB office in 1939:

> In Middlesbrough the same day (January 20th) the unemployed marched in procession through the streets several hundred strong, to the UAB offices. They were headed by a band and their banner read: "Millions a day for guns that kill – five pence a day for a child to fill". They carried a small white child's coffin which was delivered at the UAB offices and on its side were painted the words: "An extra bob may save a child – a demand that isn't false or wild – but it seems to be you'd sooner see – their bodies on your doorstep piled!"

Middlesbrough NUWM had in fact, in an 'attempt to enlist the support of the public in their campaign for winter relief', used a member to cycle with a bag to the UAB office, whereupon a group took the replica child's coffin from the bag and delivered it to the Board room in the UAB office 'without trouble'. Initially the UAB manager had refused to meet a deputation and so the branch 'took more direct methods of protesting'. Later that week a full-size coffin was carried in a demonstration to the UAB and NUWM branch secretary John Readman did manage to lead a deputation inside to discuss local 'cases of injustice'. He later told the press that the local NUWM had been thanked by the UAB for their work in 'several reconsidered cases' of winter relief applications.[9]

We have seen John Longstaff's account of how his Stockton contingent had carried a coffin with the slogan 'He Died of Starvation' at the end of the1934 Hunger March. He also described how they were used in the North, both as symbols of the effects of poverty and as focal points for an effective event. He recalled too the strategy the marchers of 1934 who were experienced demonstrators used to thwart police efforts to remove the coffin:

> … what they did was, they made these coffins out of slits of bamboo and cardboard and the cardboard was painted on one side, black. On the other side there would be a slogan, so immediately the police had broken up a coffin, within seconds, men were carrying parts, which the police didn't understand were parts of another coffin, and were now assembling these coffins again and, as such, this perplexed the police. How the hell did we get these, they didn't realise and I suppose they still don't know how those coffins were made, but there must have been at least half a dozen of those coffins that had been carried and, of course, the weather had damaged and broken some up but we are talking of London and it was the first time, as far as I understand, that the people in the south, especially the London people who had seen the coffin paraded in the manner that it was paraded …

He had learned that this was the result of police reactions to the coffin being used in demonstrations in his home area:

> … Also, little did I realize, it had become a symbol of the North, all these coffins and, of course, the police up North had broken these up, again because they became the centre point of the march, the demonstration or the meeting and, so long as a coffin was carried, then the men would march, the men would keep in discipline but the moment the coffin wasn't there, then the police could start breaking you up all over and this was one of the other reasons why they became almost fascist minded.[10]

In South Shields the police certainly took against 'coffin' demonstrations in the way John Longstaff recalls. Local Communists and NUWM activists had long referred to the Chief Constable there as 'our local Mussolini' on account of his reluctance to permit marches by radical organisations. It was claimed that South Shields was the only town in the North East where this happened. In the summer of 1939 the NUWM branch reacted to government advice to the public to stock up on food for emergency use in the event of war. They made the point that 'the unemployed should be enabled to purchase emergency food supplied for use in war time', which was a way of looking out for their interests within a critique of war preparations. When they marched from their meeting in the Market Square to the UAB office though 'the black coffin of the South Shields branch of the NUWM was a noticeable absentee'. The Chief Constable had permitted the march but banned the carrying of the coffin they had planned. In August 1939 the National Council for Civil Liberties took this up with the Chief Constable of South Shields, querying the legal basis for his banning marches under the Public Order Act. By September, of course, war had been declared and the attention of all concerned was presumably elsewhere.[11]

The North East NUWM made good use of sympathetic local MPs to raise the issues about the effect of unemployment regulations, payments of winter relief and the hardship consequences of conscription. Case histories were used to make points about national issues as well as to seek redress for the individuals and families concerned. Whereas the sole Communist MP Willie Gallacher had always, since his election in 1935, been a reliable parliamentary ally for the unemployed movement they also had some friends in the parliamentary Labour Party. A good example was Ellen Wilkinson, who in both 1938 and 1939 maintained a series of questions to the Minister of Labour about winter relief allocations. It seems that the discretion exercised by individual UAB officers over what was meant by 'hardship' varied enough on Tyneside to be a postcode-lottery when it came to grants. South Shields MP James Chuter Ede took up the case of the NUWM branch in the town when the UAB manager refused to meet their deputation about emergency food supplies.[12]

The publicity generated by the winter relief campaign enabled Donald Renton, the strategic planner behind many of the London events, to provide an upbeat report on the NUWM. This included an accurate political critique of the local trades council unemployed associations which, he claimed, had never had any meaningful leadership from the TUC and therefore 'at no time have they stood out as organs of the unemployed struggle'. Their purely local character meant they were isolated from each other and unable to make a united effort. This was in stark contrast to the branches of the NUWM which could mobilise together for a national campaign. This article went against the stream of the Party Central Committee discussions which as we have seen tended to be critical and even hostile to the NUWM. He presented the campaign as having re-energised the NUWM and argued that it gave the movement a rationale for its work with the local unemployed associations; it was to lead the 'co-operation around common action for the unemployed.'[13]

The imaginative action to publicise the campaign for winter relief envisaged by the NUWM leaders seems to have been thin on the ground in the North East, certainly in terms of press coverage. This does not necessarily mean that the local branches were dormant. A different action, but nonetheless a significant one and in keeping with the approach of the NUWM, took place in Sunderland shortly before war broke out and it is worth examining in detail. It is also part of a national picture of NUWM activity that has not been seriously explored.

The Sunderland Rent Strike

Early in June 1939 the rent collectors for the North East Housing Association arrived at the new Hylton Lane and Plains Farm Estates in Sunderland to collect the rents, which were to include a new 6d a week increase. They were probably unaware that over the previous two days well over a thousand tenants had been meeting and had agreed to withhold the increase. According to the press:

> 1,600 tenants on Sunderland's two newest housing estates ... have refused the 6d a week rent increase introduced by the NEHA ... Following meetings of tenants on the two estates last night, parties of demonstrators with banners, bells and rattles, met the rent collectors as they arrived this morning.

The demonstrators picketed the rent offices and followed the collectors about their rounds, using a gramophone horn as a megaphone to urge tenants to pay their rent but to withhold the 6d increase. Almost everyone on the two estates did that and apparently the rent strikers were good-humoured, the collectors reporting that they were not being intimidated. Several of the tenants' leaders put their case to the newspaper, stating that in 1938 the rent for a three bed-roomed house on the Hylton Lane Estate had been 8s 7d, this had been increased, and with the new proposed increase it would be 9s 10d. 'Nearly everyone on the estate is unemployed' and they could not afford it. The tenants continued that they 'hoped to force the Council to take action, since they won't do it otherwise'. Delegations from the tenants successfully petitioned Sunderland Council to hold a special meeting of the Estates Committee to hear their views. Four days into the strike this Committee agreed to recommend to the Council that it withdraw the increase on the grounds of the hardship it would cause. It was not within the powers of the Council to do this however because the NEHA would have to agree too, and so the strike continued.[14]

Complaints appeared in the *Sunderland Echo* that 'it is being turned into a political stunt ... some extreme elements are conducting a campaign on this estate'. The paper had already reported that 'W Booth, a prominent member of the National Unemployed Workers Movement', led the demonstration on the Hylton Lane Estate and that the one on Plains Farm had been led by 'Mr. J Dewar'. Billy Booth, as we have seen, was a long-standing NUWM activist in Sunderland; Jock Dewar, besides being in the NUWM was a committee member of the tenants' association and so it was probably the presence of these two individuals that prompted the complaint, to say nothing of a banner reading, 'An Injury to One is an Injury to All' in an *Echo* photograph. A left political influence was visible too on the several occasions when tenants' committee members used the approach taken in Wal Hannington's book *The Problem of the Distressed Areas,* published by the Left Book Club two years earlier, to support their case. Examples of the weekly budgets of real tenants, setting out just exactly what they had available to spend on what, were put forward to demonstrate the effects of the 6d increase would be for people living on the margin. Jock Dewar was able to quote examples of how tenants were struggling to afford vital outgoings as things were, and said that 'The provision of new houses and fresh air doesn't make up for the loss of food'. He was also able to put this in the context of the diet, income and health debates of the time, which were discussed in an earlier chapter. He used the survey evidence from the Rowntree Trust, Dr. Boyd-Orr of the Rowett Institute, and the BMA to argue that the average tenant's income was already below that needed for an adequate diet. Clearly the Sunderland NUWM at least had taken up the suggestion to use Left Book Club publications for campaign material.[15]

The Sunderland rent strike was part of what can be described as a national movement. Between June and the end of August 1939, for example, the *Daily Worker* carried reports of at least twenty-seven different tenants' disputes around the country, frequently leading to a rent strike, and in about a third of them a direct involvement by the NUWM is mentioned. Some – particularly in the East End of London – were directed at private sector slum landlords who were extracting high rents and failing to carry out even basic maintenance and repairs. Many were against rent increases imposed by Tory Councils, such as the biggest and most successful of them all, in Prime Minister Neville Chamberlain's constituency in Birmingham. Here at one point thousands of tenants, faced with the threat of legal action over non-payment of rents, marched behind a coffin carrying a 'bailiff' in effigy, which they gave a mock burial.[16]

Several Councils or private companies did resort to legal action, using bailiffs to try to serve summonses for non- payment of rent or eviction orders. There are several reports of tenants, local women, and the NUWM, standing sentry on estate entrances ready to blow warning whistles at the approach of the bailiffs. This would produce an instant picket of tenants to bar their way. There were occasional arrests and outbreaks of violence for example in Stepney, Barrhead and Enfield when police baton charges were used to clear a path for the bailiffs. Nothing like this happened during the Sunderland rent strike although the tenants' committee stated that it intended to raise money for a legal defence fund.[17]

The success of the Birmingham rent strike led to the establishment of the National Federation of Tenants and Residents, whose first national conference in July 1939 developed a Housing Charter and drafted a new Housing Act. This included increased subsidy for slum clearance, a policy also adopted by the Labour Party. The tenant victory in Birmingham had other ramifications. It gave encouragement to others, and it seems reasonable to assume that the political activists at least on the tenants' committees on the Sunderland estates would have been aware of it. The public event of the mock funeral of a bailiff – symbolising the resistance to legal action – was used in rent strikes elsewhere. Twenty years after the event Sunderland Communist Party members still remembered the coffin being carried on the rent strike demonstrations in the town and this may have been a use of the Birmingham idea. On the other hand, as we have seen, by 1939 carrying a coffin to represent the result of malnutrition was also common on NUWM demonstrations and that may also have been the source of the idea.[18]

The NEHA Secretary complained about the strike that 'there has been no outcry anywhere else, even where things are just as bad'. Certainly there seem to be no reports of rent strikes on NEHA estates elsewhere in the region, although at the start of the year a Council tenants' rent strike was threatened in Jarrow. There too slum clearance tenants could not afford their new rents. It may of course be coincidental that the Sunderland action was unique. Possibly too it was because only the Sunderland tenants included political activists who would have been aware of tenant actions in other parts of the country, and who had access to good propaganda material about income, health and housing. Besides the clear influence of the NUWM it is noticeable how the women from the estates were fully involved in the leadership. The Secretary of Plains Farm Tenants Association was Mrs. Isabella Orwin, and she with Mrs. Young and Mrs. Harty were members of the delegations that met councillors, officials and Labour Party groups. Mrs. Cotterrell from the Hylton Lane Estate Tenant's Committee was part of the deputation that led a march of 200 tenants to lobby the Estates Committee meeting at Sunderland Town Hall. On the previous day 300 women, 'some with perambulators, some with babes in arms' had marched from the Hylton Lane Estate to an open-air meeting to show their support.[19]

The women also began to take up some wider issues that were having an impact on their domestic spheres on the new estates. Mrs. Cotterrell believed that 'ever since the tenants moved into the estate everything has gone wrong'; she was concerned about the lack of shops, schools and other facilities, together with the costs of having to travel for everything. Tenants had to pay a 3d fare to the post office to collect a 10s old age pension, and 3d to get to the Public Assistance Committee to collect a 8s benefit. This experience was not uncommon in re-housing schemes in the 1930s; the collapse in agricultural land values made opportunities to build new estates on the outskirts of towns, but low-paid tenants then experienced further increases in living costs by having to travel everywhere. The women tried to take these issues up, too: Mrs. Orwin and Mrs. Young met the Sunderland Corporation Transport Manager in an unsuccessful attempt to negotiate concessionary fares for school journeys and shopping visits.[20] The background to the rent strike offers another perspective on the pressures exerted on unemployed people by government policy.

The Causes of the Dispute

The Special Areas Act had been passed in 1934 with the intention of reviving the regions sustaining high levels of long-term unemployment. The Act appointed Commissioners with a national Special Areas Fund budget of £2 million to promote the economic development of designated areas such as County Durham and Tyneside. The Commissioners were not allowed to fund public works and the Government was ideologically reluctant to direct inward investment. Therefore the Special Areas legislation and the sites for new industrial estates it created – such as in Pallion in Sunderland and on the Team Valley in Gateshead - had only a marginal effect on employment rates and the consensus of historians is that it was a hesitant and ineffective intervention.[21]

The housing issue was taken up by the Commissioner for the Special Areas, who stated in his first Report in 1935 that 'The overcrowding problem in the

Special Areas in the North East is acute and there is a pressing need for more houses to be let at low rents'. Unfortunately the National Government had, by 1933, scrapped any Exchequer subsidy for council house building. Rents for good and spacious enough accommodation continued to be beyond the reach of people who were low paid, in and out of work, or unemployed. Some Exchequer subsidy for slum clearance was available under the 1930 Housing Act, and subsidies to build to alleviate overcrowding were available under the 1935 Housing Act, but only where local authorities were making their own contributions to these projects through the rates. This, in impoverished Durham and Tyneside, they could not afford to do.

Therefore the Commissioner arranged for the constitution of the North East Housing Association as a 'Public Utility Society', a not for profit company, in December 1935. The NEHA was established for the express purpose of 'providing accommodation for members of the working classes in the North East Special Areas'. This was to be achieved by entering into arrangements with local authorities for the provision of re-housing necessitated by slum clearance and addressing overcrowding. Councils would pass to the NEHA the less than adequate subsidy they received from the Exchequer, and the NEHA could supplement this from the Special Areas Fund. The supplement would take the place of, but be no more than, the contribution from the rates that the Councils would have had to make had they built the houses themselves. By this means houses could be built and let at rents the tenants could afford.[22]

The NEHA officials explained at a meeting with the tenants the 1938 Housing Subsidies Act reduced the Exchequer subsidies available for re-housing projects, even when these were managed through public utility companies such as the NEHA. Unfortunately around half of the houses in the Sunderland project had been built before this Act, attracting a higher level of subsidy, and the rest after it, thus attracting a lower. This had increased the cost to the Association of the houses by 2s 6d per house per week, a situation that could not have been forseen in 1937. Therefore further rent increases were not unlikely. Also, the new flats to be opened in the East End of Sunderland were not attracting enough tenants, because people preferred houses, and lower rents were seen as the solution. The NEHA, with Council agreement, had pooled the total expected rental income from all the houses and arranged things so that higher rents on the Hylton Lane and Plains Farm Estates would meet the costs of the decreased subsidies and the lower rents in the East End. Those at the sharp end of the decision were not impressed. Mrs. Cotterell from the Hylton Lane Tenants' Association put the position succinctly: 'We are not here to argue the point. We are just here to tell you that we don't intend paying it'. The tenants, who were often unemployed families, had not caused the problem and refused to accept that the solution should involve further hardship on their part.[23]

A further meeting was convened in July between the NEHA, Sunderland councillors and the tenants' committees. Jock Dewar pointed out that the Ministry of Health had stated that tenants re-housed from overcrowded or slum conditions should not be financially penalised by their move; he argued for a sliding scale of rents so that the unemployed would pay less than the better off. The NEHA agreed to approach the Commissioner for the Special Areas to restore their earlier level of subsidy, and similarly the Council agreed to send a deputation to the Ministry of Health to argue this case, and to try to ensure that the future re-housing developments planned for Sunderland would attract enough central government funding to keep the rents affordable. In the short term the NEHA undertook to investigate the possibility of reviewing the maintenance charge element of the rents for the houses and new flats, in the hope of being able to withdraw the latest rent increase. Tenants maintained their campaign and when this conference was reported back to the Council two days later women were escorted from the public gallery after shouting 'we're not going to pay'. The Left Book Club Theatre Guild came from Newcastle to provide a street theatre performance of a short play originally written about the rent strikes in London, to an enthusiastic reception.[24]

Later that month and into August local politicians and senior figures in the NEHA lobbied on the tenants' behalf. A cross-party delegation of North East councillors and MPs met the Minister of Health to discuss the financing of the NEHA. In August the NEHA opened new flats in the East End of Sunderland, which became known as The Garths. A new Commissioner for the Special Areas officially opened them; he would not meet a delegation from the rent strikers but councillors made their case to him, and argued for increased subsidies to extend slum clearance and keep rents down. As one said, 'It is no good providing houses at rents people cannot pay ... the average labourer's wage in Sunderland is £2 9s a week, and if the rent is 12s there is little to live on'. Sunderland still had a large number of unemployed of whom a good many were long-term, and the major re-housing schemes still needed to meet the town's needs could not go ahead in the current circumstances. A few days later Lord Ridley, Chairman of the NEHA, met the Minister of Health and argued that new legislation was needed to restore the subsidies for slum clearance to their 1930 levels. Unless this was done re-housing in the areas of high unemployment would have to stop, because the rents would be too high. The Minister undertook to 'see what could be done'.[25]

It is not clear how the Sunderland rent strike was concluded; after the declaration of war in September 1939 the pages of the *Sunderland Echo* became completely dominated by war issues: evacuation, air raid precautions and conscription. The strike was still talked about by Communist Party members in Sunderland some twenty years later, but apparently not in the terms that would be associated with a victory.[26] It is clear that the partner organisations of the NEHA, particularly Sunderland Council, were sympathetic to the strikers' cause, and there were some efforts to find accounting ways to reduce the local rents burden, which may have worked. Possibly the strikers accepted the difficulty of resolving the issue without additional central government funding and that the NEHA was making genuine efforts to secure it. Possibly too it just petered out.

But there are two aspects in which the Sunderland rent strike can be said to be a success. After two months of their action no less a person than Lord Ridley, the government appointee tasked with chairing the NEHA, was in a face to face meeting with the Minister of Health and in effect putting the tenants' case. It is hard to imagine that this would have happened without the strike. Secondly, among the raft of emergency legislation introduced when war was declared was the 1939 Rent Restriction Act. This pegged rents at August 1939 levels in the private sector and for properties not owned by local authorities. The Council did not own the Sunderland estates and so presumably they were covered by the Act, and the tenants would have been spared the further increases they feared. The National Federation of Tenants and Residents believed that the Act was 'a tribute to the strength of the tenants' movement' which had shown the government that it could expect the same unrest as had broken out between 1914 and 1918 if rents rose as they did then.[27]

This sort of dispute, an example of what might be termed class struggle at the point of consumption rather than production, was about the household budget and a threat to the already difficult job the women had to manage the domestic spheres for which they were responsible. As we have seen, this issue had drawn women who were not working but nevertheless directly affected by unemployment, benefits and the Means Test into the struggle of the unemployed movement since the 1920s. This was another example of the NUWM taking up 'every aspect' of what was affecting poverty-stricken families.

Branch Activities and Issues

A list of NUWM branches and their secretaries in England compiled in 1938 shows 26 branches and one women's section in County Durham and Tyneside. Besides the towns that had had a presence for some time – Felling, South Shields, Gateshead, Blyth, Sunderland, North Shields and Newcastle for example – there also several branches in the colliery villages. Hetton, Murton, Boldon Colliery, Ferryhill and Coundon are among those listed, the latter being the branch with a women's section. Mr. and Mrs. Fairless were the respective secretaries, suggesting again that for women in the NUWM activism was dependent on shared politics within the family. Some surviving branch correspondence provides a snapshot of their activity towards the end of the decade.[28]

The secretary of West Hartlepool reported to Hannington that the chairman and treasurer of the branch there were 'two big Labourites' but nonetheless, apparently, valuable; the branch had problems such as lacking anywhere suitable for open-air meetings and a rapid turnover of branch officials. One reason was that work was available now for the unemployed at Catterick Camp, and they had managed to ensure that they were paid at trade union rates. Nearly 200 former members were now working there but he predicted that this would only be temporary. In the meantime they were in touch with Headquarters for legal advice for local cases and were active with advice and representation for appeals. In Bishop Auckland the branch was trying to assist those whose benefit was reduced when a family member started work, and planned to send a deputation to the local Labour Council; this, they thought, 'may be the means of wakening up the town's Rip Van Winkles'. During that same summer before the war the branches in Murton and Hetton were being formed or re-formed, obtaining premises ('3s a week including light') and liaising with the NUWM legal department. They were taking up re-housing cases and meeting with the local Council, distributing hundreds of guides to the UAB regulations, and actively helping with claims.[29]

As was mentioned in the previous chapter, the NUWM had a national campaign to promote civil defence and air raid shelter construction as public works measures to reduce unemployment; as always, they campaigned for this work to be done at trade union rates, and for the jobs to be advertised at labour exchanges so as not to exclude the unemployed. West Hartlepool, as it seems from this correspondence, had some success here and so did the Barnard Castle Branch. It received a formal commitment from the government that recruitment for labouring work resulting 'from the international crisis' would be done through the labour exchanges. In Gateshead UAB officials blamed 'Communist propaganda' when 200 unemployed men 'swarmed into the ground floor of their office' in a protest against the rates offered for ARP labouring work. This action was the 'culmination of some days of agitation, writing on pavements and the distribution of leaflets'.[30]

There are other examples of the movement reacting to very local grievances and issues. One came up in Hetton in late autumn 1938. It appears that a woman who was the Secretary of the Hetton and District Ratepayers' Association – opponents since the1920s, of course, of relief on the rates – was reported to have stated at a meeting that the local unemployed were workshy, not interested in finding jobs, and the cause of high rates. After addressing a meeting at the Hetton Miners' Hall Tommy Richardson ('Tyneside District Organiser of the NUWM') led a procession of 200 unemployed men to the woman's home. The police presence was a token one because 'there was no rowdiness'. On their arrival she admitted Richardson and members of the NUWM and the procession into her home for a meeting. Later they emerged and Richardson satisfied the waiting crowd that her views had been distorted and that she was not blaming the unemployed themselves for their situation. This tactic of a march to the home of a particular figure had been used by the NUWM in Sunderland many years earlier, and also in Stockton; it seems that her business had been subject to a boycott into the bargain.[31]

The mass walk-out from the Ministry of Labour Camp at Hamsterly was mentioned in the previous chapter. South Shields NUWM responded to it by declaring that it would seek assurances that the 40 local men who participated would not face reductions in benefit as a result. Earlier in the year Tommy Richardson and Billy Booth had tried to make use of a royal visit to Tyneside, in which the monarch was accompanied by the Minister of Labour. They were unsuccessful in lobbying their majesties to intercede with the Minister to grant them a meeting to discuss unemployed issues. In August 1939 in Newcastle, as we have seen, Jimmy Ancrum was leading a campaign against moves by the Unemployed Assistance Board to compel unemployed youths to decorate an unemployed centre in the city or lose their benefits. He won support from the prospective Labour Prospective Parliamentary Candidate for Central Newcastle, a Labour Party District Secretary, the Northumberland Miners Association and the AEU. The issue was that under the guise of training 23 young men had been required to paint the building and to Ancrum this was just another example of the 'slave camp' principle. He and his allies were pressing for trade union rates and conditions for those affected, and he reported that a 'strong branch of the NUWM has been built up for this'. This suggests again that local branches sprang up in response to a specific issue and most likely disappeared when the issue was resolved. Ancrum, Sam Watson of the DMA, and the Newcastle

Central Labour Party Secretary convened a conference, 'in spite of the international unrest' to press the TUC to take action against compulsory unpaid work projects masquerading as training schemes.[32]

The 1939 Labour Party Conference agreed a resolution that included clauses in line with NUWM policy: increase pressure on the government to abolish the training camps, increase benefit scales, and replace the Means Test with the principle of work at trade union rates or full maintenance. In fact Sam Watson, who moved the resolution on behalf of the Miners' Federation, told the conference that in County Durham the trade unions had:

> ... found valuable co-operation with the National Unemployed Workers Movement. We have found on the question of unemployment and on the question of fighting the Means Test, that this co-operation and pooling of ideas has not done anything but good for the people for whom it was intended to do good, namely the unemployed men and women and their dependents.

Watson was probably drawing on his work with activists like Ancrum as well as the sympathy of the Labour left towards the NUWM to make this point. He continued that if the movement was serious about unemployment then its organisations should consider 'some method of applying force by the working-class movement' to achieve its aims. This may have been another reference to the industrial action he had raised at the TUC Conference in 1936, but if so he was much less explicit. In adopting the resolution Conference did agree that it must be 'pressed with all the vigour of which the working-class movement is capable' but they did not discuss what exactly that might mean. The resolution left it up to Labour's National Executive to produce a plan of action with the TUC. At the final TUC Conference before the war delegates rejected a resolution to convene a conference of all unemployed associations and the NUWM with a view to building a single unemployed organisation under the TUC. This motion was obviously CP-inspired and reflected the Party leadership's approach to the NUWM. Instead the Conference urged the TUC to appoint a full-time organiser for the trades council unemployed associations to make them more effective. This of course was several years after the TUC had encouraged its affiliated trades councils to organise these associations. Renton's point about the lack of national leadership clearly had substance, and this Conference decision seems to have concentrated more on the organisational weakness of the associations rather than their direction.[33]

Peace-Time Conscription

The previous chapter looked at how the left in Britain reacted to the introduction of peace-time conscription. Young men who were called up could appeal to a local Military Training (Hardships) Committee to be excused or to have their service deferred on the grounds of the hardship their absence would cause their families. These Committees often involved representatives from the Courts of Referees. The NUWM on Tyneside seems to have taken the lead in seeing an opportunity here. Early in June 1939 Billy Booth in Sunderland wrote to Hannington on behalf of the District to ask 'what are the chances of our movement asking for the right to represent at these Committees?' Representing appellants was familiar territory for the movement and, given that the NUWM had secured the status of a bona fide organisation to represent at the Court of Referees, surely the same should apply to the Military Training Committees. In this way the NUWM could participate in opposition to peace-time conscription and at the same time 'the young men and their dependents shall find protection in our movement'.

In the course of June Tyneside District produced a covering letter for use with these Committees as well as a booklet setting out how to approach an appeal. The booklet had been produced on Tyneside in response to requests for material to help young men called up, and the recognition that this was a national issue. It covered issues such as how to organise an appeal, obtaining expenses for witnesses, and understanding the Committee rules of procedure. The aim was to postpone call-up where it could be demonstrated that hardship would be caused. As the District put it, 'One of the most important ways in which the movement must fight Chamberlain's use of the Conscription Act against the working class is on the question of hardship ... militiamen must be assured now that the movement is prepared to fight for their dependents'. According to NUWM Headquarters the publication attracted interested attention from individuals and from trade union branches around the country.[34]

Finally it should be mentioned that in 1939 the NUWM secured one of its more unsung victories. The Ministry of Labour had never published information or guidance about claims and the claims process; no leaflets, no posters, no information either about the additional grants that were available. As an NUWM leader put it, 'legal rights defined in the Act are treated as official secrets'. The NUWM had long been campaigning against this and just before the war the Ministry agreed to display posters in the labour exchanges about the additional benefits available. Successes like this, although comparatively small perhaps in the scheme of things, still represented progress for claimants as well as stages in the evolution of modern public services.[35]

The End of an Era

By the end of 1938 unemployment, even in the mining and shipbuilding towns of the North East, was noticeably lower than in previous years. In the areas of traditional heavy industry government contracts for war production were generating an employment revival, albeit one that remained patchy. This was bound to have an effect on NUWM recruitment alongside the diversion of activists' attention towards international events. Nevertheless we have seen that the organisation still had active campaigners in the North East. The last National Conference of the NUWM took place in 1939. As was mentioned in a previous chapter the organisation permitted itself some justified praise for the role played by its members in the struggle in Spain. It also pledged to resist any resentment that might grow amongst the unemployed about the Jewish refugees from Germany, Austria and Czechoslovakia obtaining work; this campaign had already been taken up by the Middlesbrough NUWM. Despite this the Conference was not complacent. There were 140 delegates but of these only 7 were women, prompting the critical observation that 'only a small number of our branches have attempted to create women's sections'. The fact that 52 of the delegates had been members for at least five years, and 62 had been members for up to a year suggests that the activists were drawn from the long-term unemployed, and that problem was persistent despite the beginnings of an armaments boom. However it was also recognised that 'the majority of the unemployed are still unorganised'. The movement clearly believed that it still had work to do.[36]

Soon after the declaration of war in September 1939, though, NUWM Headquarters decided to 'suspend the organisation for the duration' on the grounds that there would be no 'unemployment in the sense that provides a basis for a movement like the NUWM'. Contacts would be maintained, however, because mass unemployment could be predicted to emerge after the war as it had done in 1920, and the movement would be needed once more. The historian of the NUWM has concluded this decision was more to do with war time politics and lack of headquarters personnel than anything else. Unemployment did not exactly disappear overnight after the outbreak of war and the sorts of issues taken up by activists did not either. However the campaigning roles that were pursued by the members or former members of the NUWM in the early years of the war deserve to be the subject for another detailed study. In 1943 the decision was taken to formally disband the organisation, and the NUWM leaders made a declaration that can be taken as an epitaph:[37]

> We know that not a single concession has ever been granted by any government to the unemployed over the last twenty-three years which has not been the result of the agitation and work of our movement.

This is a suitable point to assess what the unemployed movements had achieved in the North East since those lobbies and demonstrations in 1920.

Notes

1   Susan Pedersen: *Eleanor Rathbone and the Politics of Conscience* (New Haven: Yale University Press 2004, pp. 280-282). For an account of this period see Archie Potts, *Zilliacus: A Life for Peace and Socialism* (London: Merlin Press 2002).

2   *Newcastle Journal* 8 May 1939; *Heslop's Local Advertiser* 12 October 1938, 12 May, 6 June and 14 July 1939; *Blaydon Courier* 6 and 13 May 1938; *Blyth News* 5 May 1938.

3   *North Mail* 26 January 1939; Poster for Bigg Market Meeting 12 February 1939, Beamish Museum; *Newcastle Journal* 8 and 19 May 1939; *Daily Worker* 18 July 1939. The scale of the sum raised by the DMA for this fund was unprecedented; see Lewis Mates, 'Durham and South Wales Miners and the Spanish Civil War', *Twentieth Century British History* Vol 17 No3 (2006, pp. 373-395).

4   *Blaydon Courier* 15 April, 11 and 18 March 1938; Donald Renton, 'The Fight Against Unemployment', *Party Organiser* Vol 1 No 6 (January/February 1939, pp. 21-25 – NLS).

5   Wal Hannington, *Never On Our Knees* (London: Lawrence and Wishart 1967, pp. 320-324).

6   Harry McShane and Joan Smith, *No Mean Fighter* (London: Pluto Press 1978, p. 235).

7   *Report of the Central Committee to the 15th Party Congress* (London: Communist Party of Great Britain 1938, pp. 24-25).

8   Richard Croucher, *We Refuse to Starve in Silence: A History of the National Unemployed Worker" Movement 1920-1946* (London: Lawrence and Wishart 1987, pp. 190-193); Wal Hannington, *Never On Our Knees* (pp. 324-329); *Northern Echo* 21 January 1939.

9   Wal Hannington, 'Black Coffins and the Unemployed' *Fact Magazine* 15 May 1939 p. 48; *Newcastle Journal* 21 January 1939; *Northern Echo* 21 and 23 January 1939.

10   John Longstaff, interview with Duncan Longstaff. John returned to London after his service in Spain and it could be that he has mixed up the demonstrations here. Hannington also refers to such police reactions to the coffin but in London in 1939 – see his *Never On Our Knees*, p. 327

11   *Daily Worker* 24 September 1932; *Shields Gazette* 12 and 14 July 1939; *North Mail* 13 July 1939; MML: Hannington Papers A viii correspondence 15 August 1939.

12   Hansard, House of Commons Debates 23 June 1938 Vol 337 cc1239, 9 and 16 February 1939 Vol 343 cc 1106 and 1871; 20 July 1939 Vol 350 cc750.

13   Donald Renton, 'The Fight Against Unemployment', *Party Organiser* Vol 1 No 6 (January/February 1939, pp. 21-25 – NLS.)

14   *Sunderland Echo* 5, 6, and 9 June 1939.

15   *Sunderland Echo* 5, 7 and 15 June 1939.

16   *Daily Worker* 2 June to 29 August 1939; on Birmingham see *Daily Worker* 2, 3, 19 and 20 June 1939.

17   *Daily Worker* 8 and 28 June, 17 August 1939; *Sunderland Echo* 8 June 1939.

18   *Daily Worker* 14 and 17 July1939; information from Mr. Billy Vincent, who joined the Sunderland branch of the Communist Party in 1958.

19   *North Mail* 5 February 1939; *Sunderland Echo* 8 and 9 June 8 1939.

20   *Sunderland Echo* 8 June and 29 July 1939.

21   Noreen Branson and Margot Heinemann, *Britain in the 1930s* (London: Granada Publishing 1973); Alan Booth, 'An Administrative Experiment in Unemployment Policy in the Thirties' *Public Administration* Vol.56 (summer 1978, pp. 139-58).

22   *First Report of the Commissioner for the Special Areas* (London: Ministry of Labour 1935, p. 32); *Second Report of the Commissioner for the Special Areas* (London: Ministry of Labour 1936, pp. 45-6); *Third Report of the Commissioner for the Special Areas* (London: Ministry of Labour 1937, pp. 92-3).

23   *Sunderland Echo* 5, 8, 9 June 1939.

24   *Sunderland Echo* 11 and 13 July 1939; Don Watson, 'To the Head Through the Heart: the Newcastle Left Book Club Theatre Guild', *North East Labour History* No.23 (1989, pp. 3-22).

25   *Sunderland Echo* 2 and 3 August 1939.

26   Information from Mr. Billy Vincent.

27   *Daily Worker* 4 and 7 September 1939.

28   List of NUWM Branches 1938 (LHASC).

29   letter from Jas Dickenson to Hannington 16 April and 3 August 1939; letter from Harry Laight 19 June 1939; letter from Thomas Bryanhill 3 August 1939, and from George Watt 19 May 1939 (MML: Hannington Papers A viii).

30   *Daily Worker* 19 June 1939; *Newcastle Journal* 10 October 1938.

31   *Durham Chronicle* 4 November 1938.

32   *North Mail* 22 February and 24 March 1939; letter from South Shields NUWM to Hannington 21 August 1939 (MML: Hannington Papers A viii); *Daily Worker* 18, 22 and 28 August 1939.

33   *Report of the 38th Annual Conference of the Labour Party* (London: The Labour Party 1939, pp. 266-267); *Report of the 71st Annual Trades Union Congress* (London: Trades Union Congress 1939, p. 12, 134).

34   Letter from Booth to Hannington 7 June 1939; North East District covering letter for Hardships Committee 27 June 1939; North East District *Notes on Military Training (Hardships) Committees* June 1939 (MML: Hannington

Papers Avii2 and Avii7).

35   Donald Renton, 'The Fight Against Unemployment', *Party Organiser* Vol 1 No 6 (January/February 1939, pp. 21-25 - NLS); article by Hannington in the *News Chronicle* 4 August 1939 (MML: Hannington Papers Avii10).

36   On local employment see *North Mail* 4 April 1939; *Report of the 11th National Conference of the NUWM 1939* (MML: Hannington D Miscellaneous); letter about refugees in the *Northern Echo* 20 January 1939.

37   Memorandum of HQ Committee Meeting 5 September 1939; HQ Committee Circular 24 April 1943 (LHASC: CP/IND/HANN/01/07); Richard Croucher, *We Refuse to Starve in Silence* (pp. 197-200).

Chapter Eleven

CONCLUSION

Size and Influence of the Movement

We have seen that the last National Conference of the NUWM acknowledged that most of the unemployed were not organised. The principal historian of the NUWM agrees that 'at best the movement never reached more than 10% of the workless at any given time'. There is also the opinion among other historians that the NUWM 'constituted only a minute fraction of the unemployed workforce' in one account and that its activities 'were marginal to the experience of the vast majority of the unemployed' in another.[1] In terms of card-carrying membership it is true that even at its peak the movement only reached a minority of those out of work. Had it actually been a mass organisation it would have been much more difficult for the TUC leadership to push it to the sidelines. Is it accurate to say though that the NUWM was 'marginal' to the experience of the vast majority of the unemployed in the North East? Certainly the organisation, like the Communist Party, was smaller in the region than in other areas of consistently high unemployment such as Scotland and South Wales, or cities like Manchester and Liverpool. However another useful approach to evaluation may be to consider the presence, influence and effectiveness of the organisation as well as the membership figures.

The reports of activities show that there were NUWM branches across Tyneside, Sunderland, Teesside, County Durham and south Northumberland. These covered the main towns and a number of the colliery villages. There is a caveat here of course in that a keen correspondent providing regular reports creates a picture of an active branch, whereas the reality may have been less than that described. Nevertheless the main parts of the region were covered at one time or another. However some of these branches came and went rather than operating consistently, and they varied in their levels of activity or political engagement. Some branches in Newcastle in the 1920s, and West Hartlepool in 1932, are examples of unemployed groups disengaging from politics. Nick Rowell talked of the rooms in Sunderland being a place 'where the unemployed could pass the time' and just passing the time was probably what many did. Not all the North East Hunger Marchers were politically minded, by any means, or at least not when they started out.

The branches were in the same position as any local sections of a national organisation where participation is voluntary: for the most part they had to rely on the limited number of people who were prepared to be active. George Orwell wrote his famous documentary essay *The Road to Wigan Pier* after NUWM contacts had guided him around the industrial north of England. He had this to say about the organisation:

> It is a movement that has been built out of nothing by the pennies and efforts of the unemployed themselves. I have seen a good deal of the NUWM, and I greatly admire the men, ragged and underfed like the others, who keep the organisation going. Still more I admire the tact and patience with which they do it; for it is not easy to coax even a penny-a-week subscription out of the pockets of people on the PAC.[2]

Subscriptions were vital to ensure that representation would be recognised but there was the tendency for claimants to drop away when their cases had been dealt with; apart from anything else, as Orwell notes even a basic subscription challenged people on the breadline. As we have seen dire poverty was a characteristic of the movement and explains its failure to sustain a newspaper and its struggle to sell political literature. As Phyllis Short recalled, there was no point having a jumble sale because no-one had any old clothes to spare.

Branches relying on the work of just a few people are obviously vulnerable when those people move on. In North Shields for example the end of a distinct NUWM branch seems to have coincided with the departure of Walter Harrison from the town and the absences of Spike Robson when at sea. John Henderson, the Gateshead NUWM secretary, had left the area for work when he volunteered for Spain. The International Brigade too, as we have seen, drew some prominent activists out of circulation. Others will have found work when even the North East economy began to revive after 1938.[3] Those branches that did have able members who were prepared to be active sustained a presence in several towns. Felling, Blyth, North and South Shields, the Blaydon Council area and Gateshead are examples, as are Sunderland and Stockton. In these towns the NUWM had a regular and visible profile in the traditional meeting places, at least for some periods in the years under study. They were able to organise demonstrations of sizeable numbers on occasion and this was done under the NUWM banner rather than that of the official movement. Their angry clashes with the police indicate more about the attitude of the authorities than they do about the unemployed, as is suggested by the reaction of 'respectable' elements who criticised the police actions. The main phase of public demonstrations over government policies was between 1931 and 1935 after which public protest by the NUWM in the region was much less, although it did not evaporate and included the mobilisation for the 1936 Hunger March. Nor did activity dry up towards the end of the decade despite improved employment and new political campaigns demanded by the international situation.

One form of evaluation is to ask what the effect would have been if the movement had not existed. On that score the credit is clearly in balance. Like Orwell, it is impossible not to admire the commitment of those who kept the NUWM going, the unpaid working-class 'lawyers' who supported the unemployed through a hostile benefits system and took up their situation with the authorities.[4] In the North East they included men who went to prison rather than accept a court's offer to avoid it if they agreed not to take part in demonstrations. Although there were occasional problems nearly all the Hunger Marchers they led reached their destination. It is, to repeat, worth speculating as to whether Jarrow Labour Party would have decided on a march to London without the example of the previous Hunger Marches before them.

The NUWM both locally and nationally did not manage to sustain women's sections, something recognised as a weakness at the time although this assumes that the women wanted to operate in separate sections in the first place.[5] It is quite understandable that historians should consider that the NUWM was 'almost entirely male in its composition'[6] but in the North East some of the exceptions were noteworthy. Phyllis Short, Mrs. Chater, Maggie Airey and probably others too emerged as speakers and organisers; they trained through involvement in the movement and became leaders in their own right. They were part of the same political community as their husbands or families, of course, and the outcomes would probably have been different had they not been. Nevertheless they were clearly committed to drawing women into activity, even though most women in the region were not unemployed workers. There were occasions when they succeeded: low benefits, the Means Test, high rents and poor facilities all challenged the domestic manager and could provide a stimulus to action. All the unemployed demonstrations in the North East included a good proportion of women, according to the press reports, and most of the deputations included some.

Another approach to judging the influence of the movement is to consider the 'shop stewards of the streets', those Communist councillors who were elected on their records as NUWM campaigners. This aspect seems to have been overlooked by historians of the national movement. To vote for a local NUWM activist, generally a respected local campaigner, standing as a Communist instead of a Labour candidate who was probably a lodge or engineering union official was to make a choice. The NUWM cannot be said to have been 'marginal' to the experience of the unemployed in Croft ward, Blyth; they elected a local activist to the Council in 1933 and he was still returned in 1946. Ancrum and Richardson also served on their Councils for an extended period. This point should not be overdone of course because only a few local authority wards in the region returned significant votes for Communist-unemployed movement candidates. Nevertheless whether it be street meetings to watch, newspaper articles and letters to read, or stories to hear it seems fair to say that the influence of the NUWM in some areas went much wider than its own membership.

Sources of Support

It was mentioned initially that at least one historian has argued that we need to know more about the sociology of unemployed movements, who exactly it was that participated in them. It is comparatively easy to construct a profile of political activists who are recorded, quoted in documents and who are visible in other political contexts at the time. It is less easy to establish a profile of those participants who tend to be hidden in descriptive terms such as 'a large crowd of unemployed' used in newspapers, or 'unemployed workers' used in the contemporary political literature. Nevertheless to understand the organisation of the unemployed in the North East an attempt should be made.

One approach again is through the local elections. Jimmy Ancrum consistently worked West ward in Felling and was elected there. In Blyth the support for Communist candidates came from the Croft ward, whilst in North Shields support for NUWM and Communist candidates was in the Central and Dockwray wards. In addition the Bridges ward in Sunderland regularly returned the unemployed activist Jimmy Lenagh during the 1920s and early 1930s. It seems fair to assume that a good proportion of the NUWM support in those towns, even if actual membership was short-lived and temporary, came from these areas. What then were their characteristics?

In North Shields Central and Dockwray wards contained the tenements that crowded down the steep bank from there to the River Tyne. The 1931 Census for Northumberland shows that these two wards had a very high number of persons per acre, Central in particular having the highest in the borough by a very wide margin. They also had the highest ratio of persons per room. This is how overcrowding shows up in the official statistics of the time; housing in the hillside tenements was notoriously bad and it was the subject of Tynemouth Borough Council's slum clearance programme in 1934. The main occupational groups were merchant seamen, dock labourers and fishermen, with some women employed on the quay. They were the poorest of the working class in North Shields: theirs were lives of low pay, casual employment and regular periods without work or with only irregular work. This area was close to Harbour View, the traditional open-air meeting place that was itself near to Council and PAC offices.[7]

In Blyth it was Croft ward, again according to the 1931 Census, that had the highest number of people per acre in the borough, and by a significant margin. It was a neighbourhood of casually employed dockworkers, and of miners and of ship repair workers. Serious overcrowding was the case too in Felling's West ward, which had twice the population density of any of its neighbours. Again both Croft and West wards had the highest ratios of people per room, which explains the high incidence of dangerous infectious disease such as tuberculosis. These were neighbourhoods of densely populated terraces abutting either docks or railway lines. Press reports of NUWM demonstrators drawn from Stockton consistently mention the South Bank area. This, like the Bridges ward in Sunderland, was the poorest part of the town and with a reputation for poverty and the worst housing. This evidence confirms the recollection of Charlie Woods that 'our support came from the poorest areas'. What more can be brought out?[8]

We have seen that on occasion Communist Party Central Committee loyalists had a low opinion of the NUWM membership in the North East and indeed of the Party in the region too. 'Lumpen-proletarian elements' said Dave Springhall of them in 1931, and Willie Allan said much the same six years later. On at least two occasions the Chief Constable of Newcastle expressed a similarly low opinion of the local participants in the Hunger Marches; as we saw he called them 'of the lodging house type' and 'corner-boy types'. In these descriptions a politically negative label is used and a socially negative one seems to reinforce it, and so their meaning needs to be explored.

The real meaning of 'lodging house type' was described earlier and it was also set out by Orwell in 1937. He described the situation of the single man living on the usual rate of 15s a week from the PAC:

The life of a single unemployed man is dreadful. He lives sometimes in a common lodging-house, more often in a "furnished" room for which he pays six shillings a week, finding for himself as best he can on the other nine…Of course he cannot feed or look after himself properly…keeping warm is almost the sole preoccupation of a single unemployed man in winter.[9]

To repeat a point made in an earlier chapter this is not a comment on the character of those men who were in this position. Local press reports of NUWM demonstrations and of some of the Hunger Marchers sometimes mention young men being noticeable participants. Obviously young men would be attracted to a lively street event such as a demonstration and would largely have met the fitness criteria for a Hunger March. They, and young women of course, were always placed at the worst end of the benefits system and this must also be considered as a factor. Therefore a local organisation that took up their cause, as the NUWCM and the NUWM did, would attract support from them. 'Corner-boys' occupied the streets with nothing to occupy their time; as with 'lodging-house types' the derogatory term blames the victim.

What of the other derogatory term, lumpen-proletarian elements? This classically referred to the semi-criminal, or casually employed underclass of the capitalist economy, or those not only unskilled but resistant to working-class organisation and political education, and who would prove to be politically unreliable. In the eyes of a Marxist-Leninist organisation such as the Communist Party on the other hand the target recruit to the NUWM would be a trade unionist, already inculcated into the value of organisation and already with some political awareness. This is seen in the instructions to local Hunger March emphasising how participants should be selected by and representing some organised group of workers. This, and the attempt to focus on the trades council unemployed associations are examples of a political construction, so to speak, of what an unemployed workers' movement should be.

The reality of course was likely to be different. The 1939 NUWM National Conference delegates as we have seen were largely drawn from the long term unemployed, and these presumably were activists. The ordinary members or supporters could well have drifted away from union membership if their unemployment became long-term. It is revealing for example that the unemployed merchant seamen in North Shields in 1931 could not afford to keep up their union dues, although the unsympathetic attitude of the NUS towards this may have been unique to the officers of that union. As we have seen the political awareness of the North East participants in the Hunger Marches could be variable and in some cases the commitment could be slight; in a small number of cases the men selected were a problem element.

In 1934 a Newcastle councillor complained that 'people have been brought up and educated on how to get PAC funds, how to live off the funds of the City'. It did not seem to occur to him, or indeed other members of his social caste, that if people had given up on themselves in this way there might be an economic explanation. They had long since given up on seeking work that did not exist but still had to seek ways to survive. A social survey of County Durham commented in the same year that the effect of widespread and prolonged unemployment meant that people were 'living always on a bare minimum without any margin of resources or any hope of improvement' and that this led to 'feelings of depression, producing an attitude of resignation'.[10] That was certainly witnessed by the NUWM activists and the struggle against it was probably the main one they took on. As George Short in Stockton recalled:

It was terrible to watch the way unemployment would sap away at the morale, you'd see it happen to people you knew, they'd give up and become completely demoralised, there's nothing worse than unemployment when it comes to eating away at the character. The main thing with the NUWM was to get the unemployed to see political solutions, try and show them how to fight, and that way to keep alive their desire and hope.[11]

Therefore the North East NUWM could well have drawn heavily on those who had not already been associated with the labour movement in any active sense, the long-term unemployed, those in the poorest areas. Paradoxically this can be seen as a success rather than the political failure the Communist Central Committee loyalists believed it to be at the time. It also makes their achievements all the more noteworthy. The movement in the region did manage to provide opportunities for activism, organisation and political education that were not otherwise available to their supporters. This was important not just for the development of the individuals concerned but for sustaining left politics in general. The value of this was demonstrated when the British Union of Fascists attempted to organise in the region. They were prevented from doing so and do not appear to have gained a footing amongst the unemployed. As we have seen the NUWM was an important element in the anti-fascist movement in the North East, including of course its ultimate expression, service with the International Brigade.

Communists, Labour and the Unions

Those who kept the branches going were almost invariably unemployed Communists who were able to make the NUWM their main political activity. The story of the unemployed movement in the North East between the wars is, as elsewhere in Britain, also the story of the Communist Party with which it was intertwined. Although in Gateshead the ILP had a consistent role through activists like Jack Cogan for the most part it was the Communists whose efforts sustained the movement. During the 1926 miners' lockout the Party in the North East established a cadre who were small in number but high in ability; they sustained the movement in the region well into the 1930s, re-inforced by others recruited when the Means Test was implemented in 1931. The politics practised by the Communists both strengthened and weakened the NUWM when it emerged as the leader of the national movement by 1929.

In the 1920s the NUWCM was an active force in Tyneside and County Durham and the movement was by no means 'close to extinction' in the North East in the mid-1920s, as the historian of the NUWM believes can be said of the country as a whole.[12] The prospect of a national dispute in the mining industry prompted action in the Durham coalfield, in the tradition of the unemployed movement, to secure the maximum concessions from the local Boards of Guardians. The left promoted Poor Law relief applications as a counter to the government and the employers' use of the 'starvation weapon'. The defeat of the miners' lockout in 1926 was an historic low point for the working class in the region but the unemployed movement helped to keep activism alive there for the rest of the decade, protesting against cuts in benefits scales, trying to resist evictions, and advocacy on behalf of individuals.

The Communist Party obviously strengthened it, in fact probably kept it going in much of the region, by the commitment of its members. It has been argued though that dependence on the line of the Communist International was crucial in preventing the NUWM from becoming a mass organisation, 'mass' here meaning to have influence on the mass of the unemployed.[13] Certainly the evidence is that the controversies over the adoption of 'class against class' lost the unemployed movement active members in the North East when that policy was pushed through. Not long afterwards the policy risked alienating good allies in the Labour left such as Harry Bolton and George Harvey, as well as the ILP. The left in the region was not so strong that it could afford divisions like these. A collision course between the Labour and trade union leaderships and the Communist milieu was inevitable after 1926, but the understandable critique of their role by the Communists extended to the entire Labour and trades union movement with little discrimination. This was the approach of the NUWM during the introduction of the Means Test, a time when its agitation would have benefited from alliances with the left of the labour movement. This did not appear to be happening until 1935 or 1936, after which there is some evidence of co-operation between the NUWM and the mainstream movement in the region.

The position of the Communist International in the early 1930s drew a distinction between 'a trade union for the unemployed' and a political organisation. This was a false division. There were plenty of examples in the North East, from the 1920s until the outbreak of war, where representing unemployed people went alongside protest and political action. Although a large amount of the activists' time was taken up with advice and representation, this had to be done before an audience for the political ideas could be built. Later of course the position was reversed, with the lead political role for the NUWM envisaged as coming from within the official movement. Wholesale conformity to either of these approaches would have finished off the NUWM as an organisation but this was avoided through adroit moves by Hannington, secure as the respected leader of a separate movement. The local activists had to hold a balance between the realities of the unemployed they were dealing with on one hand and the political expectations of the Communist Party on the other.

Interestingly, it was the adoption of quite the opposite approach to 'class against class' that alienated active NUWM members in Blyth, including one of the few Communist councillors. The only evidence or details are in newspaper letters written by Willie Allan, the Central Committee loyalist responsible for pushing the approach in the town. Therefore it is difficult to know whether the problem was over adopting a more constructive attitude to working with the Labour Party as such, or over how that was being interpreted as submergence into leadership by the Labour Party and the TUC. Some NUWM activists in the town had been engaging with the inactivity of local Labour since the early 1920s and it is not difficult to imagine their response to having this new approach imposed upon them.

The role of the mainstream labour movement, however, deserves critical assessment too. In the North East Labour certainly did organise some demonstrations and deputations about the Means Test and the UAB. The national Labour Party did have the opportunity to at least disrupt the operation of the Means Test and to cause the government problems over it. Labour councillors in the North East were certainly angry enough to do this. The 1932 Conference rejected this approach, of course, because to mandate its members to nationally co-ordinated action in such a way ran against the culture of the organisation.

The historian of the NUWM speaks of a 'plurality' of unemployed organisations and this is true of the North East.[14] The TUC encouraged trades councils to form unemployed associations and saw them as an alternative to the NUWM. There was no consensus in the movement about the value of these associations, little leadership from the TUC and whereas those in Newcastle, Jarrow and Gateshead advised and represented claimants this work was uneven. The associations were unclear from the 1920s about their role with those who were not in unions, they did not have the public presence of the NUWM, and there seems little evidence that they were keen to pursue 'every aspect of what was affecting poverty-stricken families' in the way that active NUWM branches in the region did.

The DMA certainly represented its unemployed members and acted as a mediator with the UAB; the union's success in diffusing angry situations was noted approvingly by that body. Although Durham County Council – whose prime mover was in fact the DMA – left the field to Commissioners rather than implement government policy it did not then lead a campaign against the Commissioners' work. Although the DMA through Sam Watson posed the issue of industrial action against the Means Test regulations at the TUC Conference in 1936, once that had been rejected the union fell back on resolutions, conferences and letters to express its protests. This has been judged to be in keeping with a local coalfield tradition that was strong in solidarity but lacking in militancy.[15]

The context in which the North East NUWM had to work was one of constraints, some inevitable, some inflicted on them, and some self-imposed. Nevertheless they sustained a patchy but frequently vibrant movement. It was part of an unprecedented phenomenon in British politics: a radical unemployed organisation that operated continuously for some twenty years. That it was of the unemployed themselves and not just an effort of others on their behalf was also unprecedented. It offered support and, for some at least, opportunities to develop as well as to lobby and protest at both local and national levels. In this respect the struggles of those abandoned by the economic system between the wars can provide some inspiration to those who find themselves in a similar position today.

Notes

1   Richard Croucher, *We Refuse to Starve in Silence: A History of the National Unemployed Workers' Movement 1920-1946* (London: Lawrence and Wishart

1987, p. 203; Willie Thompson, *The Good Old Cause: British Communism 1920-1991* (London: Pluto Press 1992, p. 49); Keith Laybourn, *Britain on the Breadline: A Social and Political History of Britain 1918-1939* (Stroud: Sutton Publishing 1998, p. 28).

2 George Orwell, The *Road to Wigan Pier* (London: Penguin Books 1989, p. 77).

3 North Tyneside Community Development Project Final report vol.1: *North Shields: Working -Class Politics and Housing 1900-1977* (Newcastle on Tyne: Benwell Community Project 1978, p. 32); Don Watson and John Corcoran, *An Inspiring Example: The North East of England and the Spanish Civil War* (London: McGuffin Press 1996, p. 53).

4 The one dissenting voice is Keith Laybourn, *Britain on the Breadline*, p. 40. He claims that the success rate of the NUWM appeals before the Umpires was below the average. He does not state a source for this or take account of appeals that were excluded because of lapsed membership, an issue that exercised the NUWM Headquarters. The official record, published by the Ministry of Labour as *Selected Decisions Given by the Umpire Respecting Claims for Benefit and Transitional Payments 1930-1934* (NA: LAB 29/216) does not mention whether or not an appellant was represented.

5 This point is made by Sue Bruley, *Leninism, Stalinism and the Women's Movement in Britain 1920-1939* (New York: Garland Publishing 1986, p. 119); she questions whether in fact they did.

6 Willie Thompson, *The Good Old Cause*, p. 49; a similar conclusion is drawn in Paul Bagguley, *From Protest to Acquiescence? Political Movements of the Unemployed* (London: Methuen 1991 p. 108).

7 North Tyneside Community Development Project Final report vol.1: *North Shields: Working-Class Politics and Housing*, p. 34.

8 Census of England and Wales 1931: *County of Durham*; (London: HMSO 1932); Census of England and Wales 1931: *County of Northumberland* (London: HMSO 1932).

9 George Orwell, *The Road to Wigan Pier*, p. 74.

10 *North Mail* 2 October 1934; D. Euart-Wallace, *Report of Investigation into the Industrial Conditions in Certain Depressed Areas* (London: Ministry of Labour 1934, pp. 75-6).

11 George Short, interview with Peter Brabban 1979.

12 Richard Croucher, *We Refuse to Starve*, p. 202.

13 Alan Campbell and John McIlroy, 'The National Unemployed Workers' Movement and the Communist Party of Great Britain Revisited' *Labour History Review* Vol 73 No.1 (April 2008, p. 84).

14 Richard Croucher, 'Divisions in the Movement: the NUWM and its Rivals in Comparative Perspective' in Geoff Andrews, Nina Fishman and Kevin Morgan (eds.): *Opening the Books: Essays on the Social and Cultural History of the British Communist Party* (London: Pluto Press 1995, pp. 23-44).

15 Stephanie Ward, 'The Means Test and the Unemployed in South Wales and the North East of England 1931-1939' *Labour History Review* Vol 73 No.1 (April 2008, p. 126).

BIBLIOGRAPHY

Oral History

Len Edmondson, interview by Karen Grunzweil 1999

Len Edmondson, interview by Ray Challinor 1987

Gateshead General Strike Interview Transcripts vols. 1-3

Frank Graham, interview by Jim McGurn, 1986

Frank Graham, Imperial War Museum interview (no date)

Frank Graham, interview by Don Watson 1996

Charlie Hall, interview by Kevin Morgan (no date)

Margot Heinemann, Imperial War Museum interview 1986

John Henderson, interview by Don Watson and John Corcoran 1988

John Longstaff, interview by Duncan Longstaff (no date)

Robert Maugham, Beamish Museum interview (no date)

Bobbie Qualie, interview by Peter Brabban 1979

Bill Reynolds, interview by Don Watson and Pauline Frazer 2006

Nick Rowell, interview by Peter Brabban 1979

George Short, interview by Peter Brabban 1979

Phyllis Short, interview by Peter Brabban 1979

Charlie Woods, interview by Peter Brabban 1979

Charlie Woods, interview by Don Watson and John Corcoran 1986

Newspapers and Journals

Blaydon Courier

Blyth News

Chester le Street Chronicle

The Communist

Daily Worker

Durham Chronicle

The Mineworker

Newcastle Evening Chronicle

Newcastle Journal

New Charter

North Mail

Northern Echo

Out of Work

Shields Gazette

Shields News

Stanley and Consett News

Sunday Sun

Sunday Worker

Sunderland Echo

Unemployed Leader

Unemployed Special

Woman Worker

Workers' Life

Workers' Weekly

World News and Views

Durham County Record Office

Correspondence with Chester le Street Unemployed Association 1925-1938
Durham Miners Association Executive Minutes
North East United Front March Committee Appeal
Sam Watson Papers

Gateshead Local Studies Library

Durham Miners Association Executive Circulars
Heslop's Local Advertiser
Gateshead Labour Herald
Gateshead Labour Party and Trades Council Circulars

Labour History Archive and Study Centre

Labour Party: *Report of the 32nd Annual Conference* (1932)
Labour Party: *Report of the 38th Annual Conference* (1939)
Minutes of the Central Committee of the Communist Party of Great Britain 1930-1939
Wal Hannington Papers

Marx Memorial Library

Hannington and Brown Papers
Hannington Miscellaneous
Hannington Papers
International Brigade Memorial Archive
NUWM Bulletins and Circulars

National Archives

CAB 24/37 – CAB 24/160: Reports on Revolutionary Organisations in the United Kingdom 1919-1923
HO 144/12143: March of the unemployed to London in 1929; hunger march to London in 1930
HO 144/13864: Disturbances: Workers' Defence Leagues, the Labour League of Ex-Servicemen and other organisations
HO 144/20696: Hunger March, 1936, 29th July – 23rd October 1936
HO 144/20697: Hunger March, 1936, 27th October 1936 – 19th January 1937
KV/5/112: List of persons who fought in Spain 1936-1939
LAB 29/216: Selected Decisions Given by the Umpire Respecting Claims

for Benefit and Transitional Payments 1930-1934
MEPO 2/3071: National Hunger March 1934; police arrangements and
reports of demonstrations
MEPO 2/3091: Communist Party and National Unemployed Workers'
Movement: hunger march of 1936
MEPO 2/3097: Jarrow march to London 1936
MH 79/334: Malnutrition among the unemployed: arrangements for local
investigations 1934-35

National Library of Scotland

Party Organiser
Communist Party of Great Britain: *Report of the Central Committee to the
15th Party Congress 1938*

Northumberland County Record Office

Minutes of Blyth Town Council
Minutes of Northumberland County Council

Trades Union Congress Library

Annual Conference of Trades Councils: *Reports* 1932-1939
National Federation of Unemployed Associations: *Monthly Report* July
1934
National Federation of Unemployed Associations: *Unemployment
Hardships -Don't Struggle By Yourself* (1935)
Newcastle and District Trades Council: *Annual Reports of the Executive
Council* 1930-1939
Reports of the Annual Trades Union Congress 1932 – 1939
Sunderland and District Trades Council: *Annual Reports and Balance
Sheets* 1934 -1939

Tyne and Wear Archives Service

Copy Correspondence, Superintendent at Felling to Chief Constable of
Durham
Minutes of the Felling Urban District Council
Minutes of the County Borough of Gateshead Watch Committee
Minutes of the Houghton le Spring Urban District Council
Minutes of the County Borough of Sunderland Watch Committee
Minutes of the County Borough of Tynemouth Watch Committee
Minutes of the City of Newcastle on Tyne Watch Committee
Newcastle on Tyne Dispensary: *Annual Reports* 1931-34

Welcome Institute for the History of Medicine

Committee Against Malnutrition: *Bulletins* 1934-1939

Working Class Movement Library

National Unemployed Workers' Movement: National Administrative
Committee Minutes 1930-1936
National Unemployed Workers' Movement: Reports of National
Conferences 1931-1937

Books and Articles

Alexander, Bill: *British Volunteers for Liberty: Spain 1936-39* (London:
Lawrence and Wishart 1982)
Ancrum, Jim: 'The W.I.R. and the Dawdon Lock-Out' *Labour Monthly* No
9 (1929 p.555-558)
Andrews, Geoff, Fishman, Nina and Morgan, Kevin (eds.): *Opening the
Books: Essays on the Social and Cultural History of the British Communist
Party* (London: Pluto Press 1995)
Armstrong, Keith, and Beynon, Huw (eds.): *Hello, Are You Working?
Memories of the Thirties in the North East of England* (Whitley Bay: Strong
Words Publications 1977)
Austrin, Terry, and Beynon, Huw: *Masters and Servants: Class and
Patronage in the Making of a Labour Organisation; the Durham Miners and
the English Political Tradition* (London: Rivers Oram Press 1994)
Bagguley, Paul: *From Protest to Acquiescence? Political Movements of the
Unemployed* (London: Methuen 1991)
Barron, Hester: *The 1926 Miners' Lockout: Meanings of Community in the
Durham Coalfield* (Oxford: Oxford University Press 2010)
Baxell, Richard: *British Volunteers in the Spanish Civil War: The British
Battalion in the International Brigades 1936-1939* (London: Routledge
2004)
Beevor, Anthony: *The Battle for Spain: The Spanish Civil War 1936-1939*
(London: Weidenfeld and Nicholson 2007)
Booth, Alan: 'An Administrative Experiment in Unemployment Policy in
the Thirties' *Public Administration* Vol.56 (summer 1978 p.139-158)
Branson, Noreen and Heinemann, Margot: *Britain in the Nineteen Thirties*
(London: Granada Publishing 1973)
Branson, Noreen: *Britain in the Nineteen Twenties* (London: Weidenfeld
and Nicholson 1976)
Branson, Noreen: *Poplarism 1919-1925: George Lansbury and the*

Councillors' Revolt (London: Lawrence and Wishart 1979)

Branson, Noreen: *History of the Communist Party of Great Britain Vol III 1927-1941* (London: Lawrence and Wishart 1985)

Branson, Noreen: *History of the Communist Party of Great Britain Vol IV 1941-1951* (London: Lawrence and Wishart 1997)

Bruley, Sue: *Leninism, Stalinism and the Women's Movement in Britain 1920-1939* (New York: Garland Publishing 1986)

Buchanan, Tom: *The Spanish Civil War and the British Labour Movement* (Cambridge: Cambridge University Press 1991)

Buchanan, Tom: *Britain and the Spanish Civil War* (Cambridge: Cambridge University Press 1997)

Byrne, David: 'The 1930 "Arab Riot" in South Shields: a Race Riot That Never Was', *Race and Class* No 18 Vol 3 (1977 p.261-277)

Campbell, Alan and McIlroy, John: 'Reflections on the Communist Party's Third Period in Scotland: The Case of Willie Allan' *Scottish Labour History* 35 (2000 p.33-55)

Campbell, Alan and McIlroy, John: 'The National Unemployed Workers' Movement and the Communist Party of Great Britain Revisited' *Labour History Review* Vol 73 No1 (April 2008 p.61-89)

Carr, Raymond: *The Civil War in Spain* (London: Weidenfeld and Nicholson 1986)

Census of England and Wales 1931: *County of Durham* (London: HMSO 1932)

Census of England and Wales 1931: *County of Northumberland* (London: HMSO 1932)

Clarke, J.F. and McDermott, T.P: *Newcastle and District Trades Council 1873-1973: A Centenary History* (Newcastle on Tyne: Frank Graham 1973)

Clarke, Joe: 'The General Strike in the North East' *North East Labour History* No.10 (1976 p.4-8)

Cohen, Gidon: *The Failure of a Dream: The Independent Labour Party from Disaffiliation to World War II* (London: I.B. Tauris 2007)

Cole, G.D.H: *The People's Front* (London: Victor Gollanz Left Book Club 1937)

Colledge, Dave: *Labour Camps: The British Experience* (Sheffield: Sheffield Popular Publishing 1989)

Commissioner for the Special Areas: *1ˢᵗ Report* (London: Ministry of Labour 1935)

Commissioner for the Special Areas: *2ⁿᵈ Report* (London: Ministry of Labour 1936)

Commissioner for the Special Areas: *3rd Report* (London: Ministry of Labour 1937)

Communist Party of Great Britain: *Report of the Central Committee to the 15th Party Congress* (London: Communist Party of Great Britain 1938)

Conlin, James: *Symbol of Glass: The History of the Sunderland Borough Police Force* (Sunderland: James A. Jobling Ltd 1969)

Croucher, Richard: *We Refuse to Starve in Silence: A History of the National Unemployed Workers' Movement 1920-1946* (London: Lawrence and Wishart 1987)

Croucher, Richard: 'Divisions in the Movement: the NUWM and its Rivals in Comparative Perspective' in Andrews, Geoff, Fishman, Nina and Morgan, Kevin (eds.): *Opening the Books: Essays on the Social and Cultural History of the British Communist Party* (London: Pluto Press 1995 p.23-44).

Croucher, Richard: 'History of Unemployed Movements', *Labour History Review* Vol 73 No.1 (April 2008 p.1-19)

Davies, Sam: 'The Membership of the National Unemployed Workers' Movement 1923-1938,' *Labour History Review* Vol 57 No.1 (spring 1992 p.29-37)

Davies, Sam; 'Legal Challenges to Labour Rule: Gateshead Politics Between the Wars' *North East History* No. 41 (2010 p.10-37)

Dimitrov, Georgi: *The Unity of the Working Class Against Fascism: Speech at the Seventh World Congress of the Communist International* (London: Lawrence and Wishart 1935)

Dorril, Stephen: *Blackshirt: Sir Oswald Mosley and British Fascism* (London: Penguin Viking 2006)

Douglass, David: *George Harvey: Pitman Bolshevik* (Gateshead: Follonsby Miners' Lodge Banner Association 2011)

Euart-Wallace, D: *Report of Investigation into the Industrial Conditions in Certain Depressed Areas: Durham and Tyneside* (London: Ministry of Labour 1934)

Fagan, Hymie: 'Towards the November Elections' *Party Organiser* Vol.1 No.4 (October 1938 p.19-20)

Feiling, Keith: *The Life of Neville Chamberlain* (London: MacMillan 1946)

Francis, Hywel: *Miners Against Fascism: Wales and the Spanish Civil War* (London: Lawrence and Wishart 1984)

Francis, Hywel: 'Say Nothing and Leave in the Middle of the Night: the Spanish Civil War Revisited', *History Workshop Journal* No 32 (1991 p.69-76)

Gilbert, Bentley: *British Social Policy 1914-39* (London: Batsford Press

1970)

Graham, Frank: *Battle of Jarama 1937: The Story of the British Battalion of the International Brigade in Spain* (Newcastle on Tyne: Frank Graham 1987)

Gregory, Walter: *The Shallow Grave: A Memoir of the Spanish Civil War* (London: Victor Gollanz 1986)

Haldane, Charlotte: *Truth Will Out* (London: Weidenfeld and Nicholson 1948)

Halstead, John: 'The Reminiscences of Sid Elias', *Bulletin of the Society for the Study of Labour History* No 38 (spring 1979 p.35-48)

Hannington, Wal: *The Story of the National Hunger March* (London: National Unemployed Workers' Committee Movement 1929)

Hannington, Wal: *The Problem of the Distressed Areas* (London: Victor Gollanz Left Book Club 1937)

Hannington, Wal: 'Black Coffins for the Unemployed', *Fact Magazine* (May 1939)

Hannington, Wal: *Never On Our Knees* (London: Lawrence and Wishart 1967)

Hannington, Wal: *Unemployed Struggles 1919-1936* (London: Lawrence and Wishart 1977)

Hannington, Wal: *Ten Lean Years* (Wakefield: EP Publishing 1978)

Hardy, George: *Those Stormy Years* (London: Lawrence and Wishart 1956)

Harmer, Harry: 'The Failure of the Communists: The National Unemployed Workers' Movement 1921-39' in Thorpe, Andrew (ed), *The Failure of Political Extremism in Inter-War Britain* (Exeter: University of Exeter Press 1989 p.29-49)

Holliday, Joyce: *Silverdale People* (Stafford: Staffordshire Library Service 1996)

Hopkins, James K: *Into the Heart of the Fire: The British in the Spanish Civil War* (Stanford California: Stanford University Press 1998)

Howard, Stuart: 'Dawdon in the Third Period: The Dawdon Dispute of 1929 and the Communist Party', *North East Labour History* No.21 (1987 p.3-17)

Howell, David: 'The British General Election of 1935', *Socialist History* No. 28 (2006 p.60-76)

Jump, Jim (ed.): *Looking Back at the Spanish Civil War* (London: Lawrence and Wishart 2010)

Kingsford, Peter: *The Hunger Marchers in Britain 1920-1940* (London: Lawrence and Wishart 1982)

Klugmann, James: *History of the Communist Party of Great Britain vol 2:*

1925-1926, The General Strike (London: Lawrence and Wishart 1980)

Lawther, Steve: *Emmie Lawther: A Tribute* (Gateshead: privately published 1964)

Laybourn, Keith: *Britain on the Breadline: A Social and Political History of Britain 1918-1939* (Stroud: Sutton Publishing 1998)

Lewis, John: *The Left Book Club: An Historical Record* (London: Victor Gollanz 1970)

Macintyre, Stuart: *Little Moscows: Communism and Working Class Militancy in Inter-War Britain* (London: Croom Helm 1980)

Martin, Roderick: *Communism and the British Trade Unions 1924-1933: A Study of the National Minority Movement* (Oxford: Clarendon Press 1969)

Mason, Anthony: *The General Strike in the North East* (Hull: The University of Hull Press 1976)

Mates, Lewis: 'Durham and South Wales Miners and the Spanish Civil War', *Twentieth Century British History* Vol 17 No3 (2006 p.373-395)

Mates, Lewis: *The Spanish Civil War and the British Left: Political Activism and the Popular Front* (London: I. B. Tauris 2007)

McDougall, Peter: (ed.): *Voices from the Hunger Marchers: Personal Recollections by the Scottish Hunger Marchers of the 1920s and 1930s* (2 vols. Edinburgh: Polygon Press 1990 and 1991)

McIlroy, John, McLoughlin, Barry, Campbell, Alan and Halstead, John: 'Forging the Faithful: The British at the International Lenin School' *Labour History Review* Vol 68 No1 (April 2003 p.99-129)

McIlroy, John, Campbell, Alan and Gildart, Keith (eds.): *Industrial Politics and the 1926 Mining Lockout: The Struggle for Dignity* (Cardiff: University of Wales Press 2009)

McShane, Harry, and Smith, Joan; *No Mean Fighter* (London: Pluto Press 1978)

Medical Officer of Health for the County of Durham: *Annual Report 1921* (Durham: Durham County Council 1922)

Medical Officer of Health for the County of Durham: *Annual Report 1926* (Durham: Durham County Council 1927)

Medical Officer of Health for the County of Durham: *Annual Report 1927* (Durham: Durham County Council 1928)

Medical Officer of Health for the County Borough of Gateshead: *Annual Report 1926* (Gateshead: County Borough of Gateshead 1927)

Mess, Henry: *Industrial Tyneside: a social survey made for the Bureau of Social Research for Tyneside* (London: E. Bell Ltd 1928)

M'Gonigle, G.C.M: *Poverty and the Public Health* (London: Victor Gollanz Left Book Club 1936)

Morgan, Kevin, Cohen, Gidon, and Flinn, Andrew: *Communists and British Society 1920-1991* (London: Rivers Oram Press 2007)

Mowat, Charles Loch: *Britain Between the Wars 1918-1940* (London: Methuen 1978)

Nicholas, Kate: *The Social Effects of Unemployment on Teesside 1919-1939* (Manchester: Manchester University Press 1986)

North Tyneside Community Development Project Final report vol.1: *North Shields: Working-Class Politics and Housing 1900-1977* (Newcastle on Tyne: Benwell Community Project 1978)

Orwell, George: *The Road to Wigan Pier* (London: Penguin Books 1989)

Pedersen, Susan: *Eleanor Rathbone and the Politics of Conscience* (New Haven: Yale University Press 2004)

Pemberton, John: 'Origins and early history of the Society for Social Medicine in the UK and Ireland' *Public Health Policy and Practice* Vol 56 No 5 (May 2002 p.342-346)

Pemberton, John: 'Some reflections in 2003 on the 1930s', *International Journal of Epidemiology* Vol.32 No 4 (August 2003 p.496-498)

Perry, Matt: *Bread and Work: The Experience of Unemployment 1918-1939* (London: Pluto Press 2000)

Perry, Matt: 'The Jarrow Crusade, the National Hunger March and the Labour Party in 1936: A Re-appraisal' *Socialist History* No. 20 (2001 p.40-54)

Perry, Matt: 'The Jarrow Crusade's Return: The "New Labour Party" of Jarrow and Ellen Wilkinson M.P'. *Northern History* Vol 39 No 2 (September 2002 p.265-279)

Perry, Matt: *The Jarrow Crusade: Protest and Legend* (Sunderland: University of Sunderland Press 2005)

Piratin, Phil: *Our Flag Stays Red* (London: Lawrence and Wishart 1980)

Potts, Archie: *Zilliacus: A Life for Peace and Socialism* (London: Merlin Press 2002)

Reiss, Mathew: 'Circulars, Surveys and Support: Trades Councils and the Marches of 1936' *Labour History Review* Vol.73 No.1 (April 2008 p.89-112)

Renton, Donald: 'The Fight Against Unemployment', *Party Organiser* Vol 1 No 6 (January/February 1939 p.21-25)

Rust, William: *Britons in Spain* (London: Lawrence and Wishart 1939)

Samuel, Raphael (ed.): *Theatres of the Left 1880-1935: Workers' Theatre Movements in Britain and America* (London: Routledge and Kegan Paul 1985)

Short, George: 'The General Strike and Class Struggles in the North East 1925-28', *Marxism Today* Vol 14 (October 1970 p.306-315)

Smith, David F: 'The Context and Outcome of Nutrition Campaigning in 1934' *International Journal of Epidemiology* Vol 32 No 4 (August 2003 p.500-502)

Spence, J.C: *Investigation into the Health and Nutrition of Certain Children of Newcastle upon Tyne Between the Ages of One and Five Years* (Newcastle on Tyne: Newcastle on Tyne Co-operative Society 1934)

Stevenson, John, and Cook, Chris: *The Slump: Society and Politics During the Depression* (London: Jonathon Cape 1977)

Tanner, John: 'The Only Fighting Element of the Working Class? Unemployed Activism and Protest in Sheffield 1919-24, *Labour History Review* Vol.73 No.1 (April 2008 p.145-167)

Thompson, Willie: *The Good Old Cause: British Communism 1920-1991* (London: Pluto Press 1992)

Thomson, Christopher: *'The Chester le Street Union 1926: Creativity and Defiance in a Community Under Siege'* B.A. Dissertation University of Manchester 1984

Thorpe, Andrew (ed.): *The Failure of Political Extremism in Inter-War Britain* (Exeter: University of Exeter Press 1989)

Thorpe, Andrew: 'The Membership of the Communist Party of Great Britain 1920-1945' *Historical Journal* Vol 3 No 43 (2000 p.777-800)

Todd, Nigel: *In Excited Times: The People Against the Blackshirts* (Whitley Bay: Bewick Press 1995)

Walsh, Lorraine, and Kenefick, William: 'Bread, Water and Hard Labour? New Perspectives on 1930s Labour Camps' *Scottish Labour History* Vol 34 (1999 p.14-34)

Ward, Stephanie: 'The Means Test and the Unemployed in South Wales and the North East of England 1931-1939' *Labour History Review* Vol 73 No1 (April 2008 p.113-133)

Watson, Don: 'To the Head Through the Heart: the Newcastle Left Book Club Theatre Guild' *North East Labour History* No.23 (1989 p.3-22)

Watson, Don, and Corcoran, John: *An Inspiring Example: The North East of England and the Spanish Civil War 1936-1939* (London: McGuffin Press 1996)

Watson, Don: 'Self-Help and Aid for Spain: The Hawick Workers' Mill 1936-1939' *Scottish Labour History* Vol. 34 (1999 p.119-124)

Watson, Don: 'Shop Stewards of the Streets': British Communists in Local Government 1933-1939' *Socialist History* No. 40 (2012 p.63-86)

Webster, Charles: 'Health, Welfare and Unemployment During the Depression', *Past and Present* No.105 (November 1985 p.204-230)

Wilkinson, Ellen: *The Town That Was Murdered: The Life Story of Jarrow* (London: Victor Gollanz Left Book Club 1939)

Williams, Chris: *Democratic Rhondda: Politics and Society 1885-1951* (Cardiff: University of Wales Press 1996)

Worley, Mathew: *Class Against Class: The Communist Party in Britain Between the Wars* (London: I.B. Tauris 2002)

INDEX